MW01259468

A HISTORY OF THE WORLD IN 500 BUILDINGS

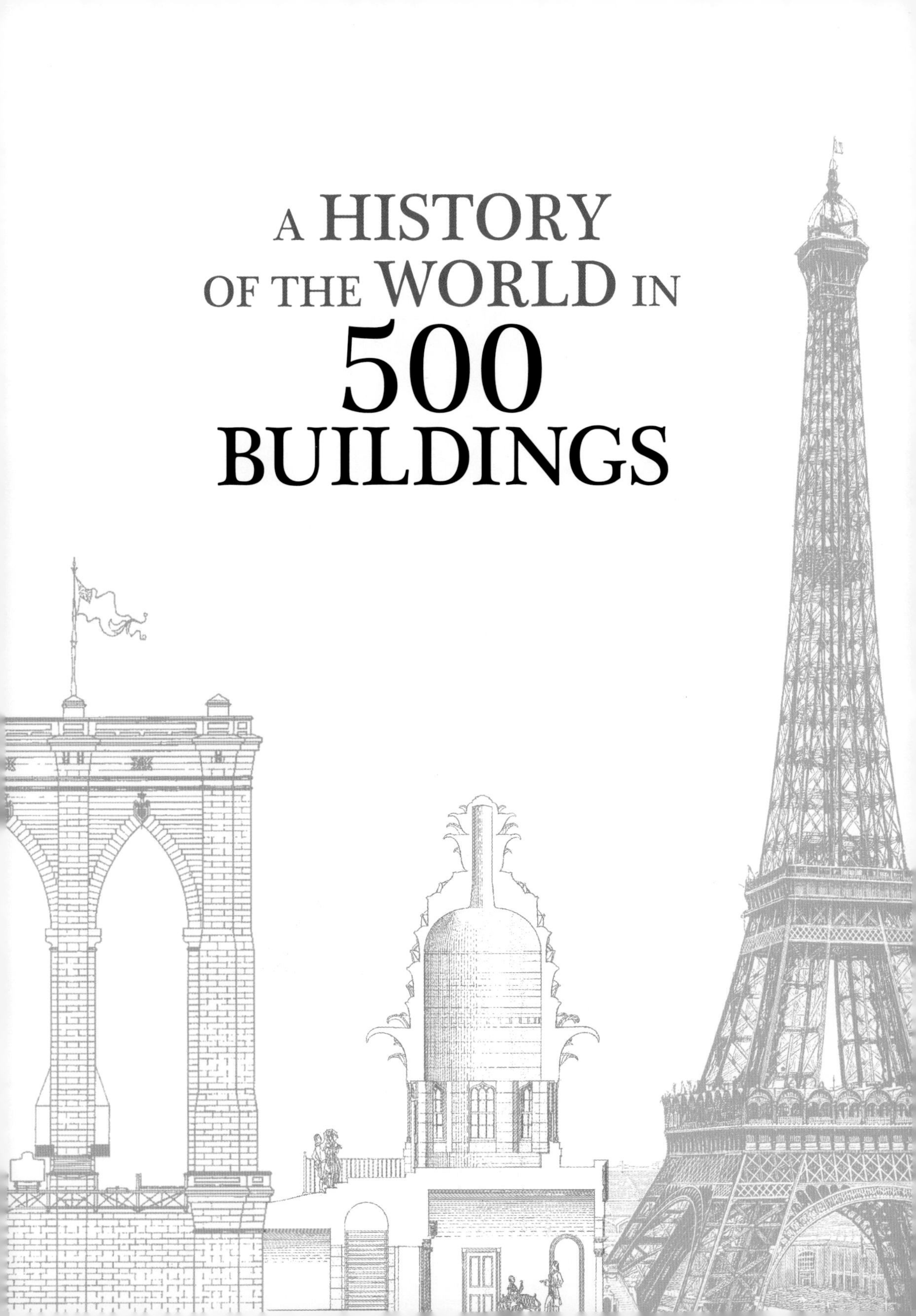

A HISTORY OF THE WORLD IN 500 BUILDINGS

THUNDER BAY
P·R·E·S·S
San Diego, California

Thunder Bay Press
An imprint of Printers Row Publishing Group
9717 Pacific Heights Blvd, San Diego, CA 92121
www.thunderbaybooks.com • mail@thunderbaybooks.com

Printers Row Publishing Group is a division of
Readerlink Distribution Services, LLC.
Thunder Bay Press is a registered trademark of
Readerlink Distribution Services, LLC.

Correspondence regarding the content of this book should be sent to Thunder Bay Press, Editorial Department, at the above address. All other inquiries should be addressed to The Bright Press at the address below.

Thunder Bay Press
Publisher: Peter Norton
Associate Publisher: Ana Parker
Editor: Dan Mansfield

Library of Congress Control Number: 2023944494

ISBN: 978-1-6672-0522-9

Conceived, designed, and produced by
The Bright Press, an imprint of the Quarto Group,
1 Triptych Place, London SE1 9SH,
United Kingdom
www.quarto.com

Publisher: James Evans
Editorial Director: Isheeta Mustafi, Anna Southgate
Art Director: James Lawrence
Managing Editor: Jacqui Sayers
Editor: Emily Angus
Project Editor: Emily Winter
Design: JC Lanaway
Picture Research: Kathleen Steeden, Jane Lanaway

Printed in Malaysia

27 26 25 24 23 1 2 3 4 5

Captions

Page 1: Brooklyn Bridge (L) (see p. 225), The Pineapple (C) (see p. 161), The Eiffel Tower (R) (see p. 235)

Page 2: The Jewel, Singapore Changi Airport (see p. 392)

Page 3: The pyramids of Egypt, 1910 (see p. 21)

Page 5: St. Paul's Cathedral cross-section (L) (see p. 155), Dymaxion House (R) (see p. 307)

CONTENTS

INTRODUCTION

Buildings have been central to the human experience since the first person noticed that a cave had some advantages over the open air in a sandstorm, heavy rain, or bone-chilling cold. More than 1.8 million years divide the first and last entries of this history. The first is the Wonderwerk cave in South Africa, where the earliest cave dwellers on record left traces, after deciding that "inside" might offer better shelter than out. The last is the "wet" animal market at Wuhan, China, notorious as the likely source of the COVID-19 pandemic that abruptly changed the world as we knew it in early 2020. The entries in between have been kept deliberately as broad as possible, including both buildings and, more loosely, structures, where people lived, worshipped, learned, and celebrated.

If you like your definitions neat and tidy, you'll find that every entry has been assigned to one (or occasionally more) of six categories. Art and Culture covers places of public entertainment, art workshops, or institutes—such as the Bauhaus—and includes the homes of great creatives, too. Infrastructure and Innovation looks at buildings and structures such as bridges, dams, and canals, which had an impact beyond their individual construction, while Politics and National Defense incorporates structures, especially military ones, that were built in support of a region, often on a boundary. Self-explanatory are Residences—where people lived—and Places of Work, where they worked. Finally, possibly the broadest category of all is Religion and Monument, which covers temples, churches, monuments built to groups or individuals, and tombs.

Some entries are obvious knockouts: no list could exclude the Pyramid of Cheops, for example, or the extraordinary moai of Rapa Nui in Polynesia. Others, though, carry their history more subtly—apparently unexceptional buildings that have seen exceptional events, such as the Stonewall Inn in New York City, or Marie Curie's research lab, still so radioactive that Parisians nicknamed it Chernobyl-

RIGHT: Xanadu (Shangdu), Kublai Khan's city, lasted only a century but lives on in romantic imagination. Samuel Taylor Coleridge created evocative images of it but today, a flat plain with just a few foundation lines, it's more reminiscent of Percy Bysshe Shelley's poem "Ozymandias."

sur-Seine. Such a variety means that every page has its surprises, small jolts as the reader moves from entry to entry, covering the whole globe, and finding some familiar histories anchoring lesser-known ones.

*"Nothing beside remains.
Round the decay
Of that colossal wreck,
boundless and bare
The lone and level sands
stretch far away."*

From "Ozymandias," by Percy Bysshe Shelley

Entries are arranged chronologically in six chapters. The first—structures that date from before AD 1000—necessarily takes some huge footsteps in time. You need seven-league boots to jump the centuries—sometimes even millennia—between developments like the first buildings with hearths, or built-in furniture (carved out of rock). Equally impressive in very different ways, the extraordinary Neolithic tomb at Newgrange in Ireland, for example, and the Pyramid of Cheops, instantly recognizable whether or not you've ever set foot in Egypt, are divided by a full seven centuries but share an instant visual and emotional impact.

As the chapters move on, however, the timeline entries quickly fall more densely. The second chapter takes the reader up to 1499, and the third to 1799. Empires rise and fall—Egyptian and Chinese dynasties, Babylonians, Greeks, Romans, and

Mayans are all celebrated through their greatest buildings or cities, and their technical innovations (and every so often—for example, with an entry for the Lupanar, Pompeii's best-known brothel—with something less elevated). The architecture of war becomes prominent, with castles and fortresses changing their design according to the weapons adversaries had developed to fight one another, moving from simple motte-and-bailey forts to the vast complex of Krak des Chevaliers. Geographical jumps supply constant contrast, too, with a Viking longship burial shown alongside an extraordinary Indian stepwell, constructed within three decades of one another, but on different sides of the world.

With the coming of the Industrial Revolution, technical developments start to take center stage from late in chapter 3. Many populations gradually move to the city from the country, and the design of workshops and factories gains an importance that it has never lost since, while vast engineering projects such as the Suez Canal transform the pace of international trade. The history of enslavement and the buildings in which humans were bought and sold, in locations ranging from Zanzibar to the southern states of the United States, find their grim place. Uprisings and revolutions can be traced through stories like that of Boston's Old Meeting House, where the Boston Tea Party was sparked, or the Bastille, whose storming saw the end of Bourbon rule in France. Individual cultural achievements also take more space—the hut from which Henry David Thoreau wrote *Walden*, the comfortable "cottage" where Jane Austen penned her greatest novels, and Yasnaya Polyana, the old-fashioned country estate that inspired Leo Tolstoy, are just some of the entries that offer a change in pace.

Chapter 5 covers the twentieth century, which contained two world wars, extraordinarily rapid scientific developments, and many buildings and structures that were witnesses to history, much of it still within living memory. The Russian revolution saw the storming of the Winter Palace, and the horrible end of the imperial family at Ipatiev House; the rise of the Third Reich prompted

"You never change things by fighting the existing reality. To change something, build a new model that makes the existing model obsolete."

Buckminster Fuller

extraordinary architectural set pieces and the horrific creation of concentration camps such as Auschwitz, and the Cold War created the Berlin Wall. Taken entry by entry, it shows how life all over the world had changed beyond recognition by the century's end.

Finally, the book's sixth and last chapter looks at some inspiring projects from the last two decades. Fittingly, as it becomes clear that humans have to live within the Earth's means or face extinction, many are innovative ecobuildings that seek to re-create a balance between nature's necessities and human needs.

"If these walls could speak . . ." goes the saying. *A History of the World in 500 Buildings* proves that not only can they speak, but that, for anyone able to listen, they can tell an engrossing story, too.

LEFT: The terrible end of the Twin Towers on September 11, 2001, and the subsequent memorial at the freshly christened Ground Zero, gave them a historical resonance that will last far beyond the life of the buildings themselves.

1 BEFORE 1000

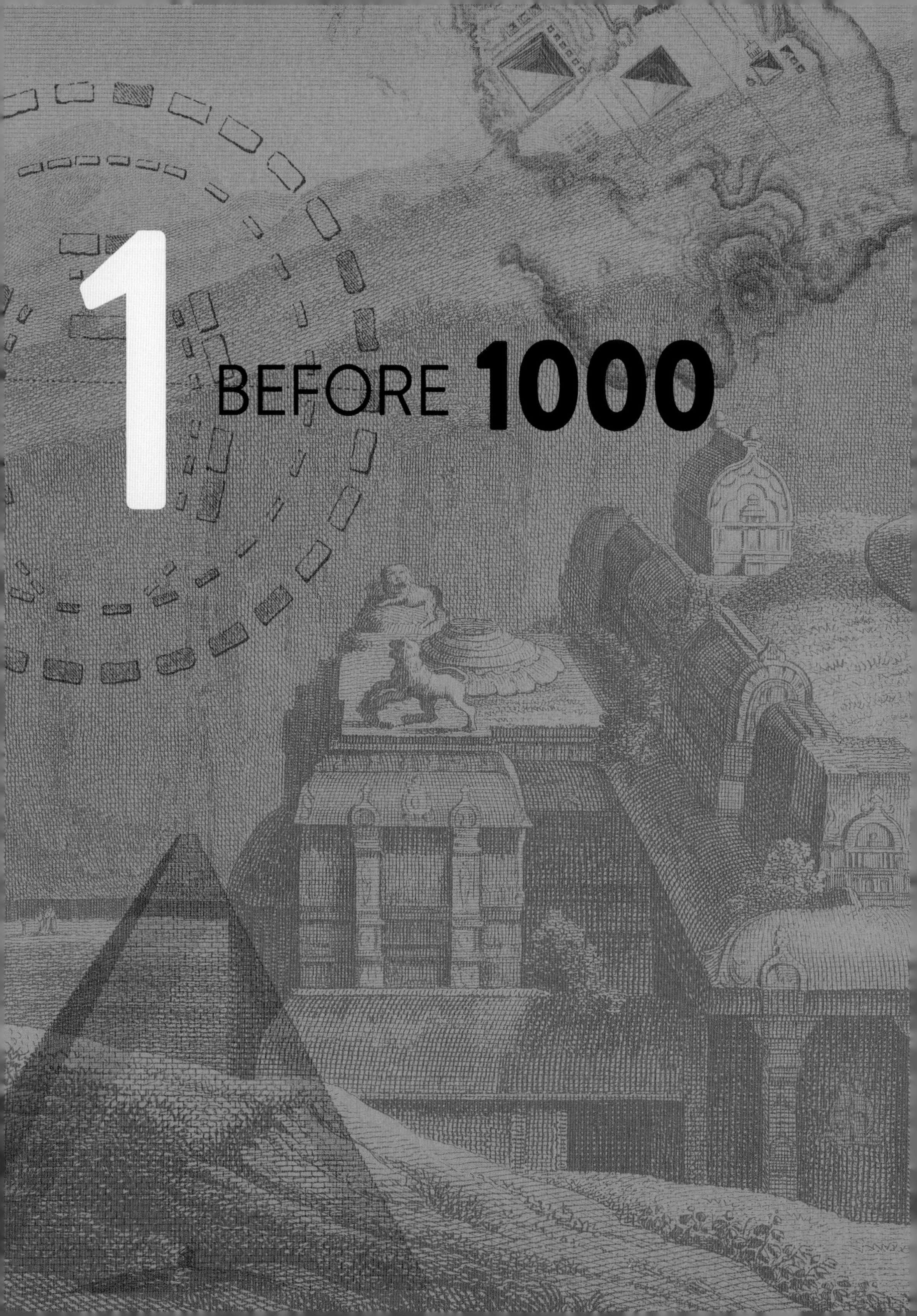

WONDERWERK CAVE

Kuruman Hills, South Africa
1,800,000 BC

The oldest shelter site yet found to have been used by humans.

This limestone cave, which reaches 459 feet into the Kuruman Hills at the edge of the Kalahari Desert, offered shelter more than 1.8 million years ago. Hundreds of generations of early humans used it as cover and protection while they went about their daily lives, making basic stone tools such as scrapers and hand axes, butchering the animals they hunted, and building fires for warmth and cooking.

All this has been revealed by minute scientific analysis of many millennia of layered deposits on the cave's floor. Very early tools, animal bones, and fire ash have been found at sites elsewhere; what makes Wonderwerk unique is that it is the first space under cover offering this kind of evidence, making it the earliest site where humans showed a preference for some form of "indoors."

BELOW: Wonderwerk Cave was rediscovered in the 1940s, when soil erosion revealed the ancient entrance.

2 RELIGION AND MONUMENT

INZALO Y'LANGA

Mpumalanga, South Africa
c. 73,000 BC

Also known as "Adam's Calendar" or the "Birthplace of the Sun," archaeologists believe that this stone circle, in the mountainous region of Mpumalanga, acted as a calendar. The stones are positioned to track the movement of the sun by means of the shadows cast on and by them. They have been dated by calculating the lineup of the three stars of Orion's Belt against them, setting its position against the 26,000-year cycle of tiny variations of the Earth on its axis.

3 RESIDENCE

KLIMONAS

Limassol District, Cyprus
9000 BC

The discovery of this Neolithic-era village offered proof that early farmers were also skilled-enough sailors to have crossed the sea from their original homes in the Middle East, bringing their crops—and possibly some animals—with them. A circular building, originally used as a granary, still held traces of emmer, an ancient crop that did not originate on the island, along with the bones of domesticated cats and dogs.

TASSILI N'AJJER

Algeria
c. 8000 BC

A strange desert moonscape marked by the evidence of humans across thousands of years.

A forest of massive columns and twisted shapes of eroded sandstone characterizes the landscape of Tassili n'Ajjer, a vast plateau in the Sahara Desert. At 44,700 square miles, it's both a national park and one of the largest archaeological sites in the world. Studies show that groups of humans lived here consistently for around 10,000 years. More than 15,000 rock engravings, together with many hand tools and evidence of ancient settlements, reveal that millennia ago, this arid area was fertile, with lakes, rivers, and vegetation, and was inhabited by plenty of wildlife, including crocodiles, hippopotamuses, elephants, and giraffes—all species that survive in the wall art, along with images of their human hunters. Over the centuries, as the climate became drier and harsher, there was a gradual drift away of both the animal and human populations.

"Its imagery documents a verdant Sahara teeming with life . . ."

Heilbrunn Timeline of Art History, Metropolitan Museum of Art, New York City

BELOW: Thousands of rock carvings reveal the fertile past of the desert landscapes of Tassili n'Ajjer.

ABOVE: The silhouetted hands were made over a period of seven millennia—perhaps an ancient form of long-term record-keeping.

5 RESIDENCE/RELIGION AND MONUMENT

CUEVO DE LOS MANOS

Argentina
c. 7000 BC

Evocative stencils offer clues to an ancient time of creative innovation.

This remote cave, deep in Argentine Patagonia, is notable not only for extensive paintings of hunting scenes, but also for the eerie outlines of hundreds of hands (*manos*) on the walls at the entrance. These paintings show a departure in ancient artistic technique, and one which called for specific tools to create. Inside the cave, most of the art was hand-drawn, or painted with fingers or sticks, but the stencils were made by blowing liquid colors—red, brown, black, white, and yellow—from a range of natural pigments through narrow pipes made from animal bone. Most are of left hands (as today, the majority of these people were right-handed), and the paintings have been dated across a long timeline of around 7,000 years, the most recent thought to have been made in around AD 700.

KNAP OF HOWAR

Orkney, Scotland
c. 3700 BC

The oldest Neolithic homestead in northwestern Europe reveals much about ancient everyday lives.

Today, Knap of Howar sits right by the sea on the small island of Papa Westray. When it was built, it would have been surrounded by flat, fertile land; its proximity to the sea is due to erosion. Two rectangular drystone buildings are set side-by-side on a slight rise, linked by a short stone passage. They were concealed by drifting sand for centuries until a winter storm in 1929 exposed them, and they were excavated during the 1930s. At first incorrectly dated to the late Iron Age, a second dig in the 1970s carbon-dated the site to around 3700 BC.

Now roofless (roofs would originally have been timber, topped by turf or thatch), the interiors have easily identifiable features: platforms, benches, partially paved floors, latches notched into the frames of low stone entryways, and upright stone slabs used as dividers. There is a large quern (used to grind grain), and hearthstones mark out a fireplace.

The site gave up plenty of clues suggesting the early Neolithic lifestyle: shells, bones, and grain fragments are evidence of a varied diet, and numerous tools, such as a polished stone axe, and hammers made from antlers and whalebone. These demonstrate that Knap's inhabitants were able to exploit what they needed from both the land and the sea.

KNOWN FOR

- Northwest Europe's oldest stone dwellings
- The first "furnished" houses found from early Neolithic times
- Proof of even older homesteads layered under the standing structure

ABOVE: The entrance tunnels are roofed in turf, as the houses themselves would have been.

RIGHT: The square compartment in the middle of the house floor marks out the hearth.

“There’s an old saying (that) if you scratch the surface of Orkney, it bleeds archaeology.”

Nick Card,
Orkney Research Center for Archaeology

7 RELIGION AND MONUMENT

GGANTIJA

Gozo, Malta
c. 3600 BC

These two Neolithic temples, held within a single boundary wall, are built from immense blocks of limestone, each weighing as much as 50 tons. Since they predate the use of the wheel, their construction represents a huge feat: the boulders were probably rolled into place on the "marbles" of rounded stone found around the site. The buildings also show traces of unusual corbel roofs, which were made from successively smaller overlapping slabs of stone.

ABOVE: This nineteenth-century engraving shows Ggantija in a more complete state than today.

8 RELIGION AND MONUMENT

NEWGRANGE

County Meath, Ireland
c. 3200 BC

A vast and atmospheric passage tomb that reveals an early understanding of astronomy.

Newgrange is the largest and most elaborate of 40 passage tombs discovered in this part of northeast Ireland. A massive, circular, turf-covered mound, its periphery is marked by huge "kerbstones" carved with complex patterns of spirals and lattices. It appears in records from the late seventeenth century, but was only thoroughly excavated between 1962 and 1975. The dig revealed an internal passage lined with stone blocks, and ending in a three-part chamber with a hollow pit containing traces of human bones and ashes. However, it was only when the so-called roofbox—a square stone opening above the passage entrance—was dug out that Newgrange's secret was revealed: the window aligns with the rise of the sun on the year's shortest day, the winter solstice, allowing a shaft of light to light up the inner chamber, first hitting the floor and then dramatically illuminating the whole space, a phenomenon lasting just 17 minutes.

RIGHT: Until you see people at Newgrange, the sheer scale of the tomb is hard to believe.

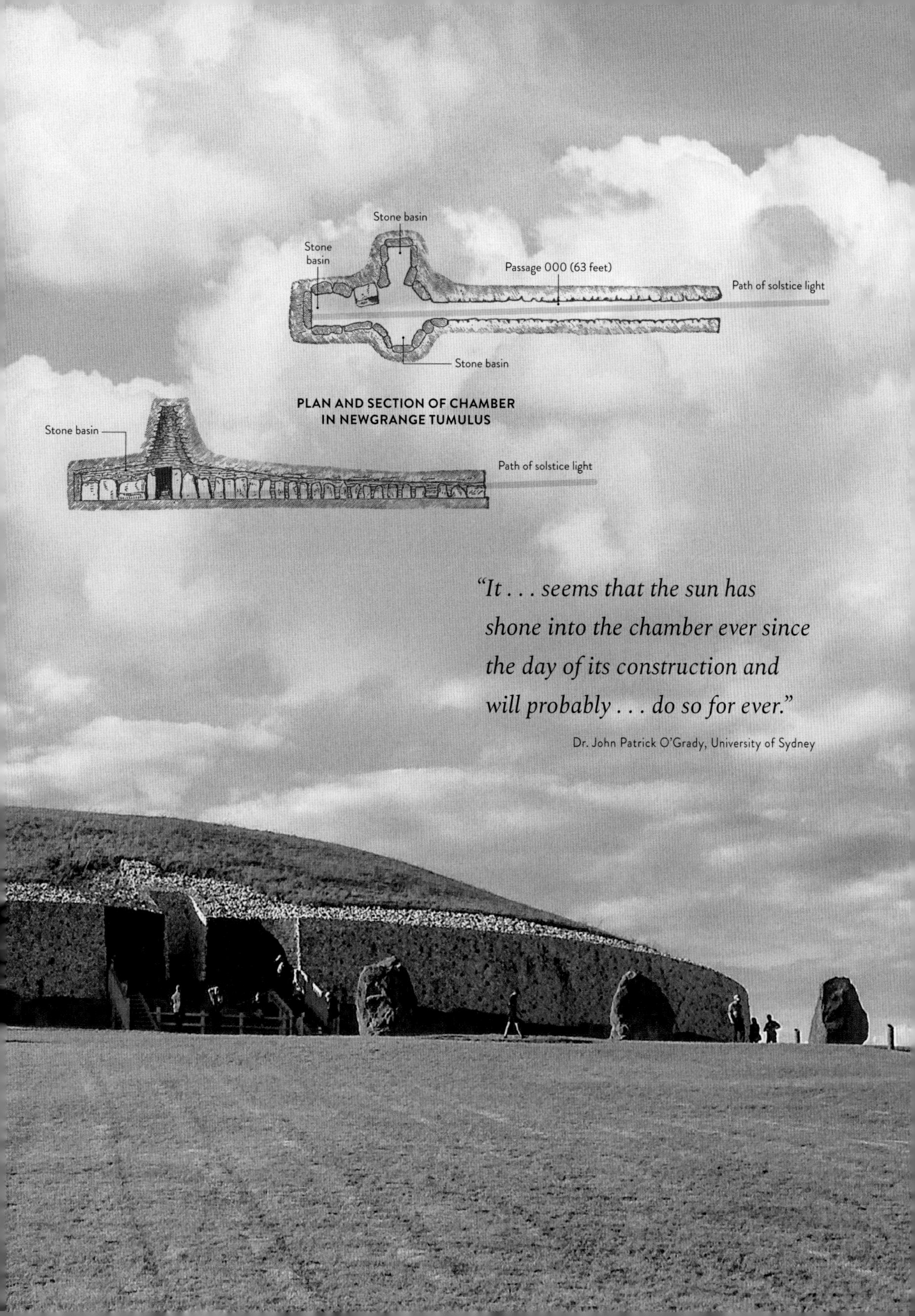

"It . . . seems that the sun has shone into the chamber ever since the day of its construction and will probably . . . do so for ever."

Dr. John Patrick O'Grady, University of Sydney

SKARA BRAE

Scotland

c. 3000 BC

The ten Neolithic buildings that make up Skara Brae are remarkably complete. Rediscovered in the mid-nineteenth century, careful excavation since has uncovered numerous stone tools and domestic objects, and also some unexpectedly sophisticated construction techniques. Among these are double-stone walls to the houses, the spaces between packed with layers of organic material—which would have helped insulate them—and a basic flushable drainage system.

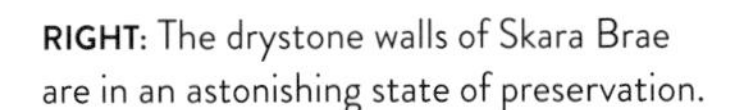

RIGHT: The drystone walls of Skara Brae are in an astonishing state of preservation.

BELOW: Single-roomed circular buildings are linked together by covered passages.

10 RELIGION AND MONUMENT

GREAT PYRAMID OF GIZA

Egypt
c. 2750 BC

Built as a tomb for the fourth-dynasty pharaoh Khufu, the 456-foot-tall pyramid is the largest of three on the Giza plateau, on the west bank of the Nile. It is believed that 20,000 workers took more than twenty years to build the Great Pyramid, using around 2.3 million blocks of stone. Originally, it was finished with a layer of white limestone, which would have made it a blinding sight in the bright desert sun.

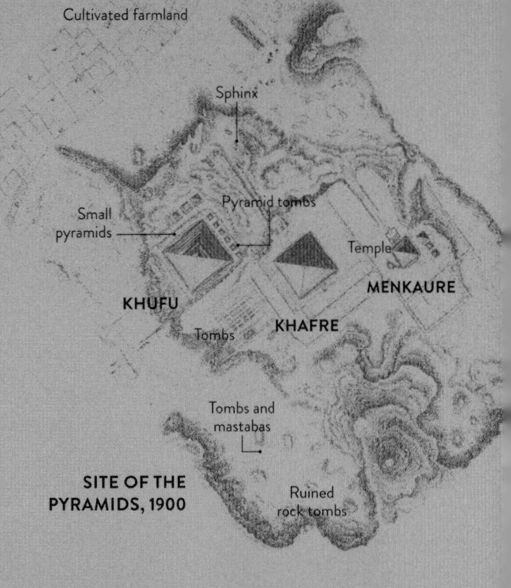

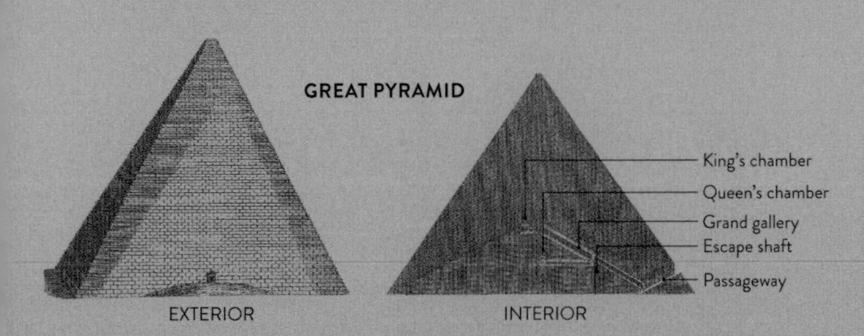

ABOVE: An aerial view shows how close the Great Pyramid of Giza, also known as the Pyramid of Khufu, on the left, is to the outskirts of Cairo today.

LEFT: So far, a number of passages and three chambers have been excavated inside the Great Pyramid.

STONEHENGE

Wiltshire, England
c. 2750 BC

An impressive centerpiece to a landscape rich in Neolithic remains.

In the Neolithic period, much of southern England was forested, so the open downland around Stonehenge made it a uniquely suitable site. Its structure took form over a thousand years. First, in around 3500 BC, was an earthwork with chalk walls. Five centuries later, large bluestone boulders were brought from Wales (a distance of more than 217 miles) to make the first stone circle. In around 2750 BC, more than 80 massive sarsen stones—local sandstone boulders—were brought from a site around 19 miles away. Gradually, over a long period, these were used to make the vast stone circle we see today, complete with lintels, slotted into place using tenon and mortise joints. The bluestones were rearranged inside.

Between *c.* 3500 and *c.* 1500 BC, Stonehenge kept its importance as a temple, a gathering place, a solar and lunar calendar, and a burial ground. Its significance faded only when metals began to gain currency for both practical and spiritual uses.

"It took five hundred men just to pull each sarsen, plus a hundred more to dash around positioning the rollers . . . Whoever was the person behind Stonehenge was one dickens of a motivator, I'll tell you that."

Bill Bryson,
Notes from a Small Island

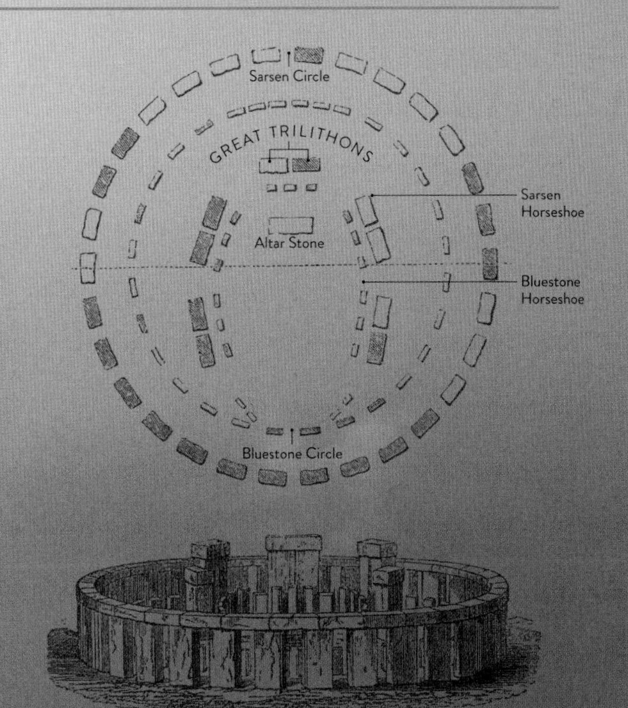

RIGHT: The configuration of the great stones at Stonehenge was altered several times during its history.

BELOW: On the left, you can see a peg on top of one of the stones, which would have helped to secure the lintel.

12 RELIGION AND MONUMENT

ZIGGURAT OF UR

Iraq
c. 2100 BC

The design, with multiple exterior staircases divided by terraces and a flattened top, is specific to the ancient city-states of the Sumerians. On top of the ziggurat, a temple to the moon god Nanna, to whom the city of Ur was dedicated, would have stood. That the ziggurat has survived is partly due to its ingenious damp-proofing—rectangular holes were bored from the outer walls through to the center to keep the unfired bricks, in the center, aired.

ABOVE: An estimated 720,000 bricks, each weighing as much as 33 pounds, were needed to build just the lowest level of the ziggurat.

13 RESIDENCE

PALACE OF KNOSSOS

Crete
c. 2000 BC

The palace was both the Minoan ruler's home and the political, economic, and religious center of this early Cretan civilization. First excavated in 1900, it proved to be a rambling complex, up to five stories high in parts, and with more than 1,500 rooms. The exquisite, stylized murals were a particular revelation, showing religious rituals, sports (notably the image of young athletes leaping a huge, charging bull), and animals (from deer to dolphins).

ABOVE: The brightly painted reconstructions at Knossos were the work of Sir Arthur Evans, who excavated the site in the early twentieth century.

TOMB OF TUTANKHAMUN

Valley of the Kings, Egypt
c. 1325 BC

A little-known pharaoh whose tomb opened the doors to ancient Egyptian life.

"Can you see anything?" "Yes, it is wonderful."

Lord Carnarvon to Howard Carter, on entering the tomb of Tutankhamun, 1922

Although Tutankhamun wasn't especially prominent among the 170 pharaohs who ruled during the 3,000-year Dynastic period, the discovery of his tomb in 1922, more than any other archaeological event, cast light on how the ancient Egyptians lived. Only 19 when he died, probably as the result of an accident, Tutankhamun's burial seems to have taken place in a tomb built for someone else, hastily customized to fit. However, this pharaoh's tomb—unlike others that have been found—had intact door seals, so the contents hadn't been looted. Every one of the 5,398 objects it contained was photographed, both as it was found and after it had been removed. This archive, covering everything from jewelry and clothing to furniture and funerary goods, has been invaluable to scholars of ancient Egypt ever since, casting light on every aspect of life in the New Kingdom, a period of political stability but also one of great artistic richness and creativity.

BELOW: Tutankhamun's tomb was found in the Valley of the Kings, among many royal tombs from 2000 BC.

15 POLITICS AND NATIONAL DEFENSE

WALLS OF TROY

Hisarlik, Turkey

c. 1250 BC

In 1871, when Heinrich Schliemann, a businessman and archaeologist, began to dig at an ancient mound at Hisarlik, in northwest Turkey, it was just one of many hypothetical sites for the "real" Troy of Homer's *Iliad*. By 1873, Schliemann had uncovered city walls and a treasure trove of objects. Many scholars agreed that he had found Troy, although the remains of nine cities overlaid one another at the site. The sixth of these was eventually identified as the closest in date to Homer's Troy.

ABOVE: The multiple layers uncovered at Hisarlik revealed a city with many stages of history.

16 RELIGION AND MONUMENT

ABU SIMBEL

Egypt

c. 1244 BC

At Abu Simbel, two temples are cut directly into the cliff face, the larger fronted by four seated statues of Ramses II, the smaller dedicated to Nefertari, the pharaoh's wife. When the Aswan Dam was planned in the early 1960s, it was clear that it would flood the site. The solution was to dismantle the temples and reassemble them on a tailor-made site 200 feet above the original.

ABOVE: Today the relocated temples look unchanged. On two days every year, the sun shines through the doorway of the larger temple, lighting up the inner sanctuary.

17 RELIGION AND MONUMENT

LA VENTA

Tabasco, Mexico
c. 1000 BC

A major center of the Olmec civilization notable for its legacy of elaborate sculptures.

Set on a slightly raised island on a marshy site near the coast of the Gulf of Mexico, La Venta was an important center of the Olmec people between *c.* 1000 and 400 BC. Its buildings, mostly made from earth and possibly wood, haven't survived the humid tropical climate. Its unique legacy is the large number of huge stone sculptures, including four massive heads with expressive features, particularly characteristic of the Olmec style. The largest is over 11 feet high and weighs more than 50 tons. A number of similarly sized long, flat stone platforms faced with elaborate figures are believed to have served as thrones for the city's ruling class.

ABOVE: Traces of paint found on the colossal stone heads indicate that they may originally have been brightly colored.

18 RELIGION AND MONUMENT

OLD TEMPLE

Chavín de Huántar, Peru

c. 900 BC

Set in a narrow valley in the Andean Highlands, Chavín de Huántar was a major social and religious center, and a place of pilgrimage for the Chavín people, a pre-Incan farming civilization. The centerpiece of the Old Temple, a network of narrow stone galleries, is a formidable 15-foot pillar sculpture of Lanzón, a human-bodied, cat-headed deity believed to have been the subject of a powerful shamanic cult.

ABOVE: The narrow galleries of the Old Temple are windowless; ceremonies would have happened in darkness, or by the light of a fire.

19 POLITICS AND NATIONAL DEFENSE

CHU STATE WALL

Henan, China

From c. 700 BC

At its peak, during the Ming Dynasty, the Great Wall of China covered 5,500 miles across the north of present-day China and southern Mongolia, but it was made up of a patchwork of earlier overlapping boundaries. Its beginnings lie with the Chu State Wall in Henan Province, when the Chu state extended its territory northwest of the Yangtze River and marked the boundary with small forts linked by walls of mud and stone.

ABOVE: The earliest parts of the Great Wall of China are basic structures built to link manned forts.

ISHTAR GATE

Babylon, Iraq

575 BC

Over 38 feet high, covered with bright-blue glazed bricks, and ornamented with reliefs of bulls and dragons, the gate, dedicated to the Babylonian goddess Ishtar, was part of a rebuilding of the city by Nebuchadnezzar II. The king was both a skilled military tactician and famously devout; much of the revamp was undertaken in the name of the gods. By the close of his reign, it was the largest city in the world and renowned for its magnificence.

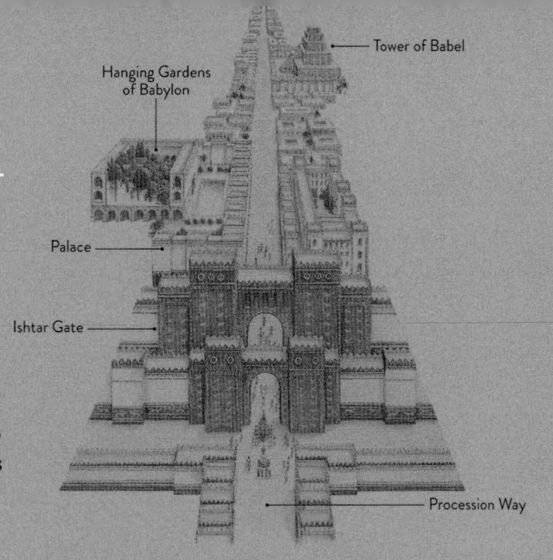

"I placed wild bulls and ferocious dragons in the gateways . . . so that people might gaze on them in wonder."

Nebuchadnezzar II, original dedication on the Ishtar Gate

BELOW AND ABOVE: In the early twentieth century, fragments of the gate collected by German archaeologists were reassembled in Berlin; the reconstruction is in the Pergamon Museum. This drawing shows how it would have looked, newly built.

21 RELIGION AND MONUMENT

TOMB OF CYRUS THE GREAT

Iran

530 BC

A small, rectangular stone chamber, unornamented, on top of an equally plain, stepped platform, is not the most imposing sight of Pasargadae, once the capital of the then-new Persian Empire and now an important archaeological site, but as the mausoleum of Cyrus the Great, first of the Achaemenid Dynasty and founder of the empire itself, it is one of the most visited, even today.

ABOVE: Despite his simple tomb, Cyrus captured more land than any other early ruler, conquering the Lydian and Medean kingdoms and the Babylonian Empire.

22 RESIDENCE

PERSEPOLIS

Iran

515 BC

Darius I moved the capital of the Achaemenid Empire to Persepolis and, with his successor Xerxes I, created a magnificent showpiece in this remote spot. Sited on a natural terrace, the palace, council meeting place, and reception hall were sculpted from limestone, featuring elegant, animal-topped columns. Visitors described the city as the grandest in the world. Less than two centuries later, in 330 BC, it was burned down by Alexander the Great.

ABOVE: Even after the city's destruction, the ruins of Persepolis remain impressive, with massive stone terraces and fine relief carvings ornamenting them.

PARTHENON

Athens, Greece
438 BC

A high point of classical architecture, copied all over the world.

Originally one of a number of city-states, Athens grew in importance under the statesman Pericles. During the Persian invasion of Athens, many of the buildings on the Acropolis, the rocky plateau at its center, were destroyed. Pericles instigated their reconstruction. The Parthenon, one of several temples dedicated to Athena, the patron goddess of Athens, was designed by Iktinos and Kallikrates, master architects. The sculptures, a key part of the scheme, were designed by Phidias.

The building was intended to appeal to the eye rather than to be mathematically "perfect." Fluted Doric columns mark the external boundary, and a three-dimensional frieze ran unbroken inside the colonnade. The temple acted as both a treasury and a home for Athena—a gold-and-ivory sculpture of the goddess was kept in an inner sanctuary.

Intact until the seventeenth century, the Parthenon was badly damaged while being used as a munitions store by the Venetians. It was subsequently looted of many of its treasures.

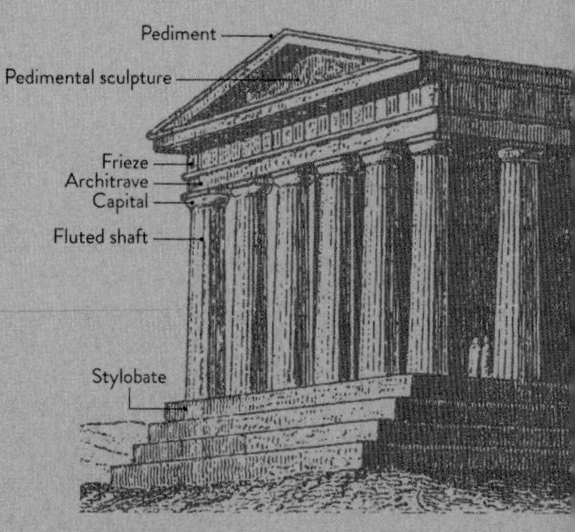

ABOVE: The Doric order, used only in mainland Greece, had three main parts: a stepped platform, columns, and an entablature.

> *"In the world over, the very name of our country is immediately associated with the Parthenon."*
>
> Melina Mercouri, former Greek minister of culture

BELOW: The Parthenon was just one of a complete scheme of buildings designed for the Acropolis in the fifth century BC.

ERECHTHEION

Athens, Greece
406 BC

A groundbreaking temple design for the most sacred site in Athens.

The Erechtheion was the final building in the redesign of the Acropolis. Its arrangement is unusual. While most Greek temples are symmetrical, the Erechtheion is built across two levels and its facades are mismatched, with a caryatid porch—itself unique—on the south side. Its columns are Ionic rather than Doric, another oddity for the period. Made from the best materials and finely finished, the design was probably a creative solution to the various roles the building had to fill.

Built over the graves of ancient kings, the Erechtheion also marks the spot where Poseidon and Athena fought over the patronage of Athens. There is a gap above the north porch, underneath which are broken slabs that are thought to mark the place where Poseidon, in fury, struck the ground with his trident. Areas in the building were dedicated to both gods, as well as a number of smaller cults. Each facade reflects the cult that particular part of the building served.

RIGHT: The most immediately recognizable aspect of the Erechtheion, the porch supported by caryatids, was probably added to the building's south side to conceal a support beam.

25 RELIGION AND MONUMENT

TOWERS OF SILENCE

Yazd, Iran
c. 400 BC

The two circular brick enclosures that top neighboring hills at Yazd are some of the oldest Zoroastrian Towers of Silence, or *dakhma*, still standing. In Zoroastrianism, human bodies become unclean after death and must be purified. The *dakhma* are sites where the dead are left exposed to the elements so that they quickly decay, and don't fall prey to *nasu*, or evil spirits. The Yazd towers were in use until the 1960s.

26 RELIGION AND MONUMENT

TOMB OF KAZANLAK

Bulgaria
c. 400 BC

The *tholos*, or beehive-shaped tomb, is in an area close to Seuthopolis, the ancient capital of the Thracians, who occupied an area covering much of present-day eastern Europe. The Tomb of Kazanlak has an antechamber linked to the burial chamber by a narrow corridor. Exquisite murals—of a procession and an elaborate scene of a couple seated at a funeral feast, waited on by attendants—decorate the corridor and the inner dome.

TOP: *Dakhma* depend on wild animals or birds of prey to strip dead bodies, and the sun to dry them—only then is the "evil" of death removed.

ABOVE: The mural of the procession in the tunnel leads to one of a wedding feast in the dome.

27 RELIGION AND MONUMENT

MAUSOLEUM OF HALICARNASSUS

Bodrum, Turkey
c. 353 BC

In the fourth century BC, Mausoleus was governor of Caria, a part of Anatolia, then under Persian rule. His tomb and memorial at Halicarnassus (known today as Bodrum) were begun in his lifetime but completed by his widow after his death. Sited on a hill overlooking the city, the structure was so impressive that it coined the word *mausoleum*, and was noted by the Roman writer Pliny the Elder in his histories.

Designed by the great contemporary Greek architects Pythias and Satyros, the huge tomb was topped by a stepped pyramid. The foremost sculptors of the day created the friezes around it, 300 freestanding works inside, and a horse-drawn chariot on its roof.

Sadly, this extraordinary building was destroyed by the seventeenth century, probably by an earthquake. Only historic accounts, together with fragments of the sculpture—including portraits believed to be of Mausoleus and his wife—remain to show how impressive it must have been.

RIGHT: A highly speculative nineteenth-century engraving of the tomb, depicting its lost glories.

28 RESIDENCE

CITADEL OF BAM

Iran
c. 320 BC

A fortified oasis city built by the Achaemenids, the Citadel of Bam was an important trading stop on the Silk Road for centuries. It was home to many industries, including silk production. Made completely from earth, it depended on a network of subterranean canals for irrigation; some of these are still in use today. It has been constantly rebuilt and remodeled—most recently after large parts of it were flattened by an earthquake in 2003.

29 RELIGION AND MONUMENT

KUSHITE PYRAMIDS

Meroë, Sudan
c. 300 BC–*c.* AD 350

A burial ground of around 200 stepped pyramids, rising out of the desert like a mirage.

During the eighth century BC, the Kushite people ruled over ancient Nubia, an area taking in much of today's Sudan and the southern part of Egypt. They were successful traders, waxing and waning in power; they ruled Egypt for a while in an era known as the "Black Pharaohs."

From around 300 BC, a burial ground arose outside the city of Meroë, which had been the Kushite capital since the sixth century BC. Pyramids marked the graves of senior nobles and royalty—both kings and queens—but here they were built during the lifetime of the subjects, so graves were ready to receive them straight after death. Between 20 to 100 feet high, the pyramids are smaller and steeper than their Egyptian equivalents. The dead were placed in chambers down staircases, underneath the pyramids, rather than being interred inside. Some pyramids also feature an ornamented internal chamber containing grave goods.

ABOVE: The Kushite rulers commissioned and oversaw the construction of their own impressive tombs.

30 RELIGION AND MONUMENT

TAPOSIRIS MAGNA

Egypt
270 BC

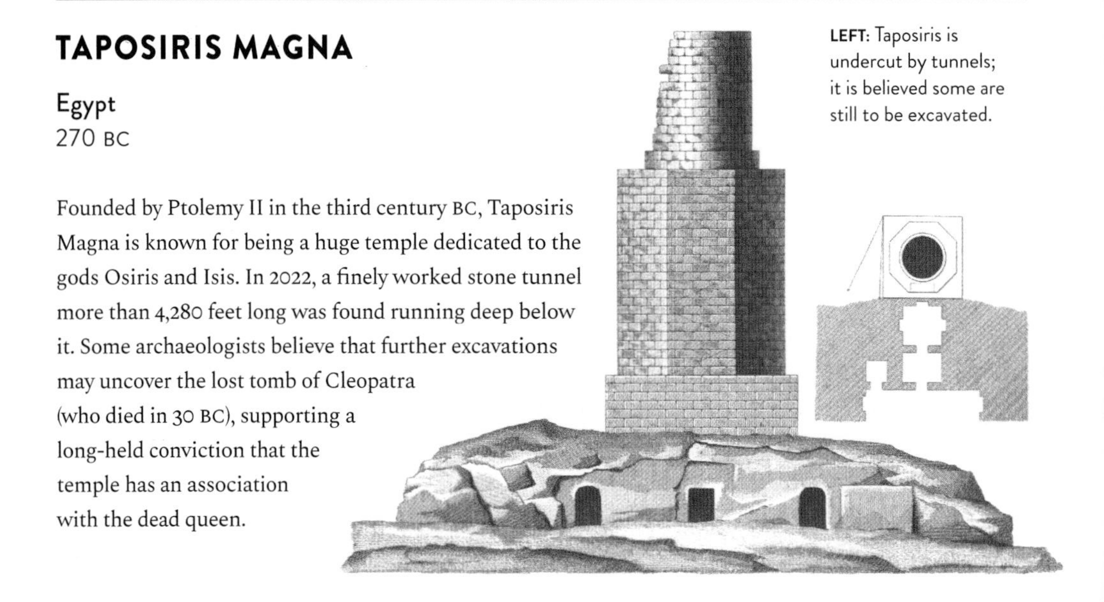

LEFT: Taposiris is undercut by tunnels; it is believed some are still to be excavated.

Founded by Ptolemy II in the third century BC, Taposiris Magna is known for being a huge temple dedicated to the gods Osiris and Isis. In 2022, a finely worked stone tunnel more than 4,280 feet long was found running deep below it. Some archaeologists believe that further excavations may uncover the lost tomb of Cleopatra (who died in 30 BC), supporting a long-held conviction that the temple has an association with the dead queen.

31 RELIGION AND MONUMENT

MAUSOLEUM OF QIN SHI HUANG

Shaanxi Province, China
210 BC

A terracotta army guards a tomb nearly four decades in the making, and yet to be excavated.

The first Qin emperor brought an end to two centuries of conflict between six kingdoms, uniting them into a single country: China. His tomb had already been under construction for years at the time of his death. The enormous complex, which has an estimated area of 20 square miles, was accidentally discovered in 1974.

So far, 2,000 of the emperor's terracotta warriors, sent with him to the afterlife, have been excavated. Each is a careful copy of a contemporary soldier with all his accoutrements. No attempt has yet been made to explore the tomb itself, a huge area topped by a flattened pyramid. A wait may pay off if archaeological science advances enough to capture all the information the tomb contains. Ancient writings make much of its splendors: it was modeled on the emperor's capital, Xianyang, with an inner and outer city, and a moat of mercury, believed to be life-giving.

32 PLACE OF WORK

STOA OF ATTALUS

Athens, Greece
150 BC

The stoa, or roofed arcade, has a surviving dedication by King Attalus and his wife from a time when Athens's agora, or main public meeting space, was being rebuilt. It was home to important temples and the city's law courts, and was a gift from Attalus to the city where he had been educated. The stoa was unusual because it had two floors (most comparable buildings had only one), and also combined a grand arcade with a double row of columns—which would have been used by Athenians to walk, talk, and do business. The 21 small shops allowed individuals to trade directly with passing citizens.

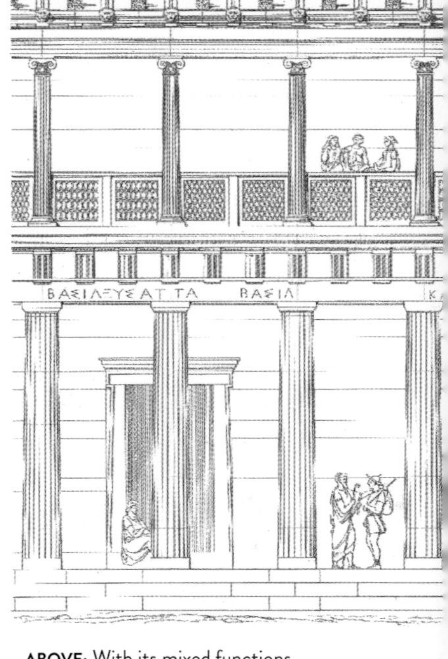

ABOVE: With its mixed functions, the stoa has been described as the world's first shopping mall.

"They built models of palaces, pavilions, and offices, and filled the tomb with fine vessels and rarities . . ."

Sima Qian, historian, 2 BC

LEFT: Soldiers of the terracotta army look entirely individual, but each was assembled from a number of parts: heads, bodies, and props.

33 RESIDENCE

HADRIAN'S VILLA

Tivoli, Italy
120 BC

Most Roman emperors retreated to country estates when they needed *otium* (time away from business), but Hadrian's Villa and Gardens were luxurious even by imperial standards. The immense site in Tivoli, close to an aqueduct, was notable for its accomplished use of water, not only for several sets of baths, but also for a complex of fountains, rills, and still pools, as well as a broad moat surrounding an artificial island.

ABOVE: What remains of the Maritime theater hints at the opulence of the vast residential complex at Hadrian's Villa, outside Rome.

34 ART AND CULTURE

COLOSSEUM

Rome, Italy
72 BC

Commissioned by Emperor Vespasian after a period of imperial unrest, the Colosseum was built by enslaved Judeans as a gift to the people of Rome, as part of a revitalization of the city. Its opening by Vespasian's successor, Titus, in 80 BC was marked by 100 days of games, mostly gladiatorial contests and animal fights. Rising to three stories and solidly built in concrete and stone, it could hold an audience of over 50,000.

ABOVE: Games and circuses were an important way for Roman rulers to display their wealth and power—and to distract from social problems.

35 RESIDENCE

KING HEROD'S PALACE

Masada, Israel
37 BC

King Herod, a client-ruler of the Roman occupiers of Judea, used the natural defenses at Masada as the site for an extensive palace, which could act as a refuge in the not-unlikely event of a revolt against his rule. Masada is an inhospitable rocky plateau overlooking the Dead Sea, accessed by a single pathway. Architects of the palace overcame the challenges, constructing a sophisticated building on hanging terraces cut out of the rock.

ABOVE: High on its plateau, Masada was believed to be almost unassailable by Herod's enemies.

36 RELIGION AND MONUMENT

MAISON CARRÉE

Nîmes, France
19 BC

Commissioned during the reign of Emperor Augustus, the Maison Carrée is the finest surviving example of a Roman temple and, since 2006, restored to its original gleaming white. It also offers today's visitors an architectural dialogue: the Carré d'Art, a contemporary art museum designed by Norman Foster, opened opposite in 1993. It was built as a counterpart to the original, with a similar footprint and columns but with reflective glass facades.

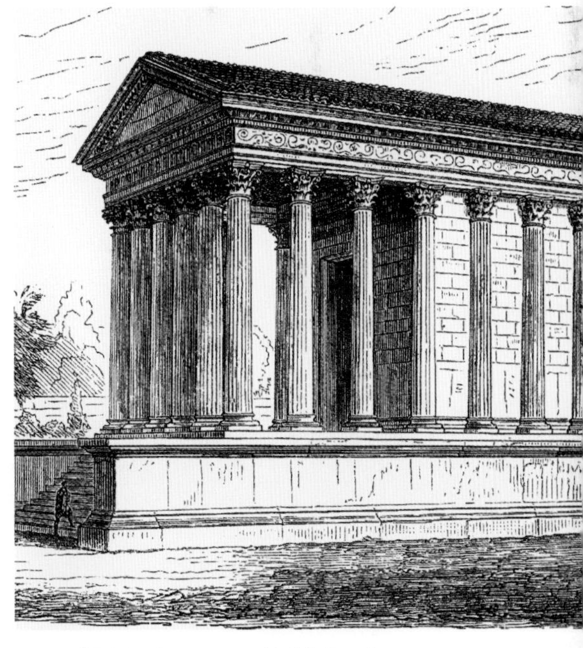

ABOVE: With its elegant, restrained design, the Maison Carrée is a model example of a Roman temple from the early imperial period.

37 RESIDENCE

FISHBOURNE ROMAN PALACE

Sussex, England
AD 75

Fishbourne, first excavated in 1960, is the largest and earliest Roman domestic villa to have been discovered in such a northerly part of the empire. It is a huge site, with a number of fine, largely intact mosaic floors. Built within 30 years of the Roman invasion, it may have been the reward for a cooperative local chieftain. Augmented and extended a number of times, it burned down toward the end of the third century.

BELOW: A seahorse, part of the "Cupid on a Dolphin" mosaic, one of several fine floors at Fishbourne.

ABOVE: The church has been in continuous use since the fourth century, seen here in 1936.

38 RELIGION AND MONUMENT

CHURCH OF THE NATIVITY

Bethlehem, Israel
AD 100

A tiny doorway leads through to the cave which, since the first century, has been widely accepted to be Christ's birthplace. The first church to be built over the site was commissioned by Constantine, the first Christian Roman emperor, in AD 339; it was replaced with a grander basilica by Emperor Justinian in the sixth century, which is now the oldest complete church in the Christian world. The building has joint guardianship, shared between the Greek Orthodox, Armenian, and Roman Catholic churches.

39 PLACE OF WORK

COLUMBARIA, BEIT GUVRIN CAVES

Israel

c. AD 100

Around 3,500 underground chambers form an extensive network underneath the ruined Roman city of Maresha. They were dug directly out of the soft ground chalk over a very long period—the earliest have been estimated to date back around 2,000 years—and used for a wide range of purposes: as workshops, houses, places of worship, and even burial rooms. Among the most elaborate are over 80 columbaria, or dovecotes, some dating to around the first century and featuring thousands of small roosting niches.

40 RELIGION AND MONUMENT

AL-KHAZNEH

Petra, Jordan

AD 100

Petra, known as the "rose-red city," was carved out of the sandstone desert cliffs by the Nabataeans, traders and entrepreneurs. Al-Khazneh is one of Petra's most elaborate buildings. Despite its name, which translates as "the Treasury," it was built as a temple and mausoleum, and dedicated to the Nabataean King Aretas IV. The Greek-influenced styling of its elaborate facade includes sculptures of Castor and Pollux at the entrance, and at the top, four eagles—symbols of the Nabataean god Dushara.

BELOW: Originally, the facades of Al-Khazneh and other buildings in Petra would have looked very different—traces show they were stuccoed and painted in bright colors.

LONGYOU CAVES

Quzhou, China
100

A mysterious feat of early engineering raises questions that can't yet be answered.

In 1992, a villager tried to drain a pond which proved to be the flooded entrance to one of the Longyou Caves. This series of vast caverns are supported by subterranean pillars, and quarried to a depth of around 100 feet. Further excavation found 35 other caves, each accessed down a vertical shaft and separated by very thin walls. Once drained, it was seen that the cave walls are entirely chiseled with a series of parallel lines, interrupted only by relief carvings. Dating placed the caves at around 2,000 years old, yet the images are in an older style, apart from one Buddhist goddess that seems much more recent.

The Longyou Caves continue to fascinate archaeologists, but they will remain a mystery until some new discovery reveals their secret. There is neither evidence that they were used by people, nor that they are grave sites. There's no sign of the stone waste from the quarrying, and there are no construction records, even in the form of local myth. No tools or artifacts were found there.

BELOW: The relief carvings at Longyou remain a puzzle; their style seems linked to an earlier era than the excavation of the caves themselves.

LUPANAR

Pompeii, Italy
100

An intimate glimpse into the darker side of life in a busy Roman town.

At the time of its destruction, Pompeii was a commercial seaside hub near the large port of Puteoli (present-day Pozzuoli). With a shifting population, taverns, bathhouses, and brothels were all in demand. With ten rooms, the Lupanar ("Wolf's den"—*lupa* being the word for both wolf and prostitute) was the largest of an estimated 25 brothels in town. The upstairs rooms, reached by an outside staircase, were larger and offered more privacy, although even these were spartan, with stone platforms for beds. The erotic wall paintings survive, although it's unclear whether they were meant to be titillating or simply showing services on offer for a clientele who might not share a common language. Most prostitutes in the Roman Empire were enslaved women, unlikely to have been there by choice; larger brothels were run by a *leno*, or manager. Numerous graffiti survive, ranging from the lewd to the poignant, offering a flavor of brothel life.

ABOVE: Relatively large, the Lupanar brothel was far from luxurious.

BELOW: Erotic paintings were commonplace in all kinds of Roman buildings, not just brothels, but those in the Lupanar are unusually varied.

Futata sum hic
("Here I am, damn it")

Graffiti scratched into the wall at the Lupanar

PONT DU GARD AQUEDUCT

Nîmes, France
100

With an elegant triple row of arches, the Pont du Gard, across the river Gardon, is part of an aqueduct that carried water from a spring at Uzes to the town of Nemausus, known today as Nîmes. The top arch carried a water channel; the challenge for Roman engineers was to manage a tiny, consistent downhill gradient. Although Uzes to Nîmes as the crow flies is 12 miles, the aqueduct measured 30 miles, falling just 55 feet along its length.

". . . from the first distant view of this noble monument, till we came near enough to see it perfectly, I felt the strongest emotions of impatience that I had ever known . . ."

Thomas Nugent, *The Grand Tour* (1749)

BELOW: From a distance, it's possible to admire the aqueduct's elegance, as well as its precision engineering.

44 INFRASTRUCTURE AND INNOVATION

ZAGHOUAN AQUEDUCT

Carthage, Tunisia
c. 110

Engineering challenges were overcome to bring water to the ancient city of Carthage.

A natural spring on the slopes near the ancient city of Zigus, present-day Zaghouan, is the starting point of this Roman aqueduct. It measured around 80 miles, making it one of the longest in the empire. A water temple in the form of a fountain was built over the opening of the spring so that water could run into its deep basin, where it was filtered and channeled to the start of the aqueduct. After that, all it took was gravity and extraordinarily precise engineering to carry it on its way. The aqueduct crossed the Meliane River on a double-arched structure, 79 feet high, but large parts of it were also laid underground, where the water ran in pipes. It remained in use for 400 years and was considered valuable enough to be restored and put back to work in the thirteenth century by the local Hafsid ruler.

45 PLACE OF WORK

MARKETS OF TRAJAN

Rome, Italy
112

A terraced complex adjoining Trajan's Forum, the markets are sometimes labeled the world's first shopping center, although they actually combined shops with living spaces for small-scale traders. The units ranged across six stories, from a double-height, vaulted hall at ground level to fishponds, which directly adjoined an aqueduct at the top. The Romans were skilled at working with concrete, making the complicated construction possible, although the facades were mostly faced with brick for a more expensive-looking finish.

ABOVE: This nineteenth-century engraving shows a section of the Zaghouan water supply system, the ruins of which still stand today. Large parts also ran in underground pipes.

46 RELIGION AND MONUMENT

PYRAMID OF THE SUN

Teotihuacán, Mexico
200

The building achievements within the eight square miles of the city of Teotihuacán were outstanding, but the Pyramid of the Sun is undoubtedly the highlight. The pyramid is built on a core of heaped stones, held by massive, stepped retaining walls. Originally, it would have been dressed with white lime, colorfully painted, and topped with an altar. Not much is known about the Teotihuacán people; even the name of the pyramid was given by the Aztecs, who took over Teotihuacán long after it was abandoned by its founding inhabitants.

ABOVE: The pyramids at Teotihuacán were part of a complex urban scheme, linked with wide avenues.

47 INFRASTRUCTURE AND INNOVATION

TOWER OF HERCULES

A Coruña, Spain
200

The sole surviving—and functional—Roman lighthouse in the world.

In the first and second centuries, trade around the westernmost parts of the Roman Empire, now the northwest coast of Spain, was on the rise. The Tower of Hercules lighthouse, built during the reign of Emperor Trajan, is sited on a natural prominence. With a height of 185 feet, it made an effective beacon combined with a lookout for the busy port nearby. Rebuilt in the eighteenth century—but retaining much of its Roman core—today's lighthouse is an enclosed stone tower, but the earlier model consisted of three open floors with either a ramp or a circular staircase leading to the top. The light was created using a huge oil lamp with a pierced-stone shade over it, through which the lit wick was threaded, and the light enlarged and reflected the polished metal surfaces that were placed around it.

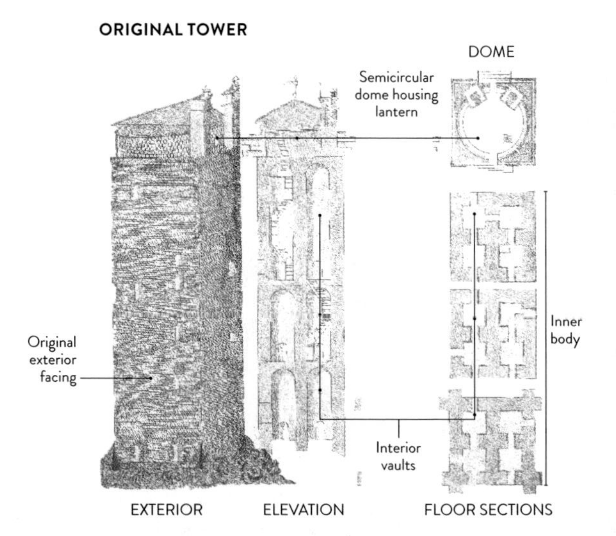

"The Galician city of Brigantia has erected a very high lighthouse for observation . . . worthy of mention as very few other things."

Cosmography, Paulus Orosius, fifth century

LEFT: The encircling wall, built in the eighteenth century, contains the lighthouse, which is Roman at its core, but was restored and raised an extra story in 1788–91.

48 RELIGION AND MONUMENT

PANTHEON

Rome, Italy
c. 200

Commissioned by Emperor Hadrian, construction on the Pantheon began around AD 118, and went through several stages, reaching its final form at the end of the second century. Its unsupported concrete dome, with an open oculus at the top, is the largest in the world. The Romans adjusted the composition of the concrete as they built, so the mixture at the top of the dome was lighter than that around the base.

49 POLITICS AND NATIONAL DEFENSE

BYRSA HILL

Carthage, Tunisia
200

Byrsa means "ox hide" in Greek; it is thought to date to the myth of the founder, Dido, who was told she could keep as much land as could be covered by a single hide. Dido cut the ox hide into tiny pieces and lay them in a circle around the whole Byrsa Hill. Carthage came under Roman rule after being defeated in 137 BC. Over the following centuries, the Romans rebuilt it and, as the managed capital of Roman Africa, it once more became an important political and trading center through the third and fourth centuries. The proconsul of Africa's quarters were sited on Byrsa Hill in the city center.

BELOW: In the fifteenth century, the rundown area around the Pantheon was cleared and paved; now it looks out onto the attractive Piazza della Rotonda.

BATHS OF CARACALLA

Rome, Italy
217

A grand public bath complex, built as a free amenity to citizens of Rome.

The 62-acre site for the Baths of Caracalla was appropriated from the estate of a well-known Roman citizen. Built in only five years, the complex had space for 1,500 people to enjoy the pre-bath massage and steam rooms; the cold, tepid, and hot baths; and the open-air swimming pool. The buildings were made of cement, faced with brick, then decorated lavishly with stucco and mosaics. They included two large libraries, one each for Greek and Roman texts, as well as halls for public meetings. Altogether, the buildings offered everything that a cultured Roman citizen could possibly want.

A subterranean network of passages was large enough for cart deliveries of wood, feeding the 50 furnaces that kept the water hot and the underfloor heating effective.

SITE PLAN

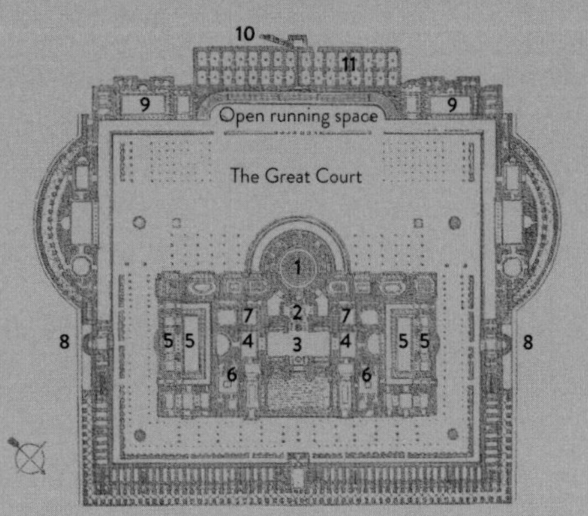

ABOVE: Seen from above, the massive scale of the Baths of Caracalla becomes apparent. Bathing was a part of civilized life, and citizens might spend time listening to philosophers debate in the theater, and then visit the library or watch some sport.

1 Caldarium (hot baths)
2 Tepidarium (warm baths)
3 Great hall/frigidarium (cold baths)
4 Halls for wrestlers
5 Palestra (open exercise spaces)
6 Oiling rooms
7 Bath services/massage room
8 Philosophers' meeting place
9 Library
10 Large aqueduct
11 Two-storied reservoir

The complex remained popular for 300 years. In 537, the Ostrogoths attacked Rome, destroying the aqueduct that filled the site's reservoir, after which the baths fell into disrepair.

GYMNASIUM AND BATH COMPLEX

Sardis, Turkey
c. 250

A grand site combining the traditions of Greece and Rome.

From the early second century, Sardis was the administrative center of the Roman province of Lydia (covering most of today's western Turkey). Built in the third century, the majestic Gymnasium and Bath Complex reflects the town's importance. It combines the Greek tradition of a gymnasium in the form of a *palaestra*, or open-air stadium, with the baths that were such a key ritual in Roman social life. The palaestra had a sanded surface for the practice of sports—such as wrestling, throwing the javelin or discus, and running. Side rooms were used both for exercise and massage. Dividing them was a hall with an elaborate three-story facade; this was reconstructed from a ruin between 1963 and 1974, and is known as the Marble Court.

The Marble Court is dedicated to the Roman emperors Caracalla and Geta. It would have been used as a rallying point for provincial citizens to show their loyalty to the Imperial Cult—the focus on the near-deity status of the emperors and the empire.

During the excavation and reconstruction, a large synagogue was discovered. It is thought to be later than the main buildings, and repurposes some of the space. Inscriptions show that there was an influential Jewish presence in Sardis.

KNOWN FOR

- A grandstanding complex for a provincial capital, reinforcing the power of the Roman Empire
- A synthesis of the physical cultures of the Greek and Roman traditions
- Incorporating the largest synagogue yet found in the ancient world

RIGHT: The grandiose facade of the Marble Court was an effective way to signal loyalty to an emperor far away in Rome.

Orandum est ut sit mens sana in corpore sano.

"You should pray for a healthy mind in a healthy body."

Juvenal, first century

52 RESIDENCE

CITY OF COPÁN

Honduras
After 250

From the mid-third century to the end of the seventh, Copán was one of the most important Mayan cities. Home to 20,000 people, it had impressive architecture, which was in a constant state of development and remodeling. The city includes five huge plazas, temples, pyramids, and the extraordinary Hieroglyphic Stairway, which is engraved with more than 1,800 glyphs, making it the longest inscription in the Mayan language ever found.

ABOVE: On the wall to the right, you can see some of the thousands of Mayan hieroglyphs at the site.

53 PLACE OF WORK

FISHMONGERS

Ostia Antica, Italy
300

Ruins of the Roman port of Ostia, at the mouth of the Tiber, reveal a wide range of commercial buildings, including a fire station and the local baths. Among them are two intact fishmongers, with wide marble tables to display the day's catch, and basins for preparing the fish. Mosaic decorations probably served as advertisements: one shows a triton, another a dolphin eating a squid.

ABOVE: Fresh fish was popular on Roman menus, and in plentiful supply at port cities such as Ostia.

54 PLACE OF WORK

AULA PALATINA

Trier, Germany
310

A rare example of a Roman basilica restored to near-perfect condition.

Augustum Treverorum, today's Trier, was a Roman colony from the first century. By the end of the third, it had become an essential political and trade center for the empire, serving as headquarters for the emperor, Constantine the Great, and nicknamed "the Second Rome." Aula Palatina was added to the existing palace as the emperor's new basilica, or audience hall, as part of a wider upgrade of the city's buildings. Although it has served several purposes—and the palace it was attached to no longer exists—Aula Palatina is the largest surviving single-room Roman building. It is laid out as a typical basilica, on a rectangular floor plan with a semicircular apse at one end, a scheme that would become standard for many early Christian churches. A double row of large windows adds to the sense of scale.

ABOVE: A nineteenth-century French engraving of Aula Palatina (top), showing the basilica before substantial restoration (above).

TEMPLE 17, SANCHI

Madhya Pradesh, India
400

A simple structure believed to be the earliest intact Buddhist temple in India.

The extensive Buddhist complex at Sanchi is best known for the large and intricate Great Stupa, but Temple 17, a much more modest building nearby, has an important place in the history of religious architecture: it is the earliest complete, unaltered Buddhist temple in India. Small and simple, measuring just 23 feet by 13 feet, it dates back to the Gupta dynasty, a high point in the region's architectural development. Built without mortar, it consists of a plain, low-roofed chamber, fronted by a porch. The latter is supported by four pillars, which are the only decorated element. Each is topped with a bell-shaped, inverted lotus flower and capitals finished with pairs of lions, carved back-to-back. Despite its simplicity, it's the forerunner of much great temple architecture to come.

BELOW: Against some of the more elegant temple buildings, Temple 17 looks almost squat. But it's the forerunner of much great architecture.

BELOW: An aerial view shows the main stupa—the round structure—and Temple 17, one of the much smaller buildings among the trees, to the left.

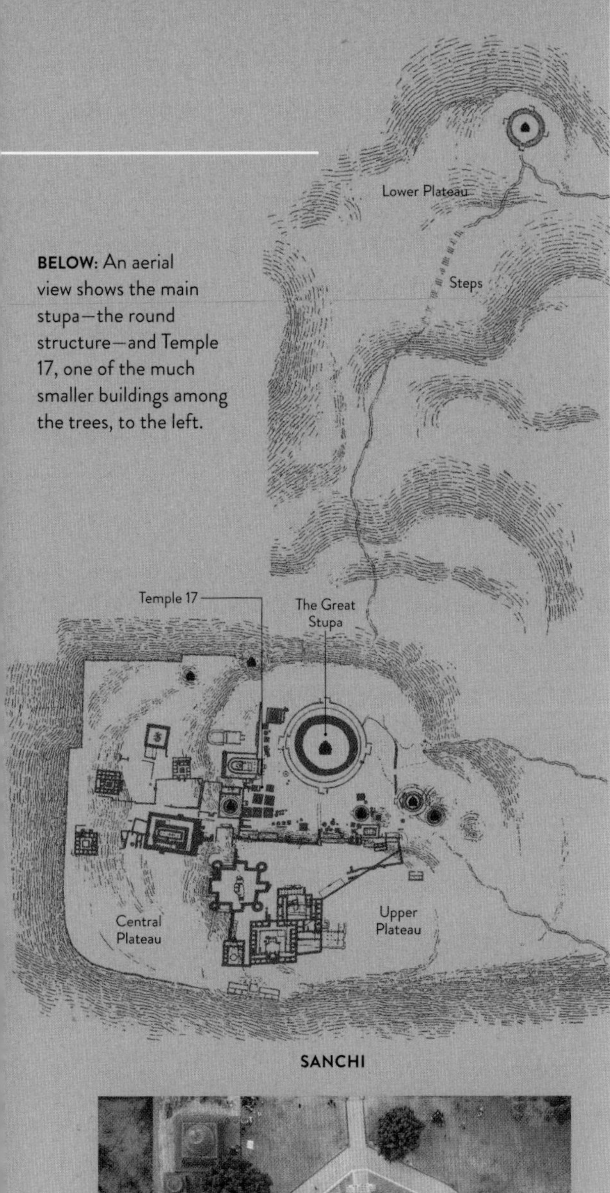

56 RESIDENCE

DERINKUYU UNDERGROUND CITY

Cappadocia, Turkey
400

The underground city is a subterranean complex carved out of the soft tuff rock, reaching depths of 250 feet across at as many as 18 different levels. Derinkuyu may have begun construction as early as the seventh century BC, but it was significantly enlarged during the Byzantine Era, eventually offering shelter to up to 20,000 people in times of conflict. Each level could be individually sealed, and large stone "doors" rolled into place to seal the main entrances.

BELOW: The rock of Cappadocia is formed out of deposits of volcanic ash. It was easy to dig by hand, creating an extensive network that was expanded over many centuries.

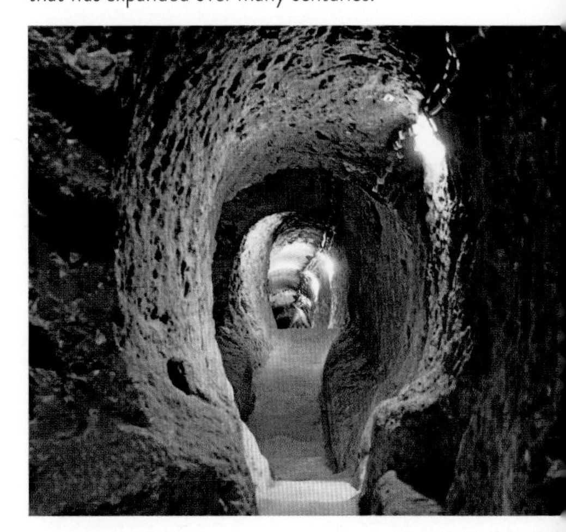

57 POLITICS AND NATIONAL DEFENSE

THEODOSIAN WALLS

Istanbul, Turkey
c. 408

The fortifications that kept Constantinople safe for eight centuries.

Rich cities are vulnerable to invasion, and the ability of Constantinople to defend itself was already being questioned when Theodosius II became emperor in 408. Two years later, after Rome had fallen to the Goths, one of his deputies was asked to create a long-term defense for Constantinople. The result was the Theodosian walls, completed in 439. Their construction was thorough: a deep ditch, 65 feet wide—which could be rapidly converted into a moat using an open-water source—surrounded a triple wall. The outermost wall doubled up as a lookout, with a walkway on top. The taller, middle wall was interrupted by towers at regular intervals from which intruders could be fired at, while the tallest inner wall, 16 feet wide, had larger towers at 70-foot intervals which could carry heavier weaponry to fire down on enemies from a greater distance.

The walls were effective. Persian, Arab, and Russian attackers laid siege to Constantinople over the following centuries, but they were not breached until 1204 during the Fourth Crusade. Finally, in 1453, they met their match in an attack by the Ottomans, and Constantinople fell.

ABOVE: The three-part construction made the walls particularly difficult to breach. The frequent castellated towers meant the inhabitants could fire at would-be invaders while remaining well-protected themselves.

MATI SI

Gansu Province, China
After 400

Believed to have been built between the fifth and seventh centuries, Mati Si, or "Horse Hoof Temple," is an extended cave temple complex consisting of multiple groups of rooms, many linked by passages, carved directly into the cliff face and furnished with statues of Buddha. They include a striking relief "pagoda," 200 feet high, which joins rooms at several levels with walkways and external terraces.

"The Mongolian classic, the Epic of King Gesar, *records that the horse of the king had set just one hoof down at Mati Si when the king rode him away. Only the hoofprint is left."*

Unattributed

BELOW: The different parts of Mati Si are linked with extremely narrow passages and precipitous staircases.

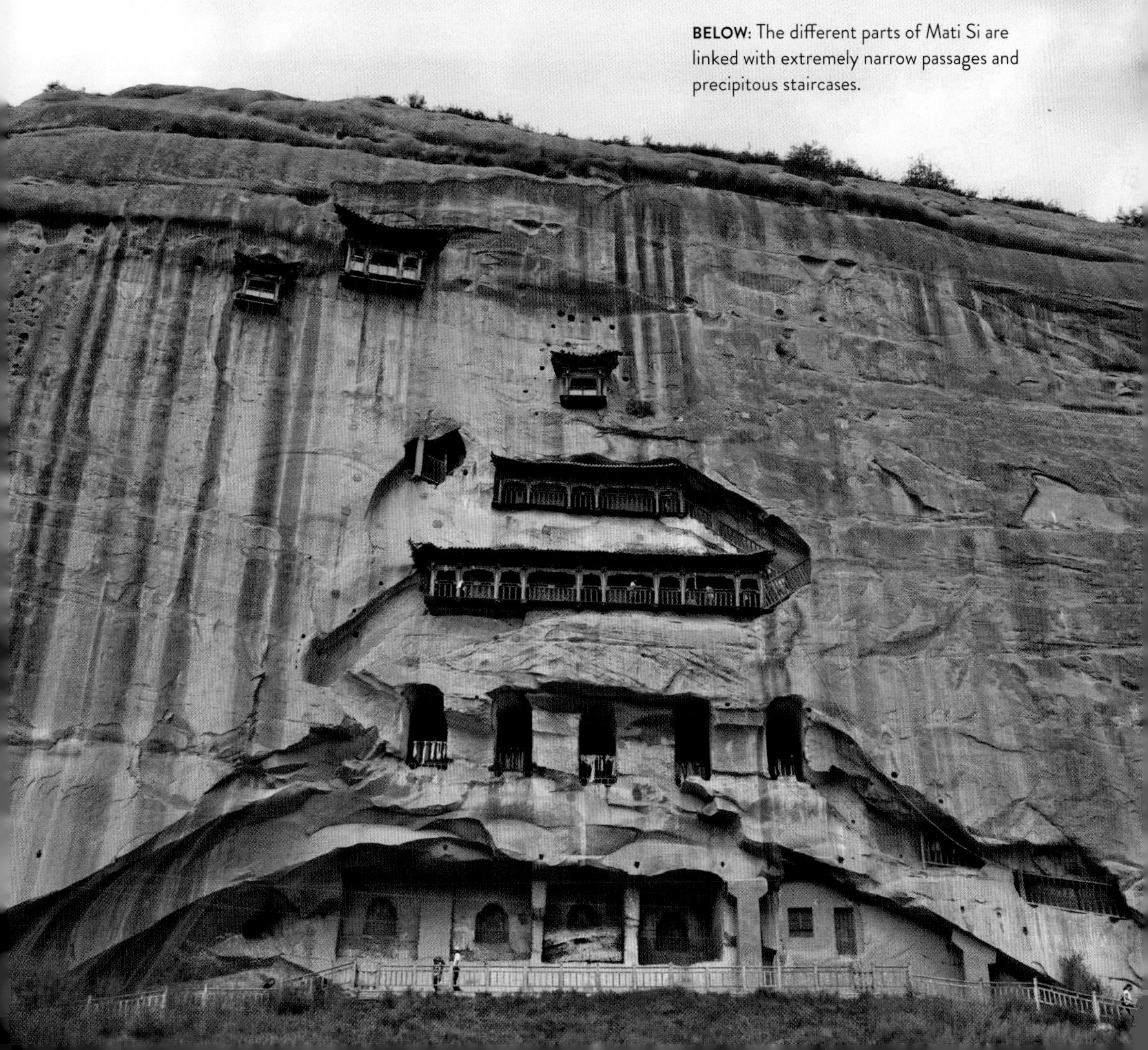

59 RESIDENCE

SITE OF THE HOUSE OF TAGA MONOLITHS

Tinian, Northern Mariana Islands
After *c.* 500

The Chamorro people originated in Southeast Asia, but were well settled on the Mariana islands by 1500 BC. Evidence from the fifth century AD suggests houses carried on wooden stilts. A-frame pole houses with steep thatched roofs were raised up on pairs of so-called latte stones, each formed of two pieces: an upright pillar capped with an inverted cup stone.

The structure was probably devised to protect the owners from wild animals or coastal flooding. Over time, size began to equate to status, and both stones and houses became larger—originally balanced on three or four pairs of pillars, some structures had many more.

60 ART AND CULTURE

ST. CATHERINE'S MONASTERY LIBRARY

Mount Sinai, Egypt
530

The oldest continually operating library in the world belongs to a small Greek Orthodox monastery built by the Byzantine emperor Justinian I on a particularly holy site, being both the place of martyrdom of St. Catherine, and also the spot where Moses saw the burning bush and heard God's voice. Its collection of icons and manuscripts is second only to that held in the Vatican Apostolic Library in Rome.

BELOW: The monastery buildings are made from gray granite and have not changed much since the sixth century.

HAGIA SOPHIA

Istanbul, Turkey
537

An enduring symbol for both Muslims and Orthodox Christians in a city that bridges East and West.

Built on the site of two earlier churches, both of which burned down, Hagia Sophia was commissioned by Emperor Justinian I, with a brief to create the most impressive church in the Byzantine Empire, using materials from all its territories. The result was a many-windowed basilica with an internal gallery and a massive central dome that, seen from the inside, seems to float. It was built in just six years, during which time the dome collapsed twice before a successful version was devised. Hagia Sophia remained a focus of Orthodoxy as the empire declined. When Constantinople fell to the Ottomans in 1453, the church was converted and used as a mosque until—in its third incarnation in 1934—it was deconsecrated and turned into a museum. In the latest controversial twist in its fortunes, Hagia Sophia was reconsecrated as a mosque in 2020 on the orders of President Recep Tayyip Erdoğan of Turkey.

BELOW: The minarets at Hagia Sophia were added in the fifteenth century, when it became a mosque.

62 RELIGION AND MONUMENT

ELLORA CAVES

Maharashtra, India
From 600

Across more than four centuries, the temples and monasteries of Ellora were built on a site over a mile long. There are 34 different buildings here, cut directly into the hard basalt rock face, and falling into three date groups: the Buddhist structures are the earliest, followed by the Hindu examples, and finally those of the Jains. Overall, the site demonstrates a religious tolerance characteristic of early Indian practice. The showpiece structure, extraordinary in both religious and engineering terms, is Kailasa, a temple dedicated to Shiva and representing Mount Kailash—his home in the Himalayas. It's a freestanding building with an elaborate tower, entirely covered with reliefs and sculptures, and cut out of the rock from the top down, calling for the removal of over 200,000 tons of stone.

63 RELIGION AND MONUMENT

HANGING MONASTERY OF HENGSHAN

Shanxi Province, China
c. 600

The Hanging Monastery looks fragile, but it has clung to the Heng mountain for at least 1,400 years and possibly longer. Its location—under an overhang and set back on a slight natural shelf—has protected it from the harshest effects of bad weather. Legend has it that it was built by a single monk, Liao Ran, in the fifth century; modern dating places it slightly later, but it's likely that it was put together over an extended period. It was built by drilling holes in the rock face and inserting poles that supported the wooden buildings which, between them, have about 40 rooms, linked by narrow passageways.

The unique feature of the monastery, however, isn't the location but the fact that it follows three different religions, with spaces dedicated to Buddhism, Taoism, and Confucianism—and the worship of all three is welcomed. One particular hall celebrates this, displaying statues of the founders of all three religions side by side.

LEFT: A group of rock temples where Buddhists, Hindus, and Jains could all worship together.

CHICHEN ITZA

Yucatán, Mexico
After 600

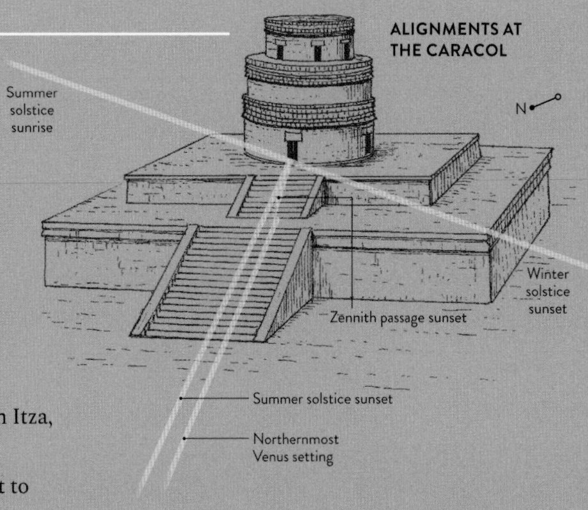

A site that shows evidence of a Mayan interest in astronomy.

The Mayan people had a sophisticated mathematical system and used a detailed calendar. One building in particular, El Caracol (meaning "the snail") at Chichen Itza, may offer evidence of some specific astronomical knowledge. Built with Puuc decoration, which dates it to the earlier phase of the city, it consists of a round tower—a rare form in Mayan architecture—raised on a plinth accessed by steps, with the remains of a collapsed smaller tower on top. Inside is a spiral staircase, which gave the building its nickname, leading up to three small openings in the deep wall. The alignment of the building and the placement of the openings have led historians to theorize that they were used to observe the planet Venus at its northern and southern extremes. Venus was important in the Mayan belief system as it was identified with the war god, Kukulkán.

BELOW: The ruins of Chichen Itza occupy 2,500 acres, and archaeologists have found evidence that it was a major center of trade, local politics, and religion, with an estimated population of around 35,000 people.

65 RESIDENCE

TIKAL

Guatemala
600

A great Mayan city set in deep forest, Tikal reached its artistic zenith between 600 and 900. It was designed on a huge scale, with a central area containing the important and ceremonial buildings, and outskirts that included residential areas. The hieroglyphics that survive on many of the buildings have helped archaeologists to put Tikal in a contemporary context, showing a pattern of communications and relationships with other Mesoamerican cities, including Teotihuacán and Copán.

ABOVE: The so-called Temple of the Great Jaguar, at Tikal, has a lintel showing a ruler sitting on a jaguar throne.

66 RELIGION AND MONUMENT

HŌRYŪ-JI TEMPLE COMPLEX

Nara, Japan
607

A temple compound containing 48 listed buildings commissioned by Prince Shōtoku, who is famous in Japanese history for championing both Buddhism (in the early seventh century—a comparatively recent import from China) and the arts. Not all the buildings survive in their original form, but the *kondo*, or great hall, which was arranged to imitate the Buddhist version of paradise, is intact and is one of the oldest wooden buildings in Japan.

LINDISFARNE PRIORY

Northumberland, England
634

The priory was founded when King Oswald of Northumbria offered the small island of Lindisfarne, off the northeast coast of England, to a group of Irish monks from Iona—with the intention of giving his kingdom a bishopric. Lindisfarne had a sustained importance in the early Christian church. St. Cuthbert, bishop there between 685 and 687, gave his name (and his relics) to the priory's shrine, and it remains a place of pilgrimage.

ABOVE: The priory is also known for having produced the exquisitely illuminated Lindisfarne Gospels in about 700, now in the British Library.

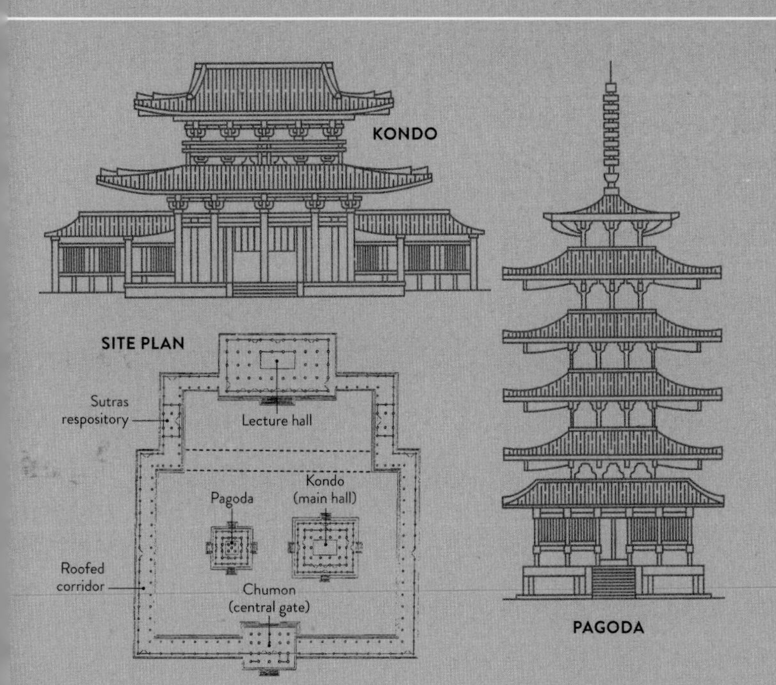

"The three treasures, which are Buddha, the Law, and the Priesthood, should be given sincere reverence, for they are the final refuge of all living things."

Prince Shōtoku (573–621)

FAR LEFT: The kondo, or great hall, is to the left of the photograph. It contains a statue of Buddha, with a likeness to Prince Shōtoku, and dedicated to his memory.

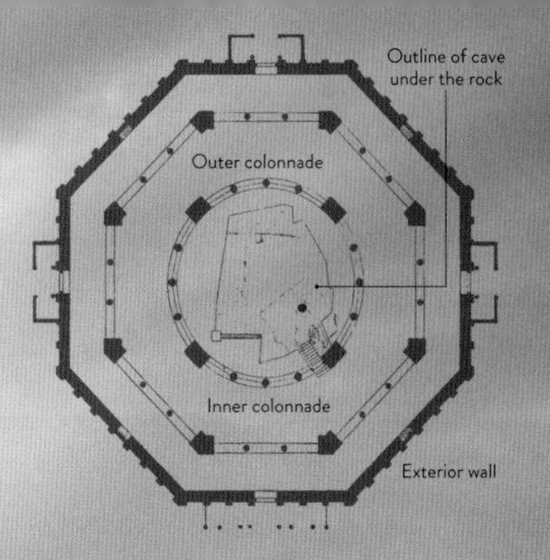

DOME OF THE ROCK

Jerusalem, Israel
684

An iconic building on a site sacred to both the Muslim and Jewish faiths.

The dome is the oldest extant Islamic monument. It was commissioned by Abd al-Malik, the fifth Ummayad caliph, during a bitter civil war, perhaps with the aim of giving his followers a local shrine to encourage loyalty. Built on Haram al-Sharif, the highest point in the old city of Jerusalem, it consists of a gilded dome sitting on a short, round drum on an octagonal base, both covered in intricate patterns of blue tiles and with plenty of windows.

The inside of the building is just as highly decorated. The focus, the rock itself, is a huge slab of stone that marks the spot where, for Muslims, Muhammad—leaving a footprint—ascended to heaven to meet his fellow prophets and to see God, and the place where, for Jews, Abraham prepared to sacrifice Isaac. Most parts of today's building have been restored, but overall, the dome has stayed faithful to Abd al-Malik's original design.

LEFT: The Dome of the Rock is particularly revered in Islam as the oldest standing monument of Islamic architecture.

69 RELIGION AND MONUMENT

DESCENT OF THE GANGES

Tamil Nadu, India
c. 690

A masterwork of naturalistic carving in the temple town of Mamallapuram in southern India.

The Descent of the Ganges, also known as Arjuna's Penance, is one of a number of sacred objects in the coastal town of Mamallapuram in southeast India. It's an immense relief carving—96 feet long by 43 feet high—made on a naturally cleft rock. The scene it shows has been debated: it may be Arjuna's Penance, a tale from the ancient *Mahabharata*, or alternatively show the legend in which the Ganges was sent down from heaven. It was probably created during the late seventh century, and a tank at the top of the rock may have been used on ceremonial occasions to reenact the river's descent, with water flowing down the natural split in the rock.

ABOVE: The teeming carving, dense with animated and lifelike figures and animals, completely covers the vast boulder: a richly told story in an age when few were literate.

The unknown sculptor has given a personality to every one of the individual animals, humans, and gods shown in the complex scene. From a cat standing on one leg imitating the yogic pose of a nearby holy man, to a family of life-size elephants sheltering their young, they have a tender, lifelike quality that far surpasses most contemporary sculpture.

70 RESIDENCE

BIRKA

Lake Mälaren, Sweden
750

Archaeological finds at Birka, a small coastal town on Björkö Island, have thrown light on the thriving trade routes that crossed the Baltic Sea between the eighth and tenth centuries. Although the port had three harbors, its buildings were modest, with simple houses built from wood and earth. However, the luxurious grave goods found locally, in particular in the tomb of one female Viking warrior, included glass and silver from Arabia, silk textiles from the Near East, and ceramics from most of north and west Europe.

71 RELIGION AND MONUMENT

GREAT MOSQUE

Córdoba, Spain
784

After the Moorish conquest of Spain, the Umayyads, cast out of their previous capital, Damascus, set up a new state, Al-Andalus. They made Córdoba its capital, and put their stamp on the city. The first Great Mosque was built on a traditional rectangular basilica structure; over the next two centuries it was extended many times. With a prayer hall filled with columns, it remains a masterpiece of Islamic style, despite its ultimate change of use to a Christian cathedral.

72 RESIDENCE

HEIAN PALACE

Kyoto, Japan
c. 794

A large, rectangular building with deep eaves, the imperial Heian Palace was built to serve both as a home for the emperor and a center for government offices at a time when the new Heian Dynasty was looking to China for ways to centralize government, and had recently moved the capital from Nara to Kyoto. The palace burned down several times and was ultimately moved to a new site in Kyoto. The Heian Shrine, an 1895 replica of part of it, can still be visited nearby.

BELOW: The columns in the magnificent prayer hall were recycled from Roman buildings, used to support numerous symmetrical arches.

MONASTIR RIBAT

Monastir, Tunisia
796

Monastir's *ribat*, or fort, was the first built—by the Abbasid Caliphate—along the coast to guard against the possibility of invasion from the sea, about a century after Islamic forces had taken over the area. Its earliest incarnation was simple: a square with 108-foot sides, solid walls, towers at three corners and a much taller watchtower at the fourth. It was built by Harthama ibn A'yan, then leader of the Abbasid Caliphate. Other local ribats modeled on it soon sprang up, most notably that at Sousse, just 13 miles away, which was built around 30 years after the Monastir Ribat, but which has remained closer to its original form. The ribat at Monastir had two substantial medieval extensions. Small private rooms were included in these early ribats for the guards—who were expected to study the Quran—as well as men of the garrison.

BELOW: The earliest Islamic fort on the North African coast forms part of an impressive defense.

AACHEN CATHEDRAL

Germany
796 (completed 1215)

The oldest cathedral in northern Europe, commissioned by the first Holy Roman Emperor.

Charlemagne ruled over a large part of western Europe in the late eighth and early ninth centuries, becoming King of the Franks in 771, and the first Holy Roman Emperor in 800. He treated Aachen as his capital. The cathedral started life as the emperor's palace chapel, also known as the Palatine Chapel. It remains inextricably linked with him and is hugely significant in German history. Its architect, Odo of Metz, was inspired by San Vitale in Ravenna, creating an impressive eight-sided dome and cupola, and a rich interior full of gilding and mosaics. The cathedral contains Charlemagne's marble throne, which would be used for the coronations of all 31 German kings between 936 and 1531, and the emperor's remains—those that aren't serving as relics elsewhere—are still kept here, in a large gilded reliquary.

The cathedral was augmented by a Gothic choir and impressive stained glass in the fourteenth and fifteenth centuries. In the nineteenth century, a tower and spire were added.

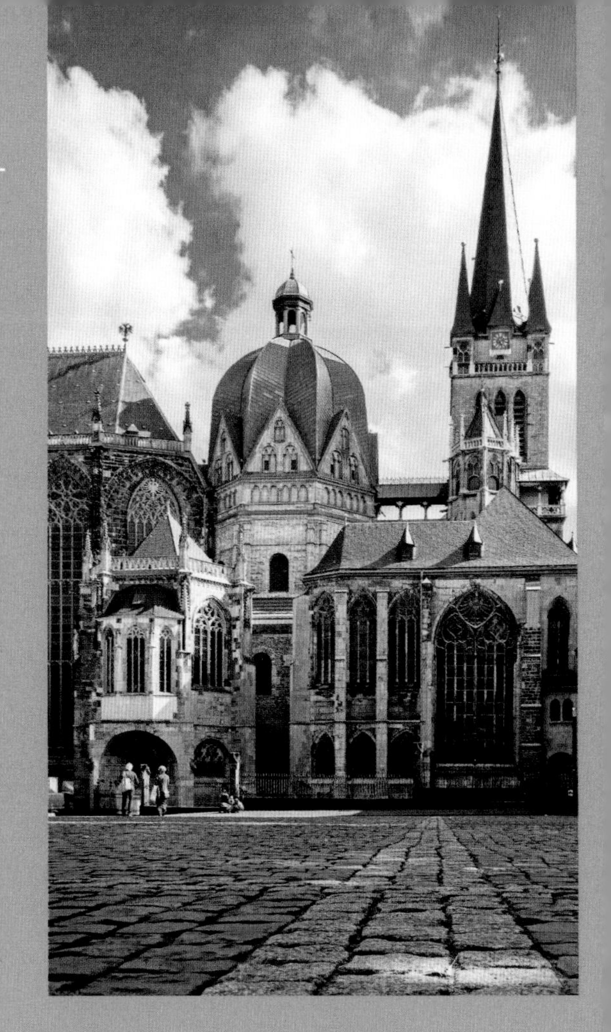

AACHEN CATHEDRAL
FLOOR PLAN

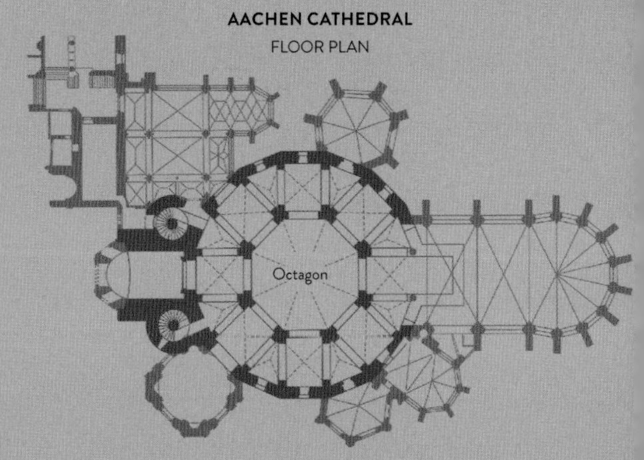

ABOVE AND RIGHT: The octagon core of Aachen Cathedral was built by Charlemagne, but complex later additions enlarged the Palatine Chapel that became the coronation church of German kings.

75 RESIDENCE

GOVERNOR'S PALACE, UXMAL

Yucatán, Mexico
c. 800

The Governor's Palace is the centerpiece in Uxmal, one of the great sites of the Mayan Classical Period. It is carved with numerous reliefs of the Mayan rain god Chaac, and may have been dedicated to him. Built on a raised platform, it is huge but low—an extended rectangle, each end separated from the main block by two triangular arches, unique in Mayan buildings and influential for many modern architects, Frank Lloyd Wright among them.

LEFT: The austere lines of the Governor's Palace have been cited as inspiration for many modernists.

76 RELIGION AND MONUMENT

ST. FIONAN'S MONASTERY

Skellig Michael, Ireland
c. 800

St. Fionan's Monastery on Skellig Michael, a rocky island located eight miles off the coast of County Kerry, was founded in the eighth or ninth century. It had residents until the thirteenth century, after which the monks left for the mainland and the island became a place of pilgrimage. This spartan existence was chosen by men who sought withdrawal from ordinary life, and was aggravated by regular Viking raids.

Over 600 rough steps led to six beehive huts, or *clochans*—living quarters—and two oratories for private prayer. All the structures were built on terraces dug from the rock and edged with stone. About a dozen monks and an abbot lived here, which also included a garden, cisterns to collect rainwater, and a graveyard. A small church was added in the eleventh century. The "beehives" were corbeled: constructed from flat stones laid in ever-decreasing circles, finished with a single stone across the top.

BOROBUDUR TEMPLE

Kedu Valley, Java
800

As the faithful climb upward, they are guided by the stories of the carvings from one plane of consciousness to the next.

Built by the Shailendra dynasty, Borobudur is the largest Buddhist temple in existence. It owes its state of preservation to the fact that it was buried under volcanic ash. The restored site is arranged to reflect the Buddhist concept of the cosmos, and laid out in the form of Buddhism's sacred flower, the lotus. The central temple consists of an immense pyramidal base, rising in terraces and topped by a vast bell-shaped stupa.

"All sentient beings are on false paths—Buddha shows them the right path."

The Flower Garland Sutra, scripture of Chinese Buddhism

BELOW: Pilgrims walked clockwise to ascend to the highest level of the temple, a symbolic journey of enlightenment.

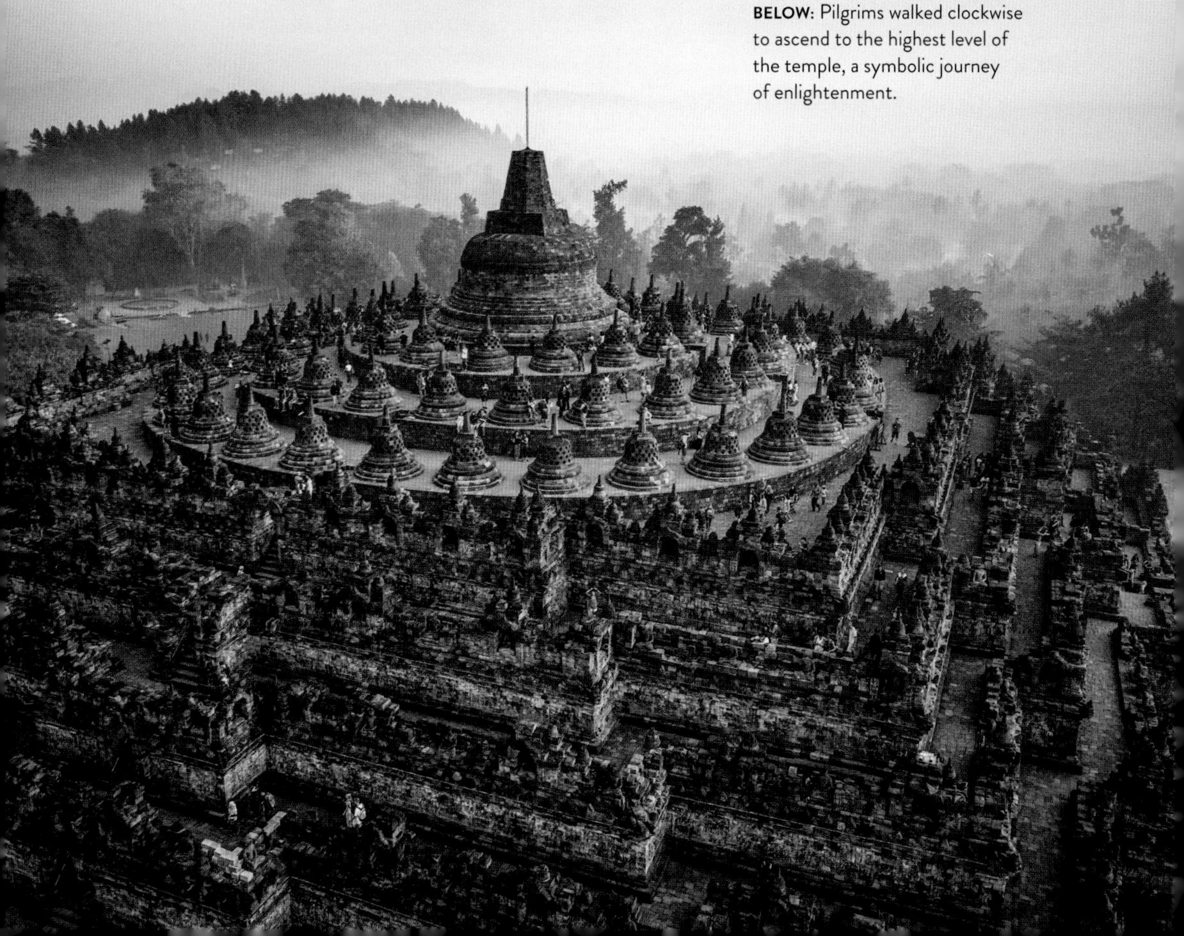

78 RELIGION AND MONUMENT

OSEBERG TOMB

Tonsberg, Norway
820

An extravagant ship burial found with its occupants and most of its contents intact.

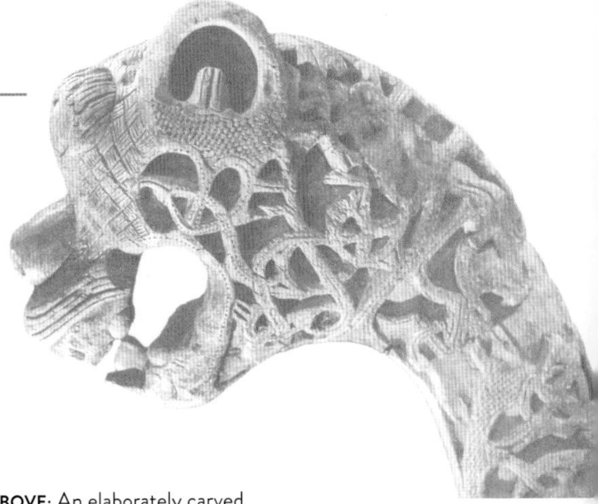

ABOVE: An elaborately carved animal head post from the contents of the Oseberg ship.

In Norse belief, boats carried their passengers to the afterlife, so ship burials were not unusual. The Oseberg Tomb, found in 1904, was one of the most important ever found in Norway.

The oak longship, or *karve*, is around 65 feet long and 16 feet wide. It is intricately carved with a prow in the form of a snake's head. It held two female bodies, laid on a bed under a wooden "tent." The damp earth preserved the wood well—not just the ship, but also an elaborate cart, three sleds, and many smaller pieces. The women—one over 70, the other around 50—have not been identified; they may have been related to one another, or one may have been the other's servant, sacrificed to the grave. The tomb had been robbed and no precious metals remained, but the other artifacts, valued belongings of a rich family, offered historians a huge amount of information about ninth-century Viking life.

ABOVE: The ship in 1904 as it was first uncovered by a team from Oslo's National Museum of Antiquities.

ABOVE: The Oseberg ship, on its way to the Bygdøy peninsula in Oslo, where it would eventually become the star exhibit in the Viking Ship Museum.

CHAN CHAN

Trujillo, Peru
850

An enigmatic citadel with strong links to the sea.

Chan Chan was the administrative center of the Chimú people, who held an area covering a large part of modern-day Peru between the ninth and fifteenth centuries. The huge adobe city includes nine "citadels," each built for a ruler, then abandoned when they died; the next ruler built their own. The Nik-An citadel, a late example, gives a sense of these structures in their heyday—most earlier ones have "melted" after centuries of heavy El Niño rains.

At Nik-An, a single gate through a 40-foot wall leads to two plazas, then to areas that were probably used as workshops and offices, and an immense reservoir. Different heights are separated by ramps, and relief friezes decorate the walls. Subjects include pelicans, fish, waves, and a diamond-lattice pattern which may represent fishing nets: the sea was important to the largely coastal Chimú, and Nik-An was probably dedicated to a sea deity.

BELOW: An aerial view of Chan Chan—a few surviving buildings give an idea of what was once a thriving fishing town close to the Pacific Ocean.

CHAND BAORI

Rajasthan, India
c. 850

A resourceful and elegant solution to storing water in a desert region.

Chand Baori, built in the ninth century in Abhaneri village, in Rajasthan, is not only the largest of around a thousand surviving stepwells, it is also the one of the most beautiful. "Baori" means stepwell, and "Chand" is for Raja Chanda, the king under whom it was built.

Today, stepwells are found mostly in India and Pakistan, where they were devised to ensure a supply of water in desert communities. Usually shaped like inverted pyramids, they're dug deep enough to extend down to the water table. They are constructed from porous stone, allowing water to seep through; at ground level, the wide mouths catch rare rainfall and subsequent runoff.

It is a 64-foot descent to the water at Chand Baori. On three walls, short flights of narrow steps are arranged in a sophisticated diamond pattern, adding up to 13 stories and 3,500 steps, divided at spots by recesses which could be used for shady rest, socialization, and religious ceremonies. The fourth side is occupied by an elaborate pavilion, reaching back into the rock face, originally used by ruling families as a retreat from the frying summer heat above.

Today, Chand Baori is primarily a tourist attraction, but in recent years historic stepwells have begun to be seen once again as the answer to local water shortages, and many that were once abandoned are being restored using traditional craftsmanship.

ABOVE: The pavilions on the stepwell's fourth side, always above water level, were used only by high-ranking families.

KNOWN FOR

- A standout example of an ancient architectural form
- Ingenious design applied to the practical problem of water storage in a desert climate
- Attracting renewed interest in the face of the challenges of climate change

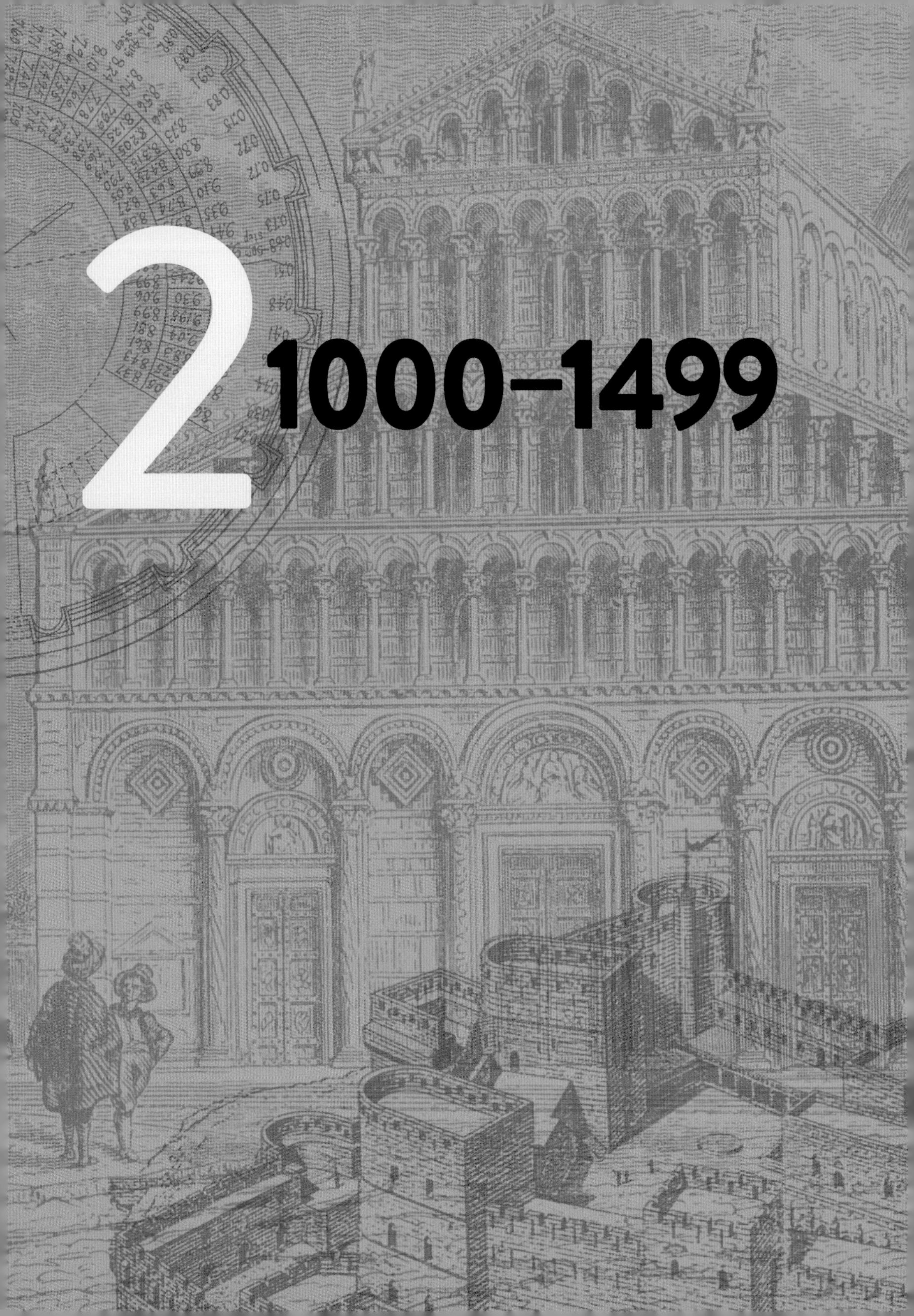

2 1000–1499

CHIEFTAIN'S HOUSE

Borg, Norway
c. 1000

The largest longhouse found in Scandinavia, home to local leaders over several centuries.

The Chieftain's House dates from the late Iron Age. It was found on Vestågøy, one of the Lofoten islands off Norway's west coast, in 1981.

The house measured 272 feet long, 39 feet wide, and 30 feet high. It was shaped like an inverted boat, with turf walls and a roof that was probably covered in wooden shingles, held up by posts. The space included living quarters, a great hall (used for communal feasting), and a byre area (for livestock), separated by partition walls. Shards of Rhineland pottery, pieces of glass, and gold-foil amulets found at the site indicate wealth. By the ninth century, Norwegians were trading extensively, finding markets for their own exports, including furs and iron. The house, in its various incarnations, had a long life and many chapters: a small version is thought to have been built in *c.* 500, which was enlarged in about 700, then abandoned early in the eleventh century, possibly because the islands' populations were growing and competition for resources was becoming too intense.

BELOW: This full-scale reconstruction of the Chieftain's House has been given a roof of wooden shingles, as speculated by archaeologists.

82 RESIDENCE

L'ANSE AUX MEADOWS

Newfoundland, Canada
c. 1000

The archaeological remains of eight buildings, made from wooden frames covered in turf, offer proof of transatlantic crossings in Viking times. The site, at the northern tip of Newfoundland, was uncovered in 1960. It was quickly identified as a Norse settlement; it appears to have been occupied for only a short period; it may have been a place where seafarers repaired their boats and restocked. It could also support the idea that the sagas of Erik the Red and Leif Erikson might have a basis in fact.

83 POLITICS AND NATIONAL DEFENSE

OCMULGEE EARTH LODGE

Macon, Georgia
1015

Earth lodges were built by the Mississippian people as centers for meetings and religious ceremonies. The lodge at Ocmulgee has been carbon-dated to the early eleventh century; although the wood and turf roof that can be seen today is a reconstruction, the inner structures are original. Around the internal wall, 47 earthen niches have been carved for seats, with another three on a raised platform in the symbolic shape of a bird of prey.

ABOVE: Over 800 objects were discovered at the site, including a whetstone, oil lamps, and bronze cloak pins.

ABOVE: The internal arrangements of this grass mound were rediscovered on excavation in 1934.

KRAK DES CHEVALIERS

Syria
1031

The great surviving fortress from the time of the Crusades.

Built for the Emir of Aleppo, Krak des Chevaliers passed to the Knights Hospitaller—the "holy warriors" of the Crusades—after the defeat of the emir in 1144. Its hilltop location meant that it could be defended from an attack from any direction. It was remodeled into one of the great medieval Crusader fortresses, with a structure of two concentric circles—an inner castle with an outer ring of massive walls, in some places 100 feet thick.

ABOVE: The massive outer walls, separated by some distance from the inner castle, made Krak des Chevaliers especially hard to breach.

BELOW: The high, remote situation ensures a 360-degree lookout for the approach of enemies.

HASTINGS CASTLE

Sussex, England
1066

One of the first of the motte-and-bailey castles, key to the success of the Norman invasion.

When William, Duke of Normandy, invaded England in 1066, he brought prefabricated wooden stockades aboard his ships. When his army arrived in Hastings, they used the local hilltop to set up a wooden motte-and-bailey structure. The motte was a steep hill, either natural or made from layers of soil and rubble, topped with a tower or keep. The bailey was a courtyard around the base, encircled by a palisade or wall. After the Saxons were defeated in the Battle of Hastings, the castle was rebuilt in stone and passed on to one of William's followers, but these quick-build motte-and-bailey castles were crucial to the Norman invasion's success. They were cheap, easy to defend, and could be strengthened or made more permanent as funds and labor became available. Between the Norman invasion in 1066 and his death in 1087, William the Conqueror built over 600 such castles in England.

ABOVE: In its first incarnation, Hastings Castle was just one of many quick-build forts with which William the Conqueror ensured victory over the Saxons.

ABOVE: Additional walls were built around the original Norman keep in medieval times, reinforcing it as a fortress.

86 RESIDENCE

TOWER OF LONDON

London, England
1078

William the Conqueror began building the castle that would become the Tower of London on a strategic site on the river Thames, near to London's port, in 1066. By 1078, the wooden building was being replaced with something permanent: the White Tower, a square Norman fortress built with imported Caen stone. Two further outer walls were added subsequently as reinforcement. By 1285, the layout was much as it remains today.

ABOVE: The city has been occupied for at least two millennia. The traditional style of the buildings makes it hard to date them precisely.

87 RESIDENCE

OLD CITY OF SANA'A

Yemen
Pre-1100

The tower houses of Yemen have been built in a similar style for centuries. They are raised from the inside, with the wooden joists of one floor providing scaffolding for the next. Between four and nine stories high, the lower floors are of stone, and the upper ones of pressed earth bricks—called *pisé*—and wood, with white patterns painted around the windows using gypsum. Sana'a is both an exceedingly ancient city and a particularly green one. Groups of traditional houses are constructed around gardens and plots designed for growing food. Sana'a is under a double threat: first, from the protracted civil war in Yemen; second, from climate change, which has led to severe rainy seasons, causing flash flooding.

ANGKOR WAT

Siem Riep, Cambodia

From 1100

Angkor Wat was built by Suryavarman II, king of the Cambodian Khmer dynasty, who planned to be interred there after his death. It is estimated to have taken over 30 years to build, and it covers more than 400 acres, laid out as a mirror of Mount Meru, the home of the Hindu gods. The temple towers symbolize the mountains of the gods' home, and a huge moat represents the sea that surrounds it. Almost every surface of the thousand or so buildings in the complex is intricately carved with depictions of gods, spirits, and animals.

At the end of the twelfth century, the Khmer kings converted from Hinduism to Buddhism, and Angkor transformed from Hindu temple to Buddhist shrine. The religious mix is still visible today.

BELOW: The largest religious building in the world, laid out to reflect the home of the gods.

HOUSE OF THE SAVIOR OF THE WORLD

Lalibela, Ethiopia
From 1100

A "new Jerusalem" built by a devout medieval king of Ethiopia.

Lalibela, in the Ethiopian highlands, is known for its eleven subterranean rock-cut churches. They are said to have been commissioned by King Gebre Mesqel Lalibela, after whom the town is named, who ruled between 1181 and 1221. The Christian king had previously made the pilgrimage to Jerusalem. However, after the Holy City fell to Saladin in 1187, his subjects could no longer do the same, so he modeled a new site on Jerusalem, as a local place of pilgrimage. Although some of the work at Lalibela has been dated a few decades earlier, there seems little doubt that the king was the prime mover in the ultimate scheme.

The churches are either rectangular or cruciform. They have been chiseled from the volcanic rock, working downward, with their roofs at ground level. Many names relate to places in Jerusalem, and the river crossing the site was christened the "Jordan." The block for each church was cut first, then hollowed out to make the interior. The slight slope on the roofs, together with drainage channels, prevents flooding in the rainy season.

The rectangular House of the Savior of the World is the largest on the site, at around 8,000 square feet. Barrel vaults have been created for decoration only—with no structural purpose—in a room cut from a single stone block. Details are precisely chiseled. Lalibela remains a popular site of pilgrimage for the Orthodox Ethiopian Church.

KNOWN FOR

- The world's largest monolithic churches, carved from solid blocks of stone
- The site's creation imitates the Holy City of Jerusalem
- Lalibela's status as a modern place of pilgrimage

"The ceiling or roof is all flat like the floor of the church, the sides also are worked in a fine fashion, also the windows and the doors with all the tracery . . . so that neither a jeweler in silver, nor a worker of wax . . . could do more work."

Father Francisco Alvarez, chaplain to the first Portuguese embassy in Ethiopia, c. 1540

RIGHT: Despite the architectural details, the church is really more like a sculpture, cut out from a block of stone.

90 RELIGION AND MONUMENT

OLD CATHEDRAL OF SALAMANCA

Spain
1102

Unusually, Salamanca has two cathedrals adjoining one another: the "new," built in the sixteenth century in late Gothic style, and the "old," the Cathedral of Santa Maria, founded at the beginning of the twelfth century. The Old Cathedral of Salamanca is particularly notable for its extraordinarily elaborate late Romanesque dome, the Torre de Gallo, which is roofed with hefty scalloped "tiles" of stone, and covered with a mass of minute detail that shows the influence of Byzantine architecture.

ABOVE: Despite its elaborate exterior detailing, the cathedral's interior is in plain Romanesque style.

91 RELIGION AND MONUMENT

PANTHEON OF THE KINGS OF LEÓN

León, Spain
1150

A part of the Basilica of San Isidoro, an important stop on the Santiago pilgrimage route, this vaulted Romanesque space is the burial chapel of the kings of León. It is a rare survival of a complete scheme, including pillars with elaborately carved capitals, and murals from the twelfth century showing episodes from the life of Christ, from the Annunciation to the Resurrection, in an exceptional state of preservation.

ABOVE: The paintings in the Pantheon are in quite exceptional condition, retaining all their bright original colors.

92 POLITICS AND NATIONAL DEFENSE

CITADEL OF CAIRO

Egypt
1176

Also known as the Citadel of Saladin, the castle sits on a naturally defended position—a limestone spur of land on the Mokattam Hill. It began life as a heavily fortified castle to repel the Crusaders. It would long outlast Saladin—it remained the seat of power for Egypt's rulers for the next seven centuries; it wasn't until the 1870s that they moved to a new palace in downtown Cairo.

ABOVE: View of Cairo in the nineteenth century, looking from Mokattam Hill down to the citadel, with the Muhammad Ali Mosque behind.

93 RESIDENCE

MESA VERDE CLIFF PALACE

Montezuma County, Colorado
1190

Cliff Palace was built in the late twelfth century by the Ancestral Puebloans—a Native American culture—in southwest Colorado. Sited under a dramatic cliff overhang, it consists of around 150 square rooms. They are constructed from wooden beams and sandstone blocks, mortared together and painted with colored earth washes. There are also 23 *kivas*—sunken, circular pits that were used for religious rituals and social group meetings. The palace was abandoned about a century later, possibly due to a prolonged drought.

ABOVE: The simple, single-room stone dwellings of the Cliff Palace were occupied by a community estimated at around 700 people.

MINARET OF JAM

Ghor Province, Afghanistan
1190

The splendid 210-foot minaret is one of the few remnants of Firuzkuh, the great capital city from which the Gurid dynasty ruled Afghanistan and parts of northern India in the twelfth and thirteenth centuries. It is set on an octagonal base, and ornamented with elaborate bands of geometric pattern and blue-glazed calligraphic verses from the Quran. After the Gurids were overthrown by the Mongols, the city was destroyed and looted; little remains today.

95 RELIGION AND MONUMENT

ALHAMBRA

Andalucia, Spain
From 1200

The Alhambra is both a palace and a fortress; it has a spectacular position on a plateau above the city of Granada. It was built by the Nasrid dynasty, Moorish rulers of Spain, to serve as a private residence and a center for court life and government administration. Its architecture and decoration represent a high point in Islamic art: the Palacios Nazaríes, the least-altered part of a subsequently much-enlarged complex, showcases an extraordinary spectrum of refined carving, tiling, stucco, waterways, and fountains.

LEFT: Isolated today, the minaret was originally in the center of a city on a thriving trade route.

96 POLITICS AND NATIONAL DEFENSE

EDINBURGH CASTLE

Scotland
From 1200

The fortress that was also the longtime home to Scottish royalty.

Its setting on a high crag, named Castle Rock, gives Edinburgh Castle good natural defenses. The mighty stone walls that enclose its large complex of buildings were built from the beginning of the thirteenth century onward, and have been much adapted and reinforced. A major royal residence between the late twelfth and mid-seventeenth centuries, it was a prize exchanged many times in battles between the English and the Scots.

ABOVE AND RIGHT: The castle predates the city below. Inside the walls, St. Margaret's Chapel dates back to the early twelfth century.

MAP OF THE CASTLE IN 1886

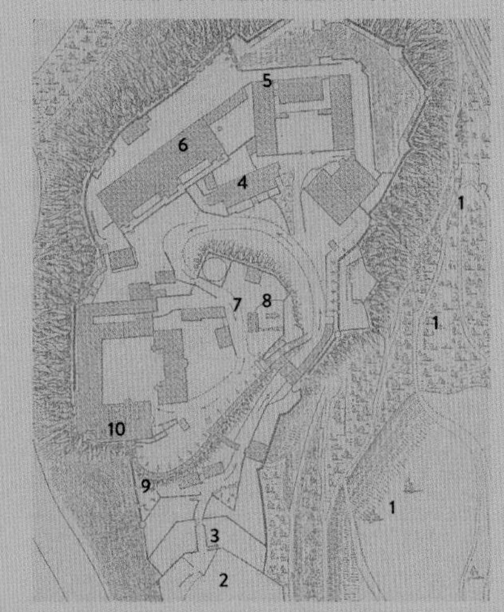

1 Princes West Gardens
2 Esplanade
3 Moat, drawbridge, and gatehouse
4 Governor's House
5 Armory and principal magazine
6 Barracks
7 St. Margaret's Chapel
8 Mons Meg
9 David's Tower
10 Old Palace

97 RESIDENCE AND NATIONAL DEFENSE

ACOMA PUEBLO

Albuquerque, New Mexico
c. 1200

Believed to be the oldest continuously inhabited pueblo in North America, Acoma Pueblo—"Sky City"—has had a community living there since between 1150 and 1250 (records vary). Sited on the top of a 357-foot-high mesa, the only access was by a stone staircase cut into the cliff. The town resisted Spanish invasion but was overcome with savagery. As a result, in 1629 a church, convent, and cemetery were forcibly built on the mesa.

BELOW: The natural defenses of the site did not prove adequate against the Spanish incomers.

98 RELIGION AND MONUMENT

CHINGUETTI

Mauritania
c. 1200

The Saharan town of Chinguetti is a *ksour*—a rest stop for trade caravans crossing the desert—and also a gathering place for Sunni pilgrims on their way to Mecca, giving it an important role as an Islamic religious center. Its mosque is built from drystone slabs without mortar, like much of the rest of the old city, and has a square minaret with turreted corners. Chinguetti also became known for its private libraries—collections of ancient manuscripts held by families, which had been copied by pilgrims and Islamic scholars passing through.

BELOW: The megaphone used for a modern call to prayer sits oddly among the traditional ostrich-egg finials on the mosque.

THE VATADAGE

Polonnaruwa, Sri Lanka
c. 1200

A shrine believed to have housed two of the most holy relics of the Buddha.

SITE PLAN

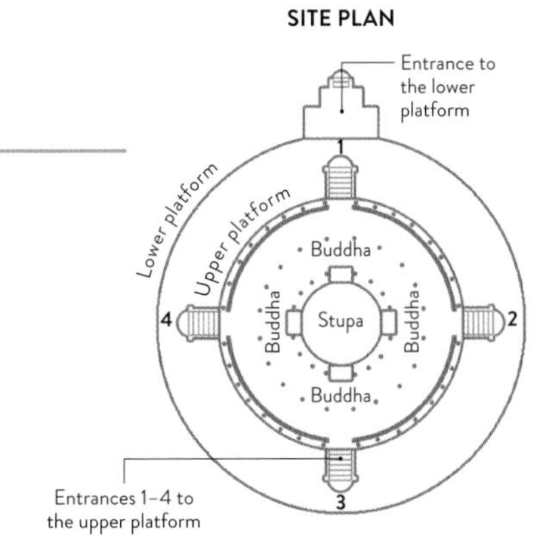

The Vatadage is one of the most sacred of a group of temples in the Old City of Polonnaruwa, capital of Sri Lanka until the early thirteenth century. Built by one king and heavily adapted by his successor, it housed one of the most sacred relics possible—a tooth from the Buddha himself. The tooth was venerated because it was believed that it conferred power on its possessor. In 1190, a second important relic was enshrined at Polonnaruwa: Buddha's alms bowl.

On a double plinth with two flights of stairs, a circular brick enclosure holds a central stupa, with four seated Buddhas around it. The stupa originally had a wooden roof, and a second floor to house the relics. At the beginning of the thirteenth century, the Vatadage was gradually abandoned. By the 1230s, Buddha's tooth had been moved, as had the seat of the new ruler, to Dambadeniya, now the island's capital.

BELOW: Statues of the Buddha face each entrance to the upper platform, which gives access to the stupa, or shrine.

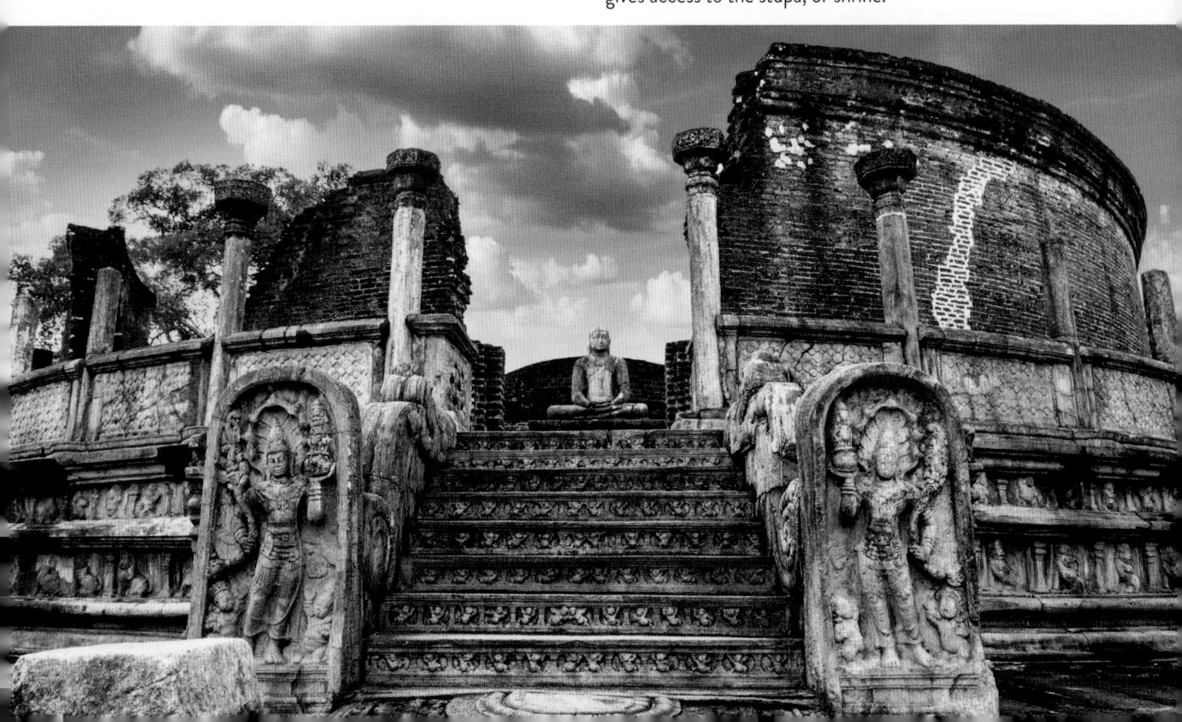

100 RESIDENCE

CASA GRANDE RUINS

Pinal County, Arizona
c. 1200

Casa Grande, the Great House, measuring 60 feet by 40 feet at the base, and rising to four stories in the center, is the largest surviving structure in a compound built by the early Ancient Sonoran Desert peoples who farmed this area of present-day Arizona. It's positioned within a vast and carefully planned irrigation system, so it may have been used as a center from which its builders could manage the fertility of their crops.

ABOVE: Casa Grande's protective roof was built in 1932, designed by the distinguished landscape architect Frederick Law Olmsted.

101 RELIGION AND MONUMENT

GEUNGNAKJEON

Andong, South Korea
c. 1200

Geungnakjeon (the Hall of Nirvana), in the Bongjeongsa temple complex, is believed to be the oldest wooden building surviving in Korea. Built during the Koryo Dynasty, it is a simple rectangular structure with an extended roof and deep eaves, enabled by column-head bracketing (sets of brackets mounted directly onto the heads of supporting columns, which enhance a building's bearing capacity), a design element influenced by contemporary Chinese architecture.

ABOVE: The elaborate brackets at Geungnakjeon are intricately painted with protective symbols.

102 RELIGION AND MONUMENT

MALAE HEIAU

Kauai, Hawaii
c. 1200

Open-air temples built for the gods of Hawaiian mythology.

Heiaus are ancient Hawaiian temples: each built for a specific use, each designed for specific people, each composed of a number of different elements. Malae Heiau is the largest of four temples, located close to one another, making up the Wailua complex. Dated to the beginning of the thirteenth century, it is a *luakini heiau*—a site dedicated to Ku, the god of war—at which sacrifices, either human or animal, might be made. As such, it could only be constructed and used by the senior chief, or *ali'i 'ai moku*, of the island.

Although Malae Heiau is ruined now, its remains are impressive in scale, covering almost two acres. It consisted of a raised platform, with an inner boundary wall 10 feet high, with stone seats around the inside. Rituals here would probably also have incorporated carved figures of the gods.

ABOVE: Watercolor drawing of a *heiau*—or temple—in use, painted by John Webber, who traveled with Captain James Cook in the 1770s.

SUN TEMPLE, KONÂRAK

Odisha, India
1250

The sun god's chariot is minutely depicted alongside scenes from the royal life of an earthly king.

Dedicated to Surya, the Hindu sun god, the temple is a complex piece of thirteenth-century Orissan architecture. Commissioned by Narasimhadeva I of the Eastern Ganga dynasty, it consists of an entrance porch, a prayer hall, and the shrine itself, with a separate dancing hall, all raised on a stone plinth. The shrine has a stepped pyramid roof, but the bulk of the building has been carved to imitate Surya's mythical chariot, with 12 pairs of wheels carved in relief along its sides, and seven huge horses to pull it (only one of the latter survives). Every surface is minutely carved—between the wheels, bands of decoration show scenes of royal life as well as dancing girls and amorous couples. Depictions of Surya are interspersed with carvings relating to Narasimhadeva himself. The temple seems to reflect on the king who commissioned it as much as on the god to whom it is dedicated.

BELOW: The "chariot" appears to be pulled on the realistically carved wheels—covered, like the rest of the temple, with decorative detailing.

104 RESIDENCE

LELUH CITY RUINS

Lelu Island, Micronesia
1250

Lelu Island sits enclosed in a bay of the larger island of Kosrae. The extensive but overgrown ruins of the buildings it once housed are made of a mixture of coral and basalt. Travelers' accounts from as late as the eighteenth century told of a complex city with individual family compounds, a canal network, and pyramid-shaped tombs. Coral dating places it back as far as the thirteenth century, but more archaeological investigation is needed to uncover its secrets.

105 RELIGION AND MONUMENT

ROYAL TOMBS OF LAPAHA

Mu'a, Tonga
1250

The Royal Tombs are located near the sea, close to the old town of Lapaha, now Mu'a. The kings of what was known as the Maritime Empire, the Tu'i Tonga dynasty, ruled from *c.* 1200 to the beginning of the nineteenth century, and most of the 39 chiefs from that period are buried here.

The tombs—called *langi*—were used only for members of the royal family, and are large, shallow pyramid structures, with three deep steps made from huge slabs. Weighing as much as 50 tons each, they were quarried in different coastal sites around Tonga and transported to the graveyard by canoe. The body was interred under the platform, while the spirit was held to rest on top. Ceremonies for members of the royal family are still held under canopies on the original platforms.

BELOW: The ceremonial graveyard of both ancient and contemporary Tongan royalty.

106 RESIDENCE

GEDI RUINS

Malindi, Kenya
1250

The remains of a sophisticated medieval town in coastal Kenya, set deep in the forest.

The ruins at Gedi are within the protected reserve of the Arabuko-Sokoke forest. One of a number of medieval Swahili sites along the Kenyan coast, Gedi has been extensively excavated since its "rediscovery" in the 1920s, revealing a well-developed town. An inner enclosure contained single-story coral-stone buildings—including courtyard houses, a more extensive "palace," and several mosques, one with a deep well—while an outer enclosure had simpler structures. Outside both are the remains of more impermanent dwellings.

The people here had extensive trading links, as remains of all kinds, including imported Chinese porcelain, Islamic pottery, beads, and coins have been found. A handful of pillar tombs—carved bases topped by a single pillar, in a specifically Swahili style—helped date the site, taking it back to at least the mid-thirteenth century, and possibly earlier.

ABOVE: The reason that the medieval town of Gedi was abandoned is unknown; it seems to have taken place over a short period in the mid-1600s.

107 POLITICS AND NATIONAL DEFENSE

CASTEL DEL MONTE

Apulia, Italy
1250

Built by Emperor Frederick II, Castel del Monte is a curious hybrid. The exterior, a rigorously geometric octagon with eight towers and a formal pedimented entrance, appears to be a fortress, yet it has none of the defenses—moat, drawbridge, ditch—typical of the mid-thirteenth century, and the interior was designed more like a luxurious hunting lodge, with fireplaces in every room, marble detailing, and some very early flushing lavatories.

ABOVE: The courtyard of Castel del Monte is open to the sky, while the rooms link through passages on the upper floors.

108 RELIGION AND MONUMENT

CHARTRES CATHEDRAL

France
1252

The earlier Romanesque cathedral burned down in 1194, leaving the way clear for a completely new Gothic building. This was built extraordinarily fast, at a time when large buildings could take centuries, meaning that the entire scheme—the soaring, airy architecture, the huge quantity of sculpture (both incorporated and freestanding), and 130 stained-glass windows—has a rare cohesion, resulting in an undisputed Gothic masterpiece.

ABOVE: The Gothic stained glass that survives at Chartres is of unparalleled quality.

109 RESIDENCE

KUBLAI KHAN'S SUMMER PALACE

Shangdu, Inner Mongolia
1263

KUBLAI KHAN

A fabled but short-lived city, where Mongol and Chinese cultures mingled.

Grandson of Genghis Khan, Kublai Khan was the first ruler of China who was not Han Chinese. When he moved the country's capital to a site on the edge of the Mongolian steppe, he planned a city that combined elements of Mongol and Chinese life. The result, Shangdu (also called Xanadu), was based around a Chinese square plan, with an inner city housing the palace, temples, and other official buildings, and an outer city for the majority of its citizens. Travelers' tales about Shangdu, with its gardens, pavilions, canals, and Mongolian-inspired hunting grounds, made the city the stuff of legend. Six centuries later, the Romantic poet Samuel Taylor Coleridge would immortalize Xanadu and its creator for a new audience with his poem "Kubla Khan."

Although its role as capital was short-lived, its mild climate kept Shangdu popular as a retreat during the summer months. However, in 1369 it was invaded by Ming forces, who would bring the Mongol Yuan Dynasty to an end. By the early fifteenth century, it was abandoned. Today, only the outlines of foundations remain.

ABOVE: Archaeologists have traced some of the legendary features of Shangdu from the outlines it left on the landscape; sadly, this is all that remains.

ŌTUATAUA STONEFIELDS

New Zealand
1300

The adaptations made by skilled gardeners to meet the challenges of a new country.

Around 750 years ago, when the first settlers from East Polynesia arrived in New Zealand, they found their traditional crops didn't thrive in the cooler conditions of their new country. The Ōtuataua Stonefields, near Auckland, revealed to archaeologists how these skilled gardeners solved the problem. Raised mounds of fertile, volcanic soil were made into impromptu walls to shelter the crops, to help retain moisture, and to warm the earth, helping yams and taro to thrive in the shorter, colder local summers.

They also developed storage pits—of which only the outlines remain—used to keep crops such as sweet potatoes, which would have overwintered in the ground in Polynesia, but which would rot in colder, damper New Zealand.

BELOW: The Stonefields show evidence of a skilled gardening culture—the methods used to support tender cropping plants echo those still used widely today.

111 RESIDENCE

CHUXI TULOU

Fujian Province, China
1300

Tulous are the fortified dwellings of the Hakka people. They take the form of ring-shaped structures built on stone foundations with earthen walls above. Each houses a family group, with shared space in the center and living quarters on the upper floors. The Chuxi Tulou cluster is one of the oldest and least-altered groups to survive. It consists of 36 individual tulous, many of them still inhabited, although mostly by the older generation, as the younger Hakka travel to the cities to work.

ABOVE: The tulous are some of the oldest continuously used dwellings in China.

112 RELIGION AND MONUMENT

DJINGUEREBER MOSQUE

Timbuktu, Mali
1327

Returning from a pilgrimage to Mecca, the gold-rich Musa I of Mali endowed Timbuktu with enough money to build mosques and found a university, gaining it a reputation as a city of devout learning. Despite its longevity, the mosque is simply built from earth, strengthened with straw and wood. Smooth, rounded outlines are achieved by coating a structure of earth bricks with layers of mud and letting them dry. Skilled craftsmen maintain the building annually, using traditional techniques.

ABOVE: Applying the mud "dressing" so that the building maintains its outlines is a skilled job.

113 RESIDENCE

DOGE'S PALACE

Venice, Italy
1340

The familiar pink colonnaded building that overlooks the water on St. Mark's Square was the seat of government when Venice had become, through trade, the richest city-state in Europe. Not only does the Venetian Gothic palace house the doge's—or leader's—private quarters, but it also homed the Great Council (Venice's parliament) and the city's judicial chambers, all under one roof.

114 RELIGION AND MONUMENT

ST. MARY'S CHURCH, ASHWELL

Hertfordshire, England
1350

St. Mary's is notable for its graffiti, offering a rare informal glimpse into daily concerns of the fourteenth century. Surviving artwork includes a sketch of old St. Paul's in London, long since burned down, rude remarks about neighbors and local clergy and, poignantly, from 1350, the year the Black Death killed 35 percent of England's population, a message in Latin which, translated, reads, "Miserable, wild, distracted. The dregs of the people alone survive."

ABOVE: An oil painting of 1706–8 by Luca Carlevarijs shows crowds assembling at the Doge's Palace as the French ambassador arrives.

THE GREAT ENCLOSURE, GREAT ZIMBABWE

Masvingo, Zimbabwe
c. 1350

The impressive remains of the largest medieval stone city built in sub-Saharan Africa.

Part of a monumental city built by the Shona people, which was continuously occupied between the eleventh and the mid-fifteenth century, the Great Enclosure was built during the site's later period. It's not known for certain what purpose its massive stone walls (33 feet high in places) served, although it's speculated that an immense tower was probably used as a granary. The symmetrical, smooth-cut and mortar-free masonry shows impressive stonecutting skills, and it has been estimated that the Great Enclosure may have taken as long as a century to build. The archaeological finds around the site include a good many metal items—both practical and decorative—and many animal bones, supporting archaeologists' belief that the economic wealth of the Shona builders of Great Zimbabwe came from the breeding and trading of cattle.

BELOW: From the early sixteenth century, Portuguese travelers—tracking the area's legendary gold trade—were impressed by the kingdom they found at Great Zimbabwe.

116 PLACE OF WORK

KHAN AL-MIRJAN

Baghdad, Iraq
1359

A *khan* is a hostel for travelers, and Khan al-Mirjan was built by Baghdad's governor at a time when the city was a major trading center. It is simply built, using brick and wood, but to an elegant design. The central courtyard is roofed with transverse vaulting—an innovation, as usually they were open to the air. Many windows ensure the inner space is very light. Individual rooms lead off the central hall on the ground floor and off a mezzanine on the level above.

The khan's most recent incarnations have been as a museum and restaurant. Currently the city's plan is to restore it as a center and library for building conservation and archaeology.

ABOVE: A spacious fourteenth-century caravanserai—like a roadside inn—surviving in the middle of modern Baghdad.

117 ART AND CULTURE

AL-QARAWIYYIN LIBRARY

Fez, Morocco
c. 1359

Freshly renovated in 2017, the halls, courtyards and arches of the fourteenth-century library are open to scholars again, as they have been for over 600 years. It houses some of the most important Islamic manuscripts in the world, many collected at the time of their writing.

The library was founded in 859 by Fatima al-Fihri, daughter of a Tunisian merchant; she was highly educated for a contemporary woman, and dedicated to broadening education in her community. When she inherited her father's fortune, she opened a mosque incorporating a religious institute and university. Her diploma, on a wooden board, is still on display.

ABOVE: An ancient library that is part of the oldest university in the world.

118 RELIGION AND MONUMENT

LEANING TOWER OF PISA

Italy
1372

Pisa's best-known architectural landmark.

The campanile of Pisa Cathedral is most famous for its tilt—almost four degrees off vertical. It took 200 years to build. Even by 1178, when the second floor was completed, it had a pronounced lean, a problem caused by soft ground and unstable foundations, and one which only worsened after its completion in 1372. The tilt hit 5.5 degrees in the 1990s, leading to urgent underpinning that corrected the angle slightly and stabilized the tower—for now, at least.

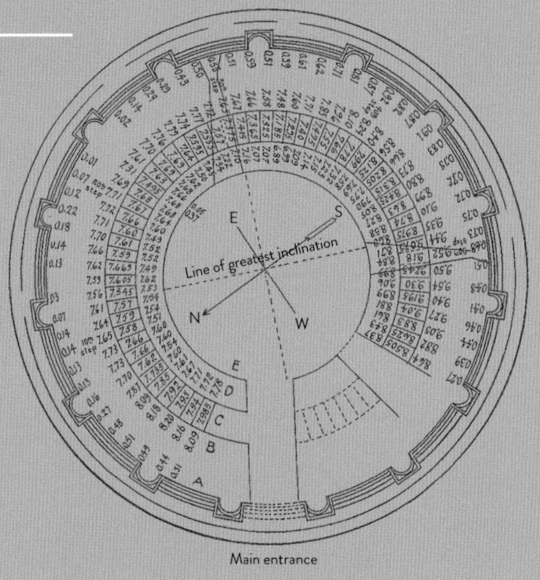

TOWER INCLINATION IN 1817

TOP: Depicted in the early nineteenth century, the tower reached its most extreme angle after 1838, when a shallow diagnostic trench caused it to lean even more. It remained standing. It was closed between 1990 and 2001, allowing structural engineers to anchor the structure without correcting its tourist-pleasing tilt.

119 PLACE OF WORK

TOWN HALL

Bruges, Belgium
1376

Until the late fourteenth century, the town halls of the self-governing cities of the Low Countries had tended to be plain and practical. The new town hall of Bruges, replacing an earlier building that had fallen into disrepair, broke the mold. Flamboyant and fashionable, it was a highly visible expression of the city's standing. Beneath a steep-pitched roof with spiked turrets, the tall, narrow windows of the facade were divided by three levels of paired niches holding statues of both biblical figures and prominent contemporary aristocrats. Inside, the Great Hall offered a suitably imposing space for meetings of the city council.

ABOVE: The late Gothic tour de force that set a new standard for civic architecture in northern Europe.

120 PLACE OF WORK

GEUNJEONGJEON HALL

Seoul, South Korea
1395

This is the audience hall of the great Gyeongbokgung Palace, which was built by the first emperor of the Joseon dynasty when the capital of Korea moved to Hanyang, now Seoul. Raised on a two-tier stone platform, the two-story building has the deep eaves and gentle roof sweep characteristic of Korean architecture, and a richly painted interior centering on the emperor's throne. Destroyed twice by fire, the first of which was during the Imjin wars with Japan in the sixteenth century, it has been meticulously reconstructed.

ABOVE: At the time it was built, the hall's main function was as a throne room, where the emperor held audiences.

MOAI

Rapa Nui (Easter Island), Polynesia
c. 1400

Depleted natural resources may answer the questions surrounding the enigmatic moai.

Archaeologists believe that the first humans to arrive on Rapa Nui were other Polynesians, although they haven't traced precisely from where. The vast stone figures, or *moai*, were part of an ancestor cult. They were carved over a long period—beginning around 1000 and ending completely in the sixteenth century—but reached a peak between the beginning of the thirteenth and the end of the fourteenth century.

KNOWN FOR

- A unique expression of ancestor worship
- Five centuries of artistic development within one expressive form
- A location where many enigmas—including *rongorongo*, a system of glyphs—remain to be solved

The finest completed examples had rusty-colored topknots made from red scoria, a local stone, and eye details made from white coral and black obsidian; at some point they had clearly been mounted on *ahu*, or platforms. But many half-finished moai were abandoned at the quarry on the side of Rano Raraku volcano, where they were carved. One theory explaining this is that as the island's limited natural resources, in particular wood, were exhausted and life became hard, the population turned from ancestor worship to a new set of beliefs revolving around a birdman cult. This may explain why so many statues had been toppled from their ahu, and also why some of the later examples have elaborate reliefs of birdmen carved on their backs, possibly during an interim period as one belief was exchanged for another.

LEFT: Many partially carved figures were found at a quarry site; some had been completed but had been toppled from their platforms.

RIGHT: Today, large numbers of the moai stand upright once more, although most are missing their contrasting red scoria topknots.

"We could hardly conceive how these islanders, wholly unacquainted with any mechanical power, could raise such stupendous figures . . ."

Captain James Cook, 1774

TANAH LOT TEMPLE

Bali, Indonesia
1400

A small sea temple with a legendary past.

Legend has it that the wooden temple complex of Tanah Lot was founded by Dang Hyang Nirartha, a holy man from Java who attained the high rank of royal priest during the late fifteenth century, and who oversaw a number of religious changes and reforms. Tanah Lot is a small rocky outcrop about 100 feet off the coast, accessible by foot at low tide. Nirartha fought his opponents here, casting off his sash, which turned into protective sea snakes, and successfully built a temple. That's the legend; in fact, the temple probably dates from a few decades before Nirartha's arrival in Bali. Nonetheless, the connection has made the temple, in its undeniably romantic setting, one of the holiest in Bali—and one of the most photographed by tourists. It is one of a string of seven sea temples, believed to give the island a ring of spiritual protection.

BELOW: Over time, the causeway that had once connected Tanah Lot to the mainland eroded and it became an island.

ULUGH BEG OBSERVATORY

Samarkand, Uzbekistan
1420

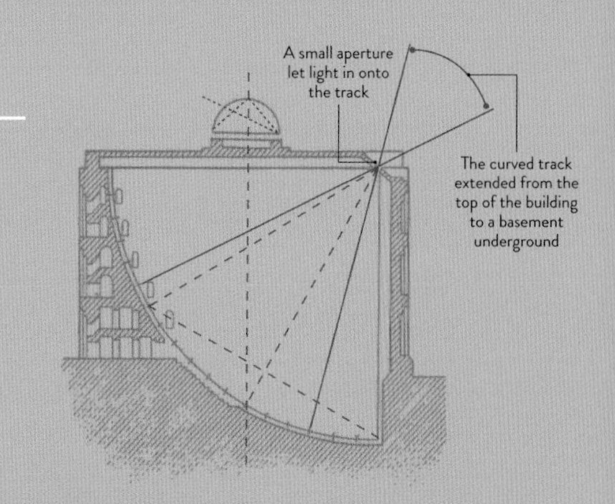
A small aperture let light in onto the track
The curved track extended from the top of the building to a basement underground

A medieval ruler's astronomical masterwork, rediscovered in modern times.

Ulugh Beg was a grandson of Tamerlane the Great, but his legacy is that of a scholar rather than a king. After a reign of just two years (he was assassinated on the orders of his own son in 1449), his observatory, on a hill outside Samarkand, was forgotten and fell into ruin; it was only rediscovered in 1908.

A round building, three stories high, it contained an immense marble arc or quadrant, the lower part cut out of the ground, the upper supported with brick pillars. Within it, a track marked with degrees and seconds was used to measure the angle of elevation of bright stars. The arc, only part of which survives, was so accurate that its readings come within a modern margin of error. Other instruments are only known through contemporary description, although Ulugh Beg's catalog of stars, transcribed during his life, outlived him.

"Another of Ulugh Beg Mirza's fine buildings is an observatory, that is an instrument for writing astronomical tables . . ."

Emperor Babur, writing of the achievements of Ulugh Beg

ABOVE: Ulugh Beg understood the importance of mounted astronomical instruments. The sextant measured the angle of elevation of the stars when their light shone through a narrow opening and hit its track, which was marked with degrees and minutes.

124 RESIDENCE AND PLACE OF WORK

FORBIDDEN CITY

Beijing, China
1420

After staging a coup, the Ming emperor Zhu Di moved China's capital to Beijing, where he built a huge palace complex, the Forbidden City, to consolidate his power. It would remain the seat of power for 24 emperors of the Ming and subsequent Qing dynasties. The outer court was dedicated to state affairs, while the inner was the imperial family's home. Between them, they contained 90 individual compounds, every building assigned a specific function within a rigorous hierarchy.

BELOW: The Forbidden City was painted red; in China, red is the color associated with power and wealth.

125 PLACE OF WORK

LAKENHALLE

Ghent, Belgium
1425

Cloth production made Ghent rich, and the Lakenhalle was planned as an imposing center for the trade—big enough for large groups to display their wares, and for inspectors to quality-check cloth. Its timing was off, however; the fine Gothic hall was still incomplete when, in the late 1430s, the boom market began to tail off, and it was never fully used for its intended purpose, housing other businesses instead, including a fencing school.

126 INFRASTRUCTURE AND INNOVATION

IL DUOMO

Florence, Italy
1436

The Gothic cathedral in Florence was already built when a competition for a dome to complete it was held. The winner, Filippo Brunelleschi, wasn't an architect by trade; many were skeptical that his design would succeed, on a site without either flying buttresses or internal supports. His innovative solution was to make a double dome, the internal one built with vertical reinforcing ribs to support the outer. The result gave the cathedral the name, il Duomo, by which it has been known ever since.

ABOVE: Brunelleschi studied Roman methods of construction to help him create the innovative il Duomo.

127 RESIDENCE

TRULLI HOUSES OF ALBEROBELLO

Puglia, Italy
1450

Dating from the mid-fifteenth century, a *trullo* is a round drystone building with a conical corbel roof, made by laying stones in increasingly smaller circles. Alberobello still has a high number of them—originally used for storehouses, the form became popular for homes when labor was cheap and materials expensive. At a time when houses were taxed, trulli could be deconstructed before a visit from the inspector, then rebuilt afterward.

ABOVE: Quick-build houses, originally devised to avoid taxes by being swiftly taken down, have become a mainstay of modern tourism in Puglia.

128 RESIDENCE/RELIGION AND MONUMENT

COUR ROYALE DE TIÉBÉLÉ

Nahouri, Burkina Faso
c. 1450

An intricately decorated ancestral village for the chiefs of the Kassena people.

The Kassena have been settled in this part of Burkina Faso, near the border with Ghana, since the mid-fifteenth century. The royal court at Tiébélé, where many Kassena people—including members of the royal family—still live, is a bravura example of their traditional architecture and its decoration. Enclosed within a low, circular wall, the houses were traditionally made of a cob mixture of straw, mud, and animal dung. They were usually windowless, with small doors and thick walls, both to keep the interiors cool and to provide shelter in times of war. The exteriors are covered in complex designs in shades of ocher, black, and white, specific to each house and family group. These are painted by the Kassena women in an annual ritual, renewed each year at the start of the dry season. Their symbolic content ranges from geometric designs to crocodiles and snakes (both considered lucky), and stylized human figures.

ABOVE: The different patterns and symbols on the buildings of the Cour Royale mark individual family groups.

PORTUGUESE CHURCH

Gorée Island, Senegal
c. 1450

The first European building on a rocky island that would become an infamous center of the slave trade.

Mural on the museum wall

The first church on Gorée Island, just off Dakar, on the Senegalese coast, was built in 1450, six years after the Portuguese discovered it in 1444. Alongside it, they built a graveyard and warehouses and began to trade. Today, a post office stands on the site of that first church; after the first European contact, the island constantly changed hands, first between the Portuguese and the Dutch, and then between France and England. It quickly became infamous as a center for the slave trade; the first official records of enslaved people being sold there date from 1536. In 1776, the House of Slaves, where slaves were kept during the wait, was built and the trade only came to an end on the island in 1815.

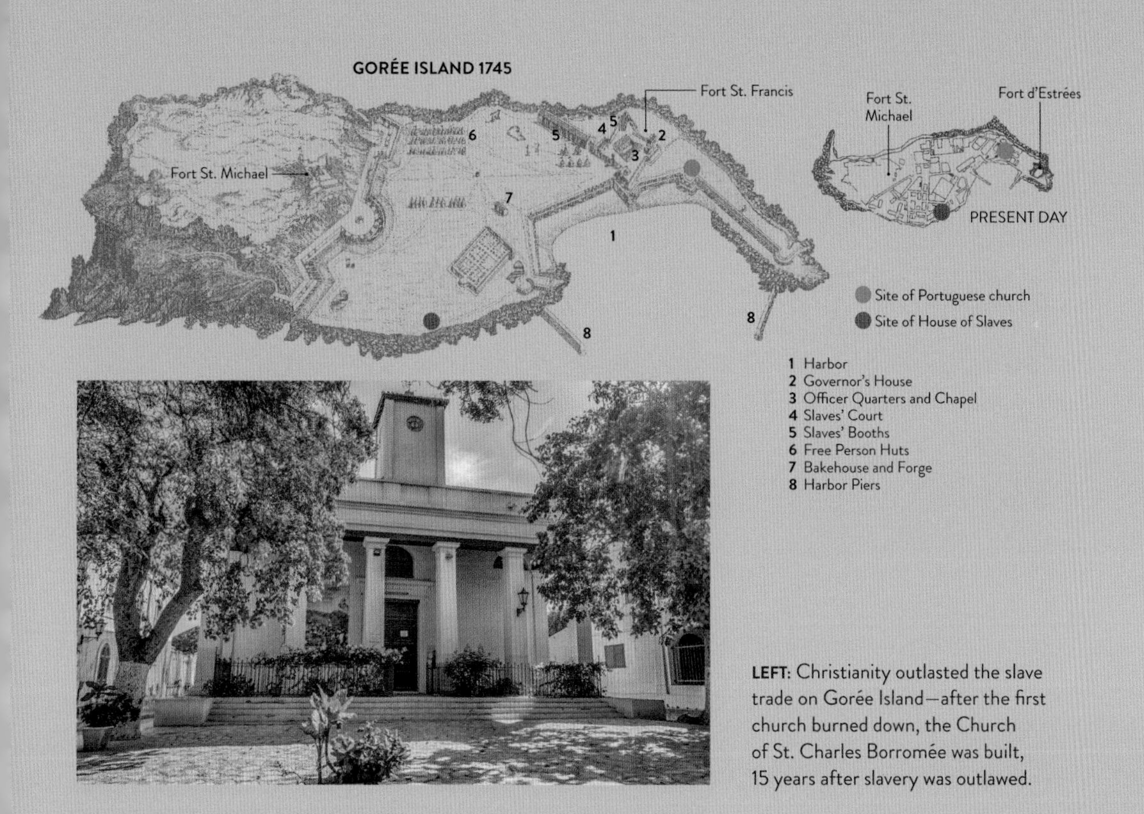

LEFT: Christianity outlasted the slave trade on Gorée Island—after the first church burned down, the Church of St. Charles Borromée was built, 15 years after slavery was outlawed.

130 RELIGION AND MONUMENT

GURDWARA JANAM ASTHAN

Nankana Sahib, Punjab, Pakistan
1469

Guru Nanak, first guru and founder of the Sikh faith, was born in Talvandi, since renamed Nankana Sahib in his honor. Born to Hindu parents, in about 1499 he experienced an enlightenment, leading him to found a new belief system that combined the best elements of Hinduism and Buddhism. Gurdwara Janam Asthan, the temple which marks his birthplace, was first built in the sixteenth century and was remodeled in the nineteenth century. It is an important site of pilgrimage for Sikhs.

131 RELIGION AND MONUMENT

CHURCH OF SAN ANDREA

Mantua, Italy
1476

When Ludovico Gonzaga, ruler of Mantua, commissioned Leon Battista Alberti to design a new church, he wanted a modern home for the town's holy relic: a cloth bearing drops of Christ's blood. Although Alberti died shortly before building began (and the church would not be completed for three centuries), the result was grand and simple: a masterpiece of restrained classicism, newly organized to suit a Christian church. The pedimented facade is centered on an enormous arch with pairs of pilasters on either side, while inside the church, the arch of the entrance extends into a deep barrel vault that runs the length of the building.

BELOW: An elegant Renaissance church with clear classical influences.

BLUE MOSQUE

Mazar-i-Sharif, Afghanistan
1481

The mosque is built on the supposed burial place of Ali, cousin and son-in-law of the Prophet Muhammad, and is the most celebrated site of pilgrimage in Afghanistan. A previous shrine was destroyed by the army of Genghis Khan. Its spectacular replacement, commissioned by Sultan Husayn Mizra, features the intricate tiling and decoration typical of fifteenth-century Islamic architecture, including two vivid blue domes.

RIGHT: The tiles constantly need to be replaced, as part of regular maintenance; one of the reasons is that they are often taken as souvenirs.

3 1500–1799

MURZUK OLD TOWN

Fezzan Province, Libya
c. 1500

An oasis town in the Sahara that became a center for both pilgrimage and the slave trade.

The foundations of Murzuk date back to the early 1300s, but the desert town only gained wider influence in the early sixteenth century, when it was taken over by the Awlad Muhammad dynasty, founded by Muhammad al-Fasi and originating in Morocco. Its new governors quickly took advantage of its location on routes between Cairo and Timbuktu and to the south, present-day Nigeria and Chad. They strengthened the town with a massive baked-brick fort, built new mosques, and, despite the punishing climate, gradually turned it into a stable commercial and political center, as well as a stop for pilgrims. Records exist showing that going north, it was a major center for the slave trade and caravans carrying "elephants' teeth" (ivory) and senna (much valued by European physicians). Traveling southward, textiles were a valued trade with sub-Saharan Africa.

BELOW: From the mid-sixteenth century, Murzuk was an essential refueling stop on the route going south into sub-Saharan Africa.

SISTINE CHAPEL

Rome, Italy
1508

A sculptor-turned-painter's frescoes transform the papal chapel into one of the great artistic masterpieces of the Renaissance.

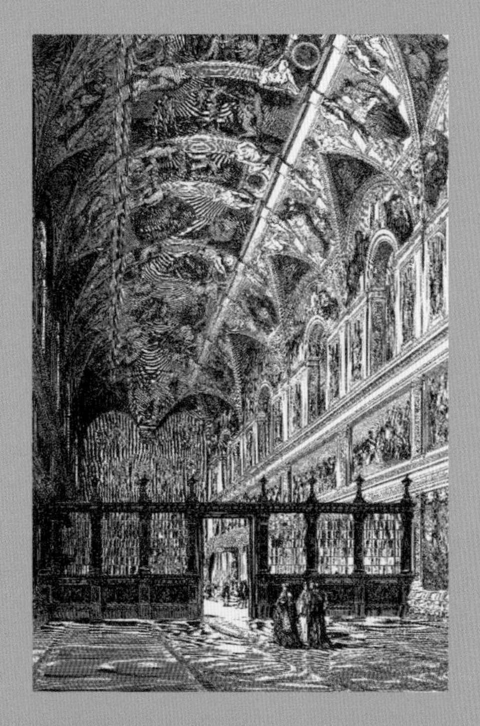

The Sistine Chapel is part of the Vatican Palace, which was completed in 1481. It is the pope's personal chapel, and is also used by the College of Cardinals to meet in a conclave when they elect a new pope. Rectangular with a vaulted ceiling, it is most famous for Michelangelo's ceiling frescoes depicting scenes from the Old Testament. Other artists, including Botticelli and Perugino, decorated the walls, but the ceiling and area directly behind the altar were entirely Michelangelo's. When hired in 1508, he was better known as a sculptor than a painter, and he suffered from crises of confidence throughout the project. The ceiling covers 12,000 square feet and was painted from scaffolding 65 feet high. On its completion, it was considered revolutionary: the biblical figures are realistic and dynamic rather than static. The iconic scene—*The Creation of Adam*—was so unusual and energetic that the first observers didn't recognize the figure of God.

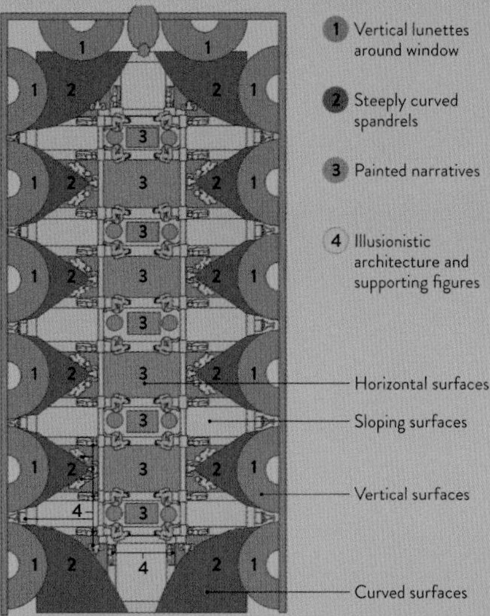

ARRANGEMENT OF THE SISTINE CEILING

"My brush, above me all the time, dribbles paint so my face makes a fine floor for droppings!"

Michelangelo, complaining to his friend Giovanni de Pistoia, about the trials of painting the Sistine Chapel ceiling, 1509 (translated by Gail Mazur)

TOP: Once completed, Michelangelo's chapel wasn't universally admired. Pope Paul IV, a successor to Julius II (who commissioned the work), complained of too much nudity, and rejected the depiction of humans interacting with God directly without the help of the Church. He suspended the artist's pension.

135 RESIDENCE

ALBRECHT DÜRER'S HOUSE

Nuremberg, Germany
1509

Dürer lived and worked in this handsome half-timbered house for nearly 20 years, from 1509. It demonstrates both his financial and artistic success. Sixteenth-century Nuremberg was a major trade hub and a center for ideas. Unlike much of northern Europe, where artists were confined to a single discipline, here they operated outside the guild system. Greater independence enabled Dürer to work at goldsmithing, engraving, and printing—as well as painting.

ABOVE: Today, the artist's house is a museum, offering insights into his life and working methods.

136 RELIGION AND MONUMENT

KING'S COLLEGE CHAPEL

Cambridge, England
1515

The finished building is a soaring example of the Late Gothic—or Perpendicular—style, which belies the problematic construction under on/off royal patronage. Commissioned by Henry VI in 1446 for his new King's College, there were to be five monarchs during the following 70 years, and King's College Chapel was finally completed under Henry VIII, in 1515. The exquisite lacelike fan vaulting—the tallest vaulted ceiling in the world—was the final element to be built.

ABOVE: Despite its stop-start construction, the completed chapel is an impressively integrated building.

137 RELIGION AND MONUMENT

ALL SAINTS' CHURCH

Wittenberg, Germany
1517

Martin Luther, scholar and priest, is buried in All Saints' Church, where he preached. It was on the wooden doors of All Saints' that Luther supposedly nailed his 95 "theses"—demands for church reform—on October 31, 1517. In his own record, Luther claimed only to have sent the theses to his archbishop; the popular church-door version may be apocryphal. But however the demands were made, it was these theses that ultimately led to the Protestant break with the Catholic Church.

ABOVE: The idea that Luther literally nailed his demands to All Saints' door is probably apocryphal.

138 RESIDENCE

CASA DOS BICOS

Lisbon, Portugal
1523

Literally the "House of Beaks," this domestic Renaissance building is a rare survivor of the Great Lisbon earthquake of 1755, and an unusual marriage of styles. The first owner, Afonso de Albuquerque, traveled in Italy for some years, and the diamond-shaped "spikes" covering the facade show the influence of the Renaissance palaces of Venice, while the fancy arched windows on the upper floors reflect the local Manueline Gothic style.

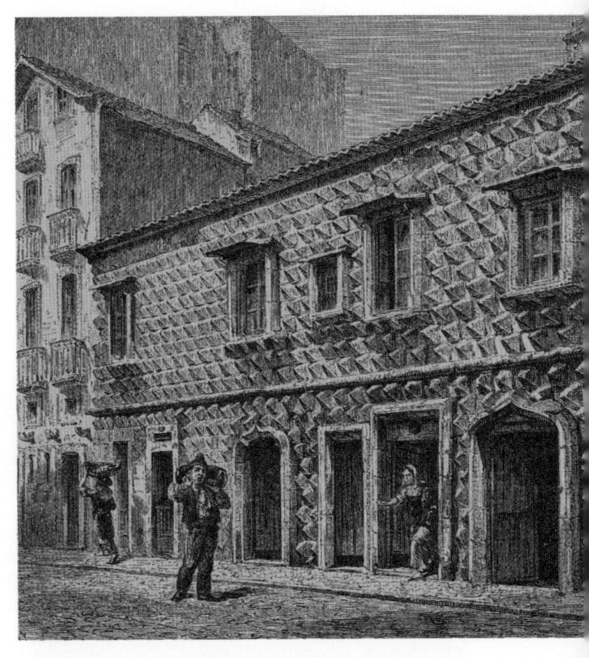

ABOVE: The unusual style of the house probably arose from the ideas collected by its well-traveled owner.

139 RESIDENCE

HAMPTON COURT PALACE

Hampton, England
1530

The vast palace was begun by Cardinal Thomas Wolsey, chief minister of Henry VIII. It was planned as a magnificent setting in which he could host the king. Before it was complete, Wolsey was disgraced when he failed to persuade the pope to annul the king's marriage to Catherine of Aragon, freeing Henry to marry Anne Boleyn. Wolsey gave Hampton Court to the king in an attempt to placate him, but died shortly after.

140 INFRASTRUCTURE AND INNOVATION

PUEBLA

Puebla State, Mexico
1532

Situated at the foot of the Popocatépetl volcano, and intended as a trade hub to link Mexico City with the port of Veracruz, on the Gulf of Mexico, Puebla was one of the first brand-new colonial towns built entirely on the grid system. It followed the European Renaissance model, arranged around a large central plaza. The result was a handsome city with many Baroque buildings, centered around an imposing cathedral.

BELOW: Puebla has impressive religious structures, such as the cathedral, and fine buildings including houses with walls covered in tiles.

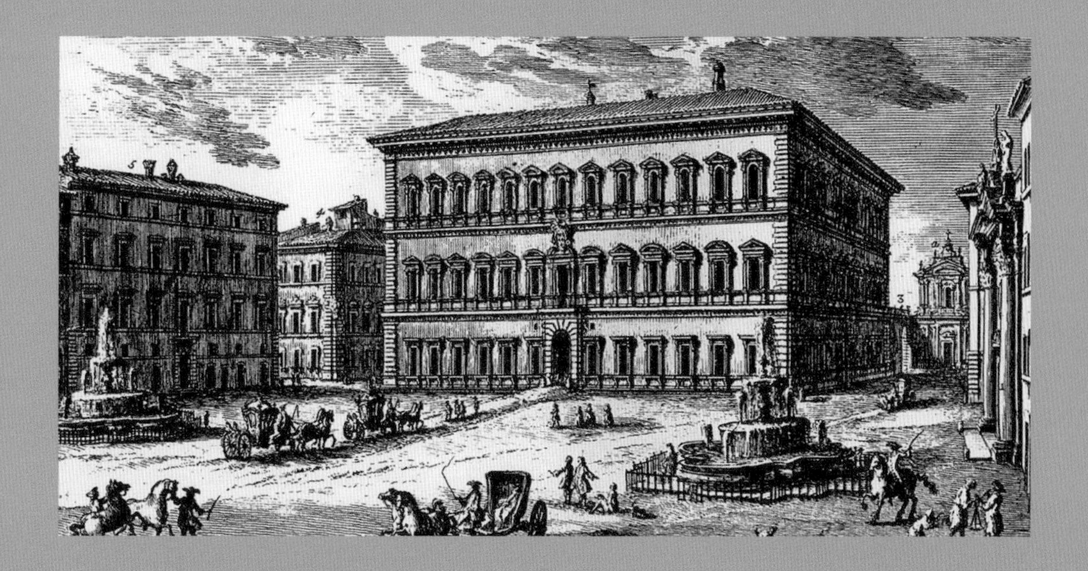

141 RESIDENCE

FARNESE PALACE

Rome, Italy
1534

The grand Renaissance home of the Farnese family, enlarged to demonstrate their growing social standing.

At the beginning of the sixteenth century, a relatively modest house owned by Augustinian monks was bought by Alessandro Farnese. In 1534, Alessandro was elected pope, becoming Pope Paul III. In the following years, the house transformed into the Farnese Palace, and was constantly altered to reflect the family's importance. Antonio da Sargallo was engaged as the architect. When he died in 1546, Michelangelo was appointed, raising the height of the first floor and adding a second, as well as designing an elaborate window and balcony above the main door. On Paul III's death in 1549, his descendants—all three of whom were cardinals—took over the project: his nephew, Ranuccio; his grandson, Alessandro Farnese il Giovane; and his great-great-grandnephew, Odoardo. From 1592, Odoardo Farnese made the palace his main home. All regularly commissioned more work; eventually, most prominent Renaissance architects and artists had contributed, inside or out, in one role or another. The result is one of the most architecturally and artistically important buildings of Renaissance Rome.

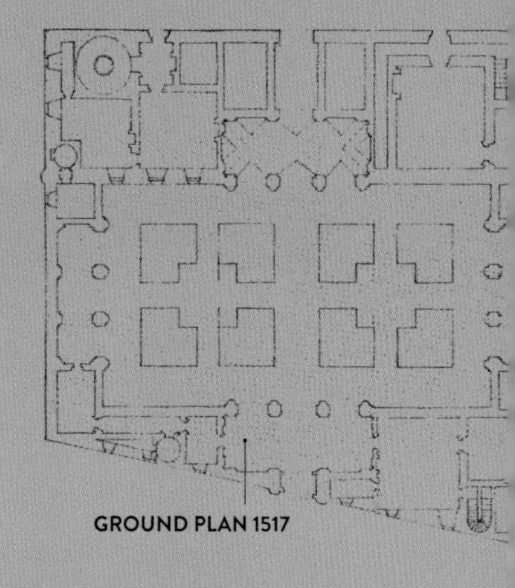

GROUND PLAN 1517

ABOVE: The completed palace had been worked on, inside and out, by so many key figures of the Italian Renaissance that it serves as a microcosm of the period's art and architecture.

142 POLITICS AND NATIONAL DEFENSE

CASTILLO DE SAN FELIPE DE BARAJAS

Cartagena, Colombia
1536

Cartagena, on the Caribbean coast of Colombia, was founded in 1533 as a critical Spanish port for Caribbean trade. Three years later, Castillo de San Felipe, the largest fortress ever built in a Spanish colony, was raised on San Lazaro Hill, overlooking the city. Designed on several levels, angled across one another, it was hard for invaders to scale. Meanwhile, a network of subterranean tunnels enabled movement between different parts of the castle.

143 RELIGION AND MONUMENT

TOMB OF VASCO DA GAMA, JERÓNIMOS MONASTERY

Lisbon, Portugal
1539

The Portuguese explorer Vasco da Gama died and was buried in 1524, on his third voyage to India. Back home, on the orders of Manuel I, king of Portugal, the magnificent Jerónimos Monastery, ornamented with maritime motifs, was under construction. It marked the site where da Gama and his crew had prayed before embarking on their first voyage. Fifteen years later, da Gama was disinterred for one final passage to Lisbon, where he was buried in this, his second grave.

ABOVE: Second time lucky: da Gama was eventually buried in an elaborate tomb in his home country, in 1539.

144 PLACE OF WORK

POTOSÍ SILVER MINE

Bolivia
1546

Silver was discovered in Cerro Rico (Rich Mountain), high in the Andes, which in the 1520s was part of the Viceroyalty of Peru. In 1546, the town of Potosí was founded below it. It took just 70 years to transform this Andean backwater to a wealthy metropolis with a population of 160,000.

The *mita*—forcible recruitment—of indigenous South Americans, augmented by enslaved Africans, formed the workforce. Terrible conditions resulted in stratospheric mortality rates: Cerro Rico was nicknamed "the mountain that eats men." At its height, the mine was producing 2,400 pounds of silver ore daily. In 1825, Potosí was liberated by the revolutionary Simón Bolívar. Today only small quantities of metal ores are mined there.

145 RELIGION AND MONUMENT

MALYAVANTA RAGHUNATHASWAMY

Hampi, Karnataka, India
c. 1550

Above the ancient city of Hampi, the hilltop temple of Malyavanta Raghunathaswamy is dedicated to the god Rama. The temple holds an important place in Hindu mythology. It is built on the spot where it is believed Rama and his brother Lakshmana waited out the monsoon before they could rescue Rama's wife, the goddess Sita, from the demon Ravana—a key story from the ancient and revered epic the *Ramayana*.

ABOVE: Among the hundreds of temples in Hampi, this is the only one with a strong link to the *Ramayana*.

FORT ST. ELMO

Valletta, Malta
1552

An early star fort in Malta proves the value of constantly evolving defensive design.

Fort St. Elmo was originally a simple watchtower, built as a lookout over the port of Valletta. In the early 1550s, Malta, then the headquarters of the Knights Hospitaller, came under threat from the navy of the Ottoman emperor Suleiman the Magnificent, and, within just six months, an impressive new fortification was built to replace the tower. Star, or bastion, forts were newly popular in the mid-sixteenth century, and Fort St. Elmo was one of the earliest. The complex outline made it less vulnerable to cannon fire—which had become increasingly accurate and powerful with developments in gunpowder—than the simple circle shape of earlier forts. The star shape meant that no large areas were left open to breach by cannon, and also offered a 360-degreee lookout. During the sustained Siege of Malta in 1565, the fort withstood constant bombardment for almost four months before its final fall.

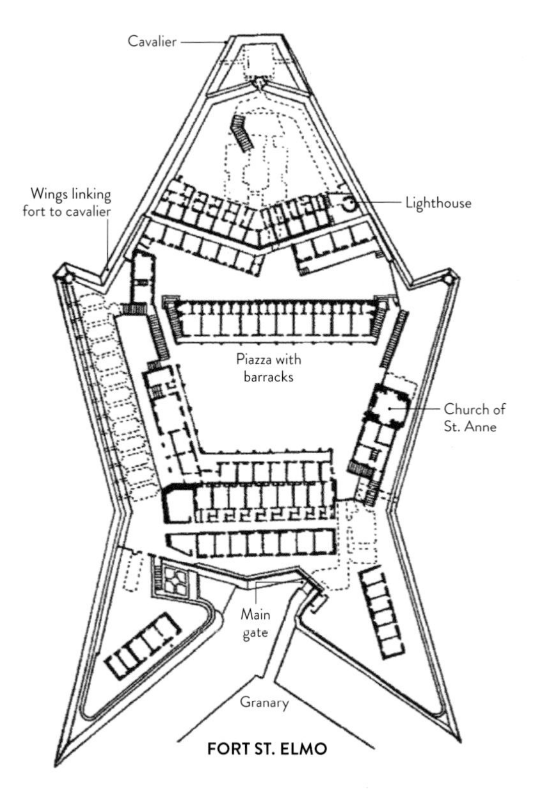

KNOWN FOR

- Being built as a result of increasingly aggressive Ottoman attacks on the island
- Playing a key role in the battle for Malta's independence in 1565
- Constant improvements and modifications, all the way up to World War II

OPPOSITE: Malta had been headquarters to the Knights Hospitaller since 1530, and Fort St. Elmo became well known after it played a key part in repelling the Ottoman forces for some time during the extraordinarily savage Siege of Malta in 1565.

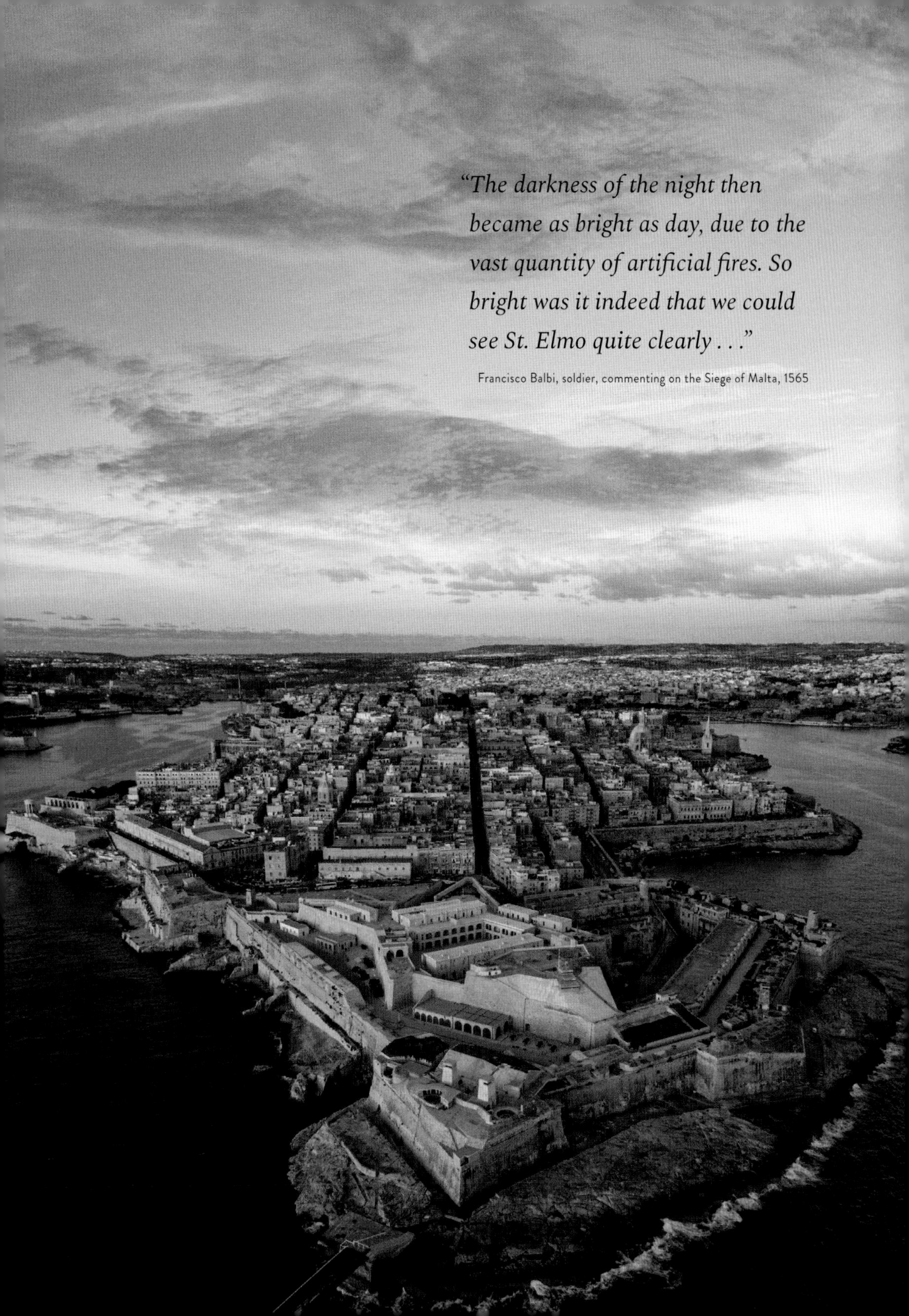

"The darkness of the night then became as bright as day, due to the vast quantity of artificial fires. So bright was it indeed that we could see St. Elmo quite clearly . . ."

Francisco Balbi, soldier, commenting on the Siege of Malta, 1565

ST. BASIL'S CATHEDRAL

Moscow, Russia
1561

The architectural icon of Moscow, built to celebrate victories in the Kazan wars.

"To Comrade Stalin. Please prevent the demolition of St. Basil's because it will cause political damage to the Soviet state."

Pyotr Baranovsky, architect, alleged text of a 1935 telegram to Stalin when the dictator threatened to have the church destroyed

The Russo-Kazan wars, between Russia and the Muslim Khanate of Kazan, had many setbacks on both sides and lasted for over a century. When Ivan IV of Russia, known as "Ivan the Terrible," finally captured Kazan in 1552, he commissioned a stone cathedral to mark the victory. For this thanksgiving church, a unique design grouped nine victories into one cathedral, with eight chapels, each one marked by its own dome, clustered around a larger, central ninth chapel. Built from brick, the cathedral—originally white with gilded onion domes—only gained its vivid colors during the seventeenth century. In 1588, a tiny chapel, the tenth dome, was built to house the tomb of St. Basil, "the Holy Fool" prophet of Moscow. It was at this point that the name of the cathedral also changed; previously dedicated to the Virgin Mary, it was renamed in honor of St. Basil.

BELOW: The cathedral was painted in red and white, and as fashions changed in the early nineteenth century, each chapel dome acquired its own vivid color scheme.

148 RELIGION AND MONUMENT

EL ESCORIAL

Escorial, Spain
1563

The largest Renaissance building in the world, El Escorial is a royal monastery built by Philip II of Spain, primarily as a mausoleum for the kings of Spain. Its long, severe facades are relieved only by a classical entrance, and although it included a library and royal apartments, its main function was as a religious building—its size and solemnity are a reminder that strongly Catholic Spain stood against the growing spirit of Protestantism in northern Europe.

ABOVE: Dedicated to San Lorenzo, the ground plan at El Escorial is rather grimly based on the grill on which the saint, in legend, was martyred.

149 RESIDENCE

QUEEN MARY'S BATH HOUSE

Edinburgh, Scotland
1565

Queen Mary's Bath House was built within the outer wall of the Palace of Holyrood House and dates back to *c.* 1565. A tiny house with two stories and a turreted roof, it's contemporaneous with the ill-fated rule of Mary, Queen of Scots, who lived at Holyrood until she was forced to abdicate in 1567. A famous beauty, she was alleged to bathe in wine to keep her complexion. The first mention of this luxurious bathing comes from John Pinkerton, an eighteenth-century antiquarian known for his fanciful "historical" accounts; consequently, the bath house became a popular tourist attraction.

Although it was probably enjoyed by Mary, it is more likely that it was a folly or summerhouse.

BELOW: An architectural oddity where the Queen of Scots is alleged to have bathed in wine.

150 INFRASTRUCTURE AND INNOVATION

STARI MOST

Mostar, Bosnia
1566

Crossing the Neretva River in the town of Mostar, Stari Most (Old Bridge) had the widest arch of any bridge at the time it was built. A masterpiece of elegant Ottoman simplicity, it was commissioned by Suleiman the Magnificent from Mimar Hayruddin, a pupil of the great Ottoman architect Sinan. It was destroyed in 1993 during the Croat-Bosniak War, but was rebuilt using some of the original stone.

BELOW: Until the early sixteenth century, the crossing was a perilous wooden bridge hung from chains. As the town grew, the need for a reliable link became urgent, and Stari Most was the result.

151 RELIGION AND MONUMENT

PARADESI SYNAGOGUE

Kerala, India
1568

A simple building with a clocktower, and an interior floored in blue-and-white tiles, the synagogue is the oldest in India. Of seven built in the city of Old Cochin, it is the only one still in use. South India was a relatively safe haven for Jewish people; one community, the Malabar Jews, had been there since the twelfth century. This synagogue was built for the Paradesi (literally "foreign") Jews, who were expelled from Spain under the Alhambra Decree in 1492.

FATEHPUR SIKRI

Uttar Pradesh, India
1569

The short-lived capital of the new Mughal Empire survives as a monument to Indo-Islamic architecture.

Fatehpur Sikri (City of Victory) was designed by the third Mughal emperor, Akbar. He chose the site because he believed it was lucky—25 miles from Agra, it was built over the village where a Sufi saint had predicted the birth of Akbar's son in 1569—and he planned a scheme for a magnificent capital city, including mosques, palaces, living quarters, and administration buildings for the court. They were all built of red sandstone between 1571 and 1573. Still considered a triumph of refined Mughal architecture, the massive walls enclose Jama Masjid, one of the largest mosques ever built.

Akbar's new capital had one major drawback: it was in an area that was short of water. Ultimately the supply couldn't meet the hugely increased needs of the city, and after just ten years Akbar relocated the capital to Lahore. Fatehpur Sikri fell into disuse, one of the reasons it remains so well preserved.

BELOW: Believing the site to be lucky, the emperor personally oversaw the building of his magnificent new capital.

"Here we see the impress of Akbar's architectural genius, as if fresh from the builder's hands."

Eustace Reynolds-Ball, travel writer, 1907

153 INFRASTRUCTURE AND INNOVATION

URANIBORG

Isle of Hven, Denmark
1576

Built to the design of the Dutch astronomer Tycho Brahe, under the patronage of Frederick II of Denmark, Uraniborg was the first custom-built observatory in Europe. After a few years, a second observatory, Stjarneborg, was added on, with ingenious adjustable domes to protect instruments from the wind. Frederick's successor didn't continue the patronage, and Brahe departed in 1597. Although the original buildings fell into ruins, detailed plans and diagrams survive.

ABOVE: Sadly, engravings such as this of the castle and observatory, published in an Amsterdam atlas in 1645, are all that remain of the innovative Uraniborg observatory.

154 RELIGION AND MONUMENT

CHURCH OF SAN GIORGIO MAGGIORE

Venice, Italy
1580

When he died in 1580, the Renaissance architect Andrea Palladio left behind *The Four Books of Architecture*—his work on building in the Classical style—and many elegant buildings, of which the Church of San Giorgio Maggiore is one of the most iconic. It takes the form of a basilica with a white marble facade, featuring a central pediment held between two halves of a lower pediment. It was incomplete on Palladio's death, and finished to his design by Vincenzo Scamozzi.

ABOVE: The Benedictine monastery church, built over an earlier building, is reminiscent of a Greek or Roman temple. The brilliant white marble glistens over the lagoon.

HIMEJI CASTLE

Hyogo Prefecture, Japan
1581

Known as the White Heron castle, the finest surviving example of a fortress from the Edo period.

The first incarnation of Himeji Castle was built in the fourteenth century, but it was extensively remodeled from 1581—at the beginning of the Edo period—by Toyotomi Hideyoshi. He was not only a powerful feudal lord who played an important role in the unification of Japan, but also an enthusiastic builder. The result combines an elegant building with an impressively inaccessible fortress. The six-story main keep has swooping pagoda roofs and is built from wood, but over a very substantial stone base. It sits at the center of a maze of paths, winding through many fortified gateways and narrow stone-walled passages—effective against any attempted invasion—and is just one of the 82 buildings within the outer wall. It's the most complete and unaltered castle of its period to survive intact.

BELOW: Its exquisite—almost delicate—appearance disguises the fact that Himeji Castle was designed as a fortress.

156 ART AND CULTURE

UFFIZI GALLERY

Florence, Italy
1581

Cosimo de Medici, Duke of Tuscany, commissioned the architect and artist Giorgio Vasari to design a complex of offices, or *uffizi*, for the administrative functions of the city of Florence. The Uffizi was extended and converted over the following 20 years to include space for the Medici family's magnificent collection of art and sculpture, making it one of the first purpose-built art galleries in the world.

LEFT: The open courtyard—or Loggiato—is the semi-enclosed space between the two long galleries that make up the Uffizi's main display space.

157 RELIGION AND MONUMENT

GOLDEN TEMPLE

Amritsar, India
1589

The foundation stone of Sri Harmandir Sahib (Home of God), now commonly called the Golden Temple, was laid in 1589, probably by Guru Arjan, the fifth of the ten gurus of the Sikh faith. It marked the lakeside spot where Guru Nanak, founder of the faith, had chosen to meditate: a significant site for the holiest shrine for Sikhs. The natural lake had already been reconstructed as a large artificial pool, which was drained to create the first version of the temple, accessed along a walkway and deliberately placed on a lower level than the buildings around it, which include an assembly hall and a dining hall, to symbolize the importance of humility. The original building was a simple brick structure; destroyed in successive Afghan invasions in the eighteenth century, it was rebuilt several times. Today's familiar version of the temple, covered in gold foil, was built in the early nineteenth century.

ANATOMICAL THEATER OF PADUA

Padua, Italy
1595

The world's first permanent anatomical theater for teaching through the dissection of corpses.

"This is a place where the dead are pleased to help the living."

Dedication at the entrance of the Anatomical Theater

Human dissection revolutionized medicine during the Renaissance. It had been understood as a source of medical knowledge for centuries, but it was only from the mid-fifteenth century that portable wooden "theaters" became popular for public dissections, attended both by professionals—doctors, surgeons, and students—and interested members of the public. The permanent anatomical theater built in the University of Padua was the idea of the anatomist and surgeon Girolamo Fabrici d'Acquapendente, and enabled regular dissections to become part of medical education. The theater centered on a table in the middle of a large oval space, with six tiers of seats above it, accommodating around 250 spectators. The city authorities supplied the cadavers, usually the bodies of executed criminals or patients who had died in the hospital. Padua's theater, which remained in use until 1872, became the model on which others were built all over Europe.

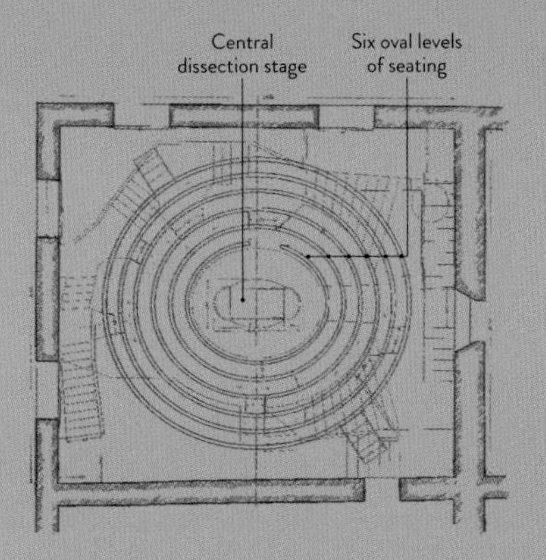

RIGHT: The theater was built in the shape of an inverted cone, with tiers of steeply ranked seats. The first two or three rows, with the best view, were reserved for students of anatomy, while interested members of the public could pay to sit up high.

GARH PALACE

Rajasthan, India
1607

A fantastical palace marks the loyalty of one ruler to the Mughal Empire.

From 1570, Kota was a vassal kingdom of the Mughal Empire under Akbar, and subsequent rulers gained and lost favor—and by implication both land and power—according to how much support they gave subsequent emperors. Rao Ratan Singh supported Emperor Jahangir in a number of military conflicts, and was substantially rewarded, enabling him to begin construction of Garh Palace. Located on a precipitous site in the town of Bundi, the extraordinary finished building is a major feat of structural engineering and has the appearance of being carved directly out of a near-vertical rock face. A steep path approaches the main gateway, which is carved with huge elephants. Subsequent rulers in Bundi extended the site and added smaller structures within the main compound, including Chitrashala, ornamented with fine murals from the eighteenth century. Although it's no longer inhabited, Garh Palace remains one of the most impressive examples of Rajput architecture.

BELOW: The building, on such a precipitous site, is so accomplished that it awed nineteenth-century travelers viewing it for the first time.

160 RESIDENCE

JAMESTOWN

Williamsburg, Virginia
1607

The first English settlement in America, Jamestown was built on a peninsula a little way up the James River, avoiding possible attack from the coast, but also offering local mooring for the settlers' own boats and far enough away from the territory of the Powhatan people. The town would survive for less than a century. After a range of catastrophes, a fire in 1698 finally saw the township moved to Williamsburg.

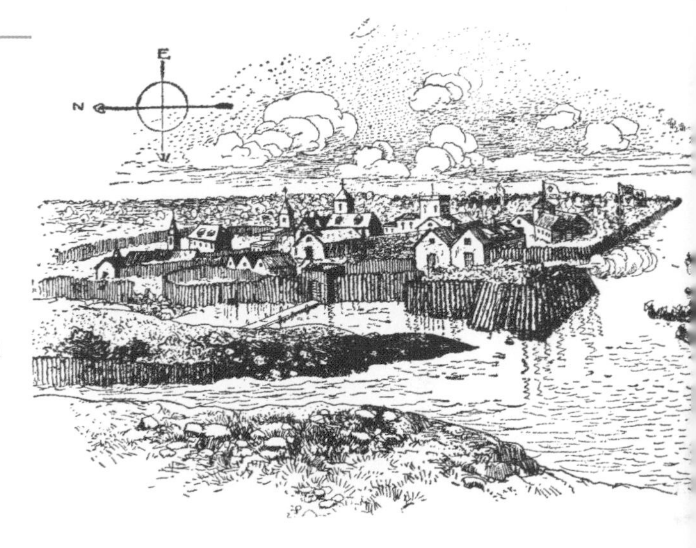

ABOVE: A fire in 1698, which destroyed its statehouse and prison, precipitated the final move from Jamestown.

161 POLITICS AND NATIONAL DEFENSE

PALACE OF THE GOVERNORS

Santa Fe, New Mexico
1610

A low adobe building with an external gallery supported by wooden posts, the Palace of the Governors is the oldest surviving colonial building in the United States. Built by Don Pedro de Peralta, the first royal governor of the Spanish colony of Nuevo Mexico, which then covered a vast area of today's southern states, it remained a center of local government until 1885, under successive Spanish, Mexican, and American regimes.

ABOVE: Initially used by local Pueblo Indians, the palace later housed Confederate forces during the Civil War. Since 1909, the palace has been open to the public as the New Mexico History Museum.

POINT COMFORT

Hampton, Virginia
1619

The basic fortification where the first enslaved people arrived in America.

Despite its name, Point Comfort, a peninsula reaching out into Chesapeake Bay, was, in 1619, a small, impoverished settlement with basic defenses—probably consisting only of a fenced cabin and some cannons—to repel possible attacks from the sea. Point Comfort gained its place in the history books when the *White Lion*, a Dutch ship, docked there carrying 20 enslaved Africans. They had been brought on board in Angola by Portuguese slavers when the original ship was captured. The colonists of Point Comfort gave the crew food in exchange for the Angolans, a transaction noted by John Rolfe, recorder general of North Virginia. Slavery was already widespread in Latin America and the Caribbean, but this marked the moment when Point Comfort became notorious as the site of the first recorded case of slavery in North America.

ABOVE: The first enslaved people brought ashore in America were traded with the colonists for food.

ABOVE: One of the first mentions of "Poynt comfort" is on a map published in 1624 in *The Generall Historie of Virginia, New-England, and the Summer Isles.*

163 RESIDENCE

NAN MADOL

Pohnpei, Micronesia
Pre-1628

The enduring questions about a unique island city built on a coral reef.

Built between the twelfth and early seventeenth centuries, Nan Madol has just as many myths attached to it as the better-known Easter Island. Located off the island of Pohnpei, it consists of 93 artificial islands built directly onto coral, linked by a network of canals. The building blocks are "logs" of basalt—brought from Sokeh, 25 miles away—laid in a crisscross pattern to make walls weighing hundreds of tons. Nan Madol was a center for the rulers of the Saudelaur dynasty, for whom rank and standing seem to have been rigidly imposed. It incorporated both their homes and a number of ceremonial buildings. It was gradually abandoned from 1628, when the dynasty came to an end.

With only oral tradition to rely on, archaeologists are still unraveling the mysteries of the city, in particular how such huge volumes of basalt could have been moved such a distance without modern technology.

ABOVE: One of the greatest mysteries of Nan Madol is how its inhabitants raised such substantial structures on unstable foundations.

KAABA

Mecca, Saudi Arabia
1631

The holiest shrine in Islam, visited by millions during the annual hajj pilgrimage.

Pre-Islamic in its earliest form, the Kaaba (Arabic for "cube") was allegedly built by Abraham—a prophet for both Muslims and Christians—and his son Ishmael. The original wooden shrine of 608 was rebuilt, but the Prophet Muhammad removed the idols, retaining only the Black Stone, which is believed to have been given to Abraham by the angel Gabriel. After this the Kaaba became a focus of faith for Muslims, established as Islam's holiest shrine.

In 1631, after the Kaaba and its surroundings were wrecked by a flood, it was rebuilt in the incarnation that has lasted ever since: a square granite building, 33 feet high, with the Black Stone set in a frame on one corner, the whole draped in a black silk-and-cotton cloth, or *kiswa*, embroidered with golden calligraphy. It is set in a courtyard in the center of the Al-Masjid al-Haram mosque. During *hajj*, the pilgrimage to Mecca which every devout Muslim is required to undertake at least once in their lifetime, pilgrims circle it counterclockwise seven times, as cited in the rules for pilgrimage set down by Muhammad himself.

"Turn your faces to the Holy Mosque and wherever you are, turn your faces to that part."

The Quran (2:144), instructing Muslims to face Mecca when they pray

LEFT: A view of the Kaaba at the height of the annual hajj pilgrimage.

BELOW: This nineteenth-century engraving of the Kaaba shows the courtyard and galleries of the mosque that surround it.

KNOWN FOR

- Its status at the center of the hajj, the vast annual pilgrimage to Mecca
- A long history, which saw it transform from a shrine venerated by pagan nomads to a focus of the Islamic faith
- The fact that every Muslim faces toward Mecca and the Kaaba when they pray

165 RESIDENCE

FASIL GHEBBI

Gondar, Ethiopia
1636

Gondar is a fortified city—including homes, churches, and monasteries—at the center of which is the fortress of Fasil Ghebbi, built as a palace for the Christian Ethiopian emperor Fasilides. Emperor Fasilides claimed direct descent from the biblical King Solomon and the Queen of Sheba. The eclectic palace is built in a mix of styles, including European Baroque and Moorish. It marks the point at which Ethiopian rulers abandoned a previously semi-nomadic existence and settled in one place.

BELOW: Fasil Ghebbi remained the center of Ethiopian government until 1864; in the 1890s, the capital moved to Addis Ababa.

166 RESIDENCE/RELIGION AND MONUMENT

POTALA PALACE

Lhasa, Tibet
1649

The holiest site for Tibetan Buddhism at the highest palace in the world.

The Potala Palace is a *dzong*, or fortified monastery, built into the side of Mar Po Ri, or Red Hill, a holy mountain in Lhasa, the Tibetan capital. A huge administrative and spiritual complex, it combines the White Palace, which served as the winter home of the Dalai Lamas between 1649 and 1959, and the Red Palace, the center of religious study and prayer.

The eight golden roofs above the Red Palace mark the stupas of the eight Dalai Lamas for whom it is also a mausoleum. Built under the fifth Dalai Lama, the palace is an impressive feat of structural engineering: it is 13 stories deep, with foundations reinforced with copper, an early form of protection against earthquakes.

After the fourteenth Dalai Lama traveled into exile in 1959—following suppression of the Tibetan national uprising by the Chinese—the Potala Palace was converted into a museum. It remains a strongly spiritual site for Buddhists.

RIGHT: The Potala seen here from the south in 1904.

BELOW: The Red Palace is behind—and surrounded by—the White Palace, and is the most important religious center in Tibet.

FARRIS WINDMILL

Cape Cod, Massachusetts
1650

The story of the Farris Windmill reflects the shortage of specific skills in the early colonies. Built in the mid-seventeenth century, it was moved three times from its original site on the north side of Cape Cod. Dismantling it wasn't simple, but with specialist mill-makers in short supply, it was easier to relocate than to build a new mill. Its final move, in 1936, was to Greenfield Village, Henry Ford's heritage museum.

BELOW: The small European population of colonial America lacked skills in trades, such as mill-making, so this windmill—now part of a museum—is well traveled.

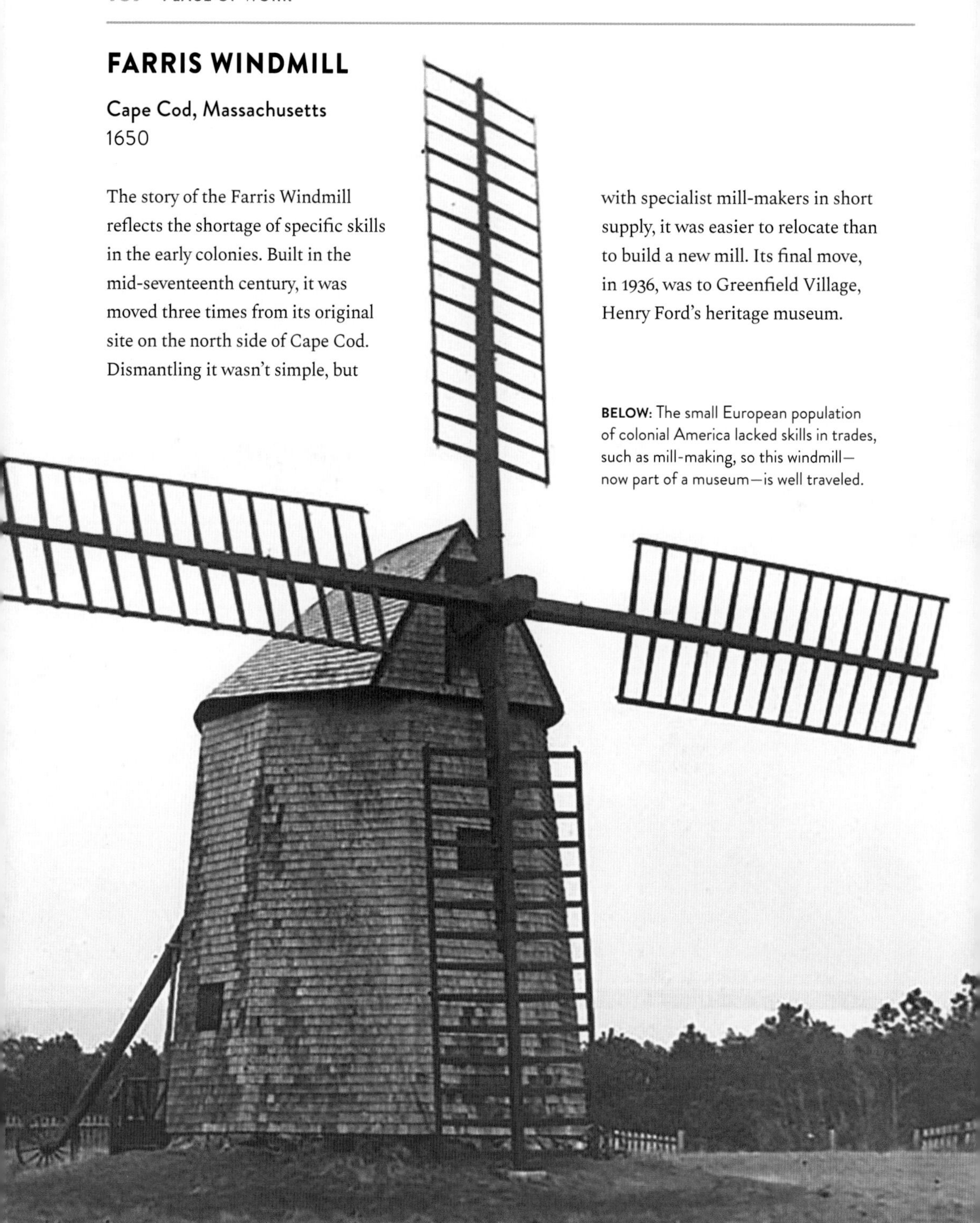

ROYAL PALACES OF ABOMEY

Dahomey, Benin
1650

The royal houses of one of the most powerful—and best organized—kingdoms in West Africa.

Built from wood and a straw-and-mud mix, ornamented with bas reliefs, the twelve palaces at Abomey, in southern Benin, were the homes of the Fon rulers of the Dahomey Empire, each of whom built their own palace as they succeeded. The Fons were the largest group in an area that was home to many different peoples; they were often at war, both expanding their territories and taking captives. The latter were either used as agricultural labor or sold to European slavers—sales that played an important part in the Dahomey economy.

From the mid-seventeenth century, the kings had absolute power over their subjects. They ran a formidable army, including an elite female corps, but also managed an efficient bureaucracy: couples were split up, with the men running their own properties away from court, and the women serving at court and issuing directives to their distant partners.

BELOW LEFT: Relief panels on the outside of the palace buildings are brightly colored.

BELOW: Inside, the finely carved stools of the royal families are still displayed.

169 INFRASTRUCTURE AND INNOVATION

KHAJU BRIDGE

Isfahan, Iran
1650

The two-story brick-and-stone structure was commissioned by Abbas II, the seventh shah of Iran. It has 23 arches with sluices under them to control the flow of the Zayanderud River, an upper story for heavy traffic, a lower story shady enough for traders to use all day, and a pavilion for the emperor's use in the center. The elegant result—one of the first bridges designed to fulfill multiple functions—is a high point of Persian architecture, and it is still in use today.

ABOVE: The multi-functional bridge is still in use. Traffic travels above, with a thriving trade arcade beneath.

170 POLITICS AND NATIONAL DEFENSE

FORT JAMES

Kunta Kinteh Island, Gambia
1651

Sitting in the middle of the wide Gambia River, tiny Kunta Kinteh Island was well situated for commerce. Ships could dock here, and the river runs directly from the interior to the Atlantic: a perfect artery for trade. Once Fort James had been built, around ten years after the first traders arrived in 1651, it quickly became a center for the slave trade in particular, successively owned by the Dutch, British, and French.

BELOW: A small but useful docking point at a key entry point to the African continent.

TAJ MAHAL

Agra, Uttar Pradesh, India
1653

The highest achievement of Mughal architecture in one perfectly conceived and executed whole.

Shah Jahan was an accomplished builder. When the Taj Mahal was begun in 1632, he had already built Delhi's Red Fort and embarked on the great Jama Masjid mosque. Built as a mausoleum for the emperor's second wife, Mumtaz Mahal—and famously a celebration of the couple's love—the Taj is also a reminder of the artistry of the Mughal Empire, and of the traditional Persian concept of a building as one element in an overall scheme.

Planned as a complete composition centering on the mausoleum, the site includes a gated outer wall, a mosque, and a *jawab*—a building mirroring the mosque and maintaining the arrangement's symmetry—as well as gardens with raised walks, channels, and a pool. The mausoleum was ornamented using the workmanship available to the vast wealth of Shah Jahan, from artists in *pietra dura*, who inlaid semiprecious stones, to master calligraphers, who engraved 22 passages from the Quran.

BELOW: A rare example of a building that is as impressive from a distance as it is at close quarters.

172 RESIDENCE

BILLIOU-STILLWELL-PERINE HOUSE

Staten Island, New York
1662

Pierre Billiou arrived in the Dutch colony of New Amsterdam in 1661, one of a group of 19 French Huguenots fleeing from persecution in their native Flanders. Peter Stuyvesant, the local governor, granted him a plot of land, and it was here that he built his first small stone house. Less than 20 years later, when the British ousted the Dutch—and New Amsterdam became New York—the house was owned by Thomas Stillwell, Billiou's son-in-law, who became a member of the Colonial Assembly of the British colony. Stillwell added to the house in around 1680; at this time a second small stone dwelling was built with a separate entrance. Three later clapboard additions in the eighteenth and early nineteenth centuries were joined on, without altering the original house. It is the only remaining domestic building that marks the earliest history of both Dutch and British colonies.

173 RELIGION AND MONUMENT

CATHEDRAL OF CUSCO

Cusco, Peru
1668

Built on the site of an ancient Incan temple, the location of the Cathedral of Cusco was deliberately chosen by the Spanish to subjugate the local people and replace their existing faith with Catholicism. Inca workers—forced to labor on the huge new Renaissance-Baroque church—left behind some of their own sacred symbols, among them the jaguar carved into the doors. Although construction began in 1559, the cathedral was only finally consecrated in 1668.

ABOVE: The early history of New York City, told by a single house.

HOUSE OF THE SEVEN GABLES

Salem, Massachusetts
1668

Although the House of the Seven Gables is best known because of Nathaniel Hawthorne's novel of the same name, the story behind the real house is that of a thriving port and successful trade with the East Indies. The parents of John Turner—its original owners—had come from England, and Turner was born into quite humble circumstances in Salem in 1644. By 1668, he was a seagoing captain and had made enough money to buy the land, knock down the previous house, and build something more suitable for him and his wife. It was adjacent to the wharf from which his cargoes came and went. At the time of his death at the age of 36, Turner was one of the richest men in Salem: he owned 200 acres, six houses, and several ships. Two more generations of Turners would enlarge the house to the many-gabled form that's recognizable today.

SKYTSBORG TOWER

St. Thomas, U.S. Virgin Islands
1679

St. Thomas became a Danish colony in 1671, after years of changing hands between different powers in the Caribbean. The round stone tower known as Skytsborg (meaning "Sky Tower") was built shortly afterward. The late seventeenth century was the golden age of piracy in the Caribbean, so the position of Skytsborg, on the peak of Government Hill, served as a lookout point and was able to provide advance warning to the fortified harbor below.

RIGHT: The rubble masonry tower was part of a network of defensive fortifications; its nickname is "Blackbeard's Castle."

PALACE OF VERSAILLES

Versailles, France
1682

A palace that, in size and splendor, reflected the power of the Sun King.

The site of a hunting lodge built by Louis XIII—about ten miles southwest of Paris—Versailles was chosen by his successor, Louis XIV, as the location for a palace set in extensive gardens, which he planned as the new center of both court and political life.

In 1682, work far from complete, Louis moved his government from Paris to Versailles. There were advantages: it kept the king at a distance from popular unrest in Paris; it obliged the aristocracy to visit Versailles regularly—making revolts fomented in the provinces unlikely—and the grandeur of the palace was a strong reminder of the monarch's authority.

Finally completed in 1710, Versailles was the birthplace of a new type of French Classicism, combining elements of Baroque and Rococo style. Incorporating set pieces such as the Ambassadors' Staircase and the Hall of Mirrors, it had involved the great architects of the age, including Louis Le Vau, François d'Orbay, and Jules Hardoin-Mansart.

RIGHT: The central Marble Courtyard of the palace is laid out with black and white tiles imported from the castle of Vaux-le-Vicomte.

BELOW: The formal Baroque garden, designed for Louis XIV by the landscape architect André le Nôtre.

177 POLITICS AND NATIONAL DEFENSE

FORT FREDERICKSBURG

Fredericksburg, Ghana
1683

The German fort that became a stronghold for an Ahanta chieftain.

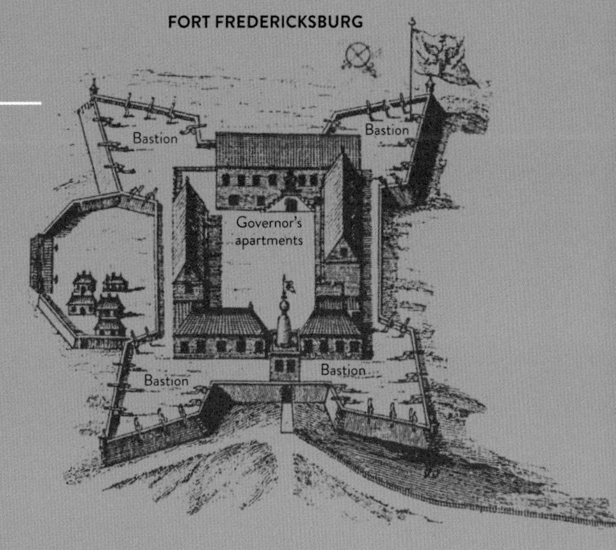

ABOVE: Sited on a natural elevation with all-around views, Fort Fredericksburg offered natural defenses, whether it was held by European or Ahanta traders.

Built on the orders of Prince Frederick of Brandenburg, Fredericksburg is the only German fort on Ghana's Gold Coast. Although the area already had a heavy British and Dutch trading presence, it wasn't strongly fortified. When the Germans left, selling their interest in the fort to the Dutch in 1717, Fredericksburg was quickly occupied by one of their former allies, a local Ahanta chief—named variously in records "John Conny" or "January Canoe." For seven years he withstood Dutch efforts to reclaim the fort, doing a brisk trade with all comers, regardless of their country or affiliation, and offering competitive prices on their two main exports: gold and enslaved people. By the time the Dutch regained Fredericksburg in 1724, he had become a local hero, and he still has a place in Caribbean folklore, marked by an annual celebration of "Johnny Canoe" day.

TIGER'S NEST MONASTERY

Paro, Bhutan
1692

One of the most sacred—and inaccessible—sites in the mountain kingdom of Bhutan.

The Paro Taktsang (Tiger's Nest) Monastery was founded around a set of caves where, in the eighth century, the Indian Buddhist sage Guru Rinpoche, or Padmasambhava, was known for spreading the teaching of Buddhism through the Himalayas. He was considered almost as holy as the Buddha himself. It is said he meditated here for three years, three months, three days, and three hours. It is the best known—and considered the holiest—of 13 monasteries built on the meditation sites of Padmasambhava. In legend, he was flown to the site—10,200 feet up in the mountains above the Paro valley—on the back of one of his followers, who had transformed herself into a tiger for the occasion, giving the monastery its name. The monastery's foundation stone was laid in 1692, by a leader of Bhutan, Gyalse Tenzing Rabke, himself believed to be a reincarnation of Padmasambhava. Four modest temples were built around the cave complex, and the caves were decorated with paintings and house sacred relics.

Although the seventeenth-century buildings were destroyed by fire in 1998, the monastery was restored by 2005 to the original plan and using the same materials, under the patronage of the king of Bhutan.

LEFT: A highly inaccessible site has helped to preserve the mystique of the Tiger's Nest.

179 PLACE OF WORK

SALEM COURTHOUSE

Salem, Massachusetts
1692

The setting of an explosion of witch-hunting hysteria.

By the time the first Salem witch trial took place here in May 1692, in a special court convened by Governor William Phips, accusations had gone on for weeks and witch-hunting hysteria had taken over the community.

The trials can be set in a wider context. They came at a stressful time: the previous harsh winter, an outbreak of smallpox, and the arrival of refugees from King William's War—a conflict between the French and the English—were all putting the colony's resources under strain. Accusations made by three girls, that local women were using witchcraft to give them fits, ignited the spark. At trial, "spectral evidence," from dreams or visions, was accepted as proof. Of the 200 accused, 19 people were hanged; one refused to plead and was crushed to death. Witch-hunting hysteria abated the following year. By 1697, the judges were issuing apologies for the horror they had been caught up in.

> *"[We] do hereby declare that we justly fear that we were sadly deluded and mistaken, for which we are much disquieted and distressed in our minds and do therefore humbly beg forgiveness . . ."*
>
> The Apology of the Salem Jury, 1697

ABOVE RIGHT: Reverend George Burroughs, denounced as "king of the witches," was hanged on August 19, 1692.

BELOW: The trials saw many hysterical denunciations—and probably also included an element of score-settling.

180 POLITICS AND NATIONAL DEFENSE

CASTILLO DE SAN MARCOS

St. Augustine, Florida
1695

The oldest masonry fortress on mainland America, San Marcos was built by the Spanish founder of the town of St. Augustine. It was built from *coquina*, a soft limestone that was a local material, which became popular for fortifications because it was effective against cannon fire, absorbing shocks rather than shattering. Although San Marcos was successively occupied by the British and the Americans after the Spanish ceded Florida to the United States, it was never successfully captured.

ABOVE: The soft coquina stone proved to be surprisingly effective in resisting cannon fire.

181 RELIGION AND MONUMENT

SAN IGNACIO MINÍ (JESUIT MISSION)

Misiones, Argentina
1696

One of around 30 Jesuit missions founded in the Province of Paraguay (covering parts of present-day Argentina, Brazil, and Paraguay), San Ignacio Miní incorporated schools and a hospital, as well as a church, built in Spanish Baroque style but ornamented with motifs from the local Guarani culture. Jesuit conversions in this region were largely successful; the mission even housed a printing shop where Christian texts were printed in the Guarani language.

ABOVE: The mission would have supported a population of 3,300. The remains of a central square, church, priest's house, cemetery, and dwellings are still visible.

NYATAPOLA TEMPLE

Bhaktapur, Nepal
1702

The earthquake-resistant temple in Nepal marks the site of a divine dispute.

Sited on the main square of Bhaktapur, this brick-and-wood Hindu temple is the tallest in Nepal. Despite its delicate, elegant appearance, it has also withstood a number of strong earthquakes over its three centuries. Built as a five-tiered pagoda, it is dedicated to the Siddhi Lakshmi, a manifestation of the warlike goddess Durga. Local legend ascribes special power to the temple because it was the site at which Lakshmi defeated Bhairava, a particularly fearsome god related to Shiva. Bhairava has a shrine on the same square; when, in a rage, he threatened to kill humankind and end civilization, Lakshmi threatened him back and won the fight because her temple was by far the most powerful. On account of this, Nyatopola Temple is considered so holy that only priests can enter its inner shrine.

ABOVE: Nyatapola, seen here on the left, is widely believed to be earthquake-proof, largely on account of its spiritual pedigree.

ST. PAUL'S CATHEDRAL

London, England
1710

A masterpiece of English Baroque that changed the skyline of London.

When the architect Sir Christopher Wren was charged with building a new cathedral for London—to replace the Gothic building damaged in the Great Fire of 1666—he was also given the job of replacing 51 of the capital's other churches. New St. Paul's would take 35 years to build; work on the foundations began in June 1675, but elements of the design were constantly revised as the building went up. Between 1690 and 1695, for example, a brick cone was inserted between the inner and outer domes for stability, and to allow an increased span. The final elements, the western towers, were completed in 1710.

The cathedral, and the companion city churches, re-created London as a modern city, completely changing its silhouette. At 365 feet high, St. Paul's was visible from anywhere in the city, surrounded by the forest of spires and towers of the other Wren churches.

BELOW: Detail of *The Thames from Somerset House Terrace toward the City*, by the Italian painter Canaletto, in 1750–51. It shows how imposing the newly completed St. Paul's Cathedral was on the cityscape.

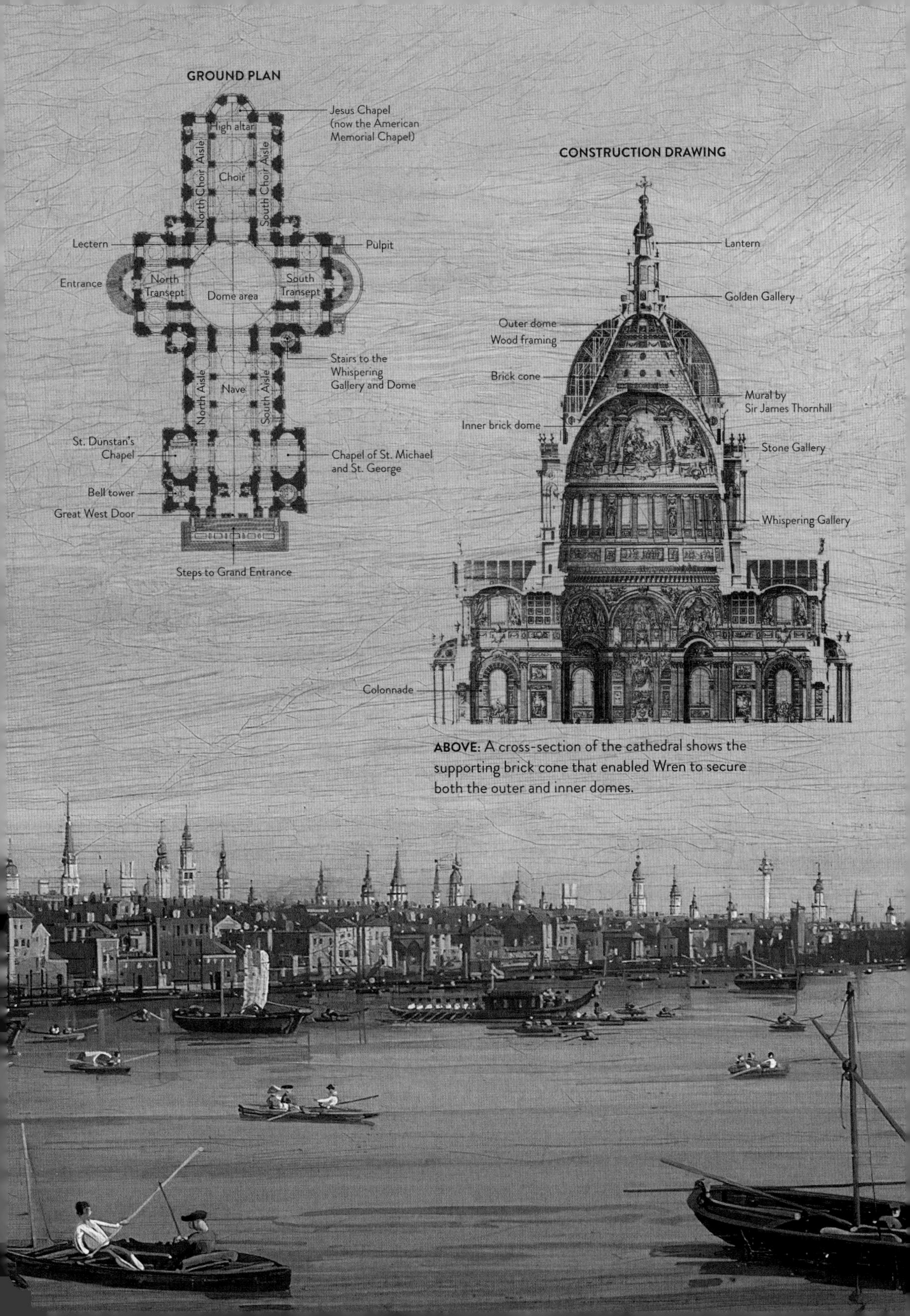

ABOVE: A cross-section of the cathedral shows the supporting brick cone that enabled Wren to secure both the outer and inner domes.

CHURCH OF THE TRANSFIGURATION

Kizhi Island, Russia
1714

A virtuoso example of the traditional church architecture of Russia.

Contained on a small island, the church served a scattered congregation in the rural and thinly populated area around Lake Onega, in Karelia. Built to commemorate Peter the Great's victory over Sweden, and topped with 22 shingled cupolas, it is a tour de force of the wooden architecture that is a strong part of the cultural inheritance of Russia. It is built entirely without nails, and with extraordinarily precise craftsmanship.

BELOW: The legend of the mysterious Nestor—who built the church, then vanished—reinforced the idea that Kizhi exhibits almost supernatural woodworking skill.

185 RELIGION AND MONUMENT

FORT ST. LOUIS

Kahnawake, Canada
1725

The Jesuit mission that settled at Kahnawake overlooks the Laurence River on the outskirts of present-day Quebec. It had moved several times, accompanying their converts—a group of Iroquois who were semi-nomadic and left their farming lands as they became depleted. Although the French government had granted the Jesuits rights to manage the land and protect the converts, in reality they acted more as landlords: granting land to European settlers and collecting dues in return. This gave rise to jealousies across the varied communities, including the local people and the incoming settlers. After a few years at the location, the community built first a wooden stockade, then a protective stone wall, enclosing both the Iroquois homes and the mission, church, and school buildings of the Jesuits.

186 INFRASTRUCTURE AND INNOVATION

MORGAN LEWIS WINDMILL

St. Andrew, Barbados
1727

By the late seventeenth century, Barbados—a British colony reliant on enslaved labor—had replaced tobacco as its primary crop with sugarcane, answering the European demand for sugar. Originally one of many, the Morgan Lewis Windmill, built from roughly cut stone and "cemented" with a local mortar—made from egg white mixed with coral dust—is the last working example of a sugar mill, used to extract juice from the cane.

BELOW: A fort built for the protection of both Jesuit missionaries and their Christian Iroquois converts.

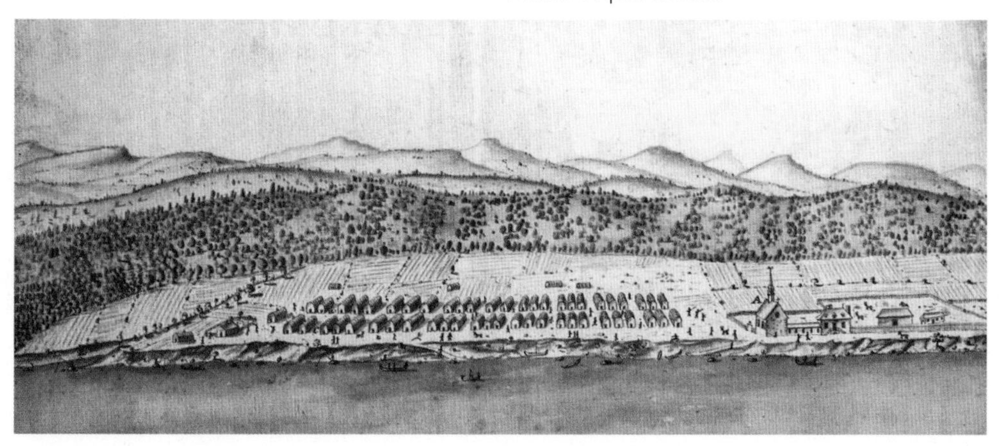

187 ART AND CULTURE

TRINITY COLLEGE LIBRARY

Dublin, Ireland
1732

In the 1680s, Trinity College, the most venerable academic institution in Dublin, was badly damaged by the occupying forces of James II during the Jacobite wars. After William III's victory in 1690, rebuilding happened slowly, but the London Parliament eventually agreed to finance a new library. The vast, impressive result was built by Thomas Burgh, responsible for a number of other notable buildings in Dublin—including the Old Custom House.

ABOVE: The magnificent scale of the new library dwarfed its predecessor.

ABOVE RIGHT: The church is a reminder of the legacy of the Jesuit influence on the Chiloé Archipelago.

188 RELIGION AND MONUMENT

SANTA MARÍA DE LORETO

Achao, Chile
c. 1740

The many islands that make up the Chiloé Archipelago were the subject of an intense conversion effort by Jesuit missionaries over the first half of the eighteenth century, when the area was under Spanish rule. Missionaries traveled briskly from place to place, often spending only a brief time in each. As the number of conversions grew, the simple thatched structures that were originally built to offer shelter to the priests and their congregations gave way to wooden churches that reflected the carpentry skills of the local population. Santa María de Loreto in Achao, on the island of Quinchao, is one of the most intact churches from the period, a tour de force built entirely from wood, and using pegs—not nails.

189 PLACE OF WORK

FANEUIL HALL

Boston, Massachusetts
1742

Faneuil Hall was named for Peter Faneuil, a wealthy merchant and slave trader who built it as a gift to Boston. Faneuil Hall was a central market and meeting place: the open market was on the ground floor and the assembly hall on the upper one. In the 1760s and 1770s it was nicknamed "the Cradle of Liberty" because prominent Sons of Liberty, including Samuel Adams and James Otis, met there on the eve of the American Revolution.

190 RESIDENCE/ART AND CULTURE

SANSSOUCI PALACE

Potsdam, Germany
1747

A small, elegant Rococo palace in a park filled with follies, Sanssouci (which means "carefree") was built by Frederick the Great of Prussia. It was designed as a retreat where he could relax, indulge his passion for the arts, and entertain the great minds of the day. (Voltaire was given his own apartment, but he never stayed there.) Although sometimes compared to Versailles, its intimate scale and lightness of touch puts it in a class of its own.

ABOVE: Comprised of exotic features such as vine- and fig-planted terraces, and a Chinese folly, the gardens of Sanssouci were as important to Frederick as the palace.

191 PLACE OF WORK

JACOB HOOY

Amsterdam, Netherlands
1747

When Jacob Hooy opened his first stall at Amsterdam's Nieuwmarkt, selling all the spices necessary for the kitchen and medicine chest, the Dutch East India Company had been trading for almost 150 years and his small business was just one in a city that was an important hub in the European spice trade. By 1747, he was installed in a shop at Kloveniersburgwal 12, which is still trading—the oldest spice store in Europe.

192 RESIDENCE

NO. 9 GETREIDEGASSE

Salzburg, Austria
1756

Wolfgang Amadeus Mozart was born in a modest apartment on the second floor of the townhouse at No. 9 Getreidegasse, in the archbishopric of Salzburg, where his father, Leopold, was music master to the court. Mozart's status as a prodigy led to him touring most of the European courts before he was eight years old. He came to regard Salzburg as provincial, much preferring Vienna, but after his death, the city took posthumous possession, regarding him as a favored son.

193 ART AND CULTURE

THE PINEAPPLE

Dunmore, Scotland
1761

A pineapple-topped garden folly added a particularly fashionable touch to the Earl of Dunmore's glasshouses, which were used to grow delicacies for the table. Pineapples were rarities in northern Europe. In 1668, Charles II served one at dinner to impress the French ambassador, and it remained a status symbol in the mid-eighteenth century, known to be expensive to import and hard to grow. Aristocrats cultivated them under glass; those not rich enough to buy them could hire one for a special occasion.

ALCÁZAR DE SEGOVIA

Segovia, Spain
1762

The Alcázar took its current form in the mid-fifteenth century as a large, well-defended medieval castle with a distinctive shiplike outline. In 1762, Carlos III of Spain, following a Europe-wide trend, opened a military training academy there. At the end of the seventeenth century, most European countries had begun to recruit permanent armies rather than relying on call-ups, and there was a resulting need for institutions to train them in specific military sciences.

LEFT: Military academies to train professional soldiers were a new, progressive development in the late eighteenth century.

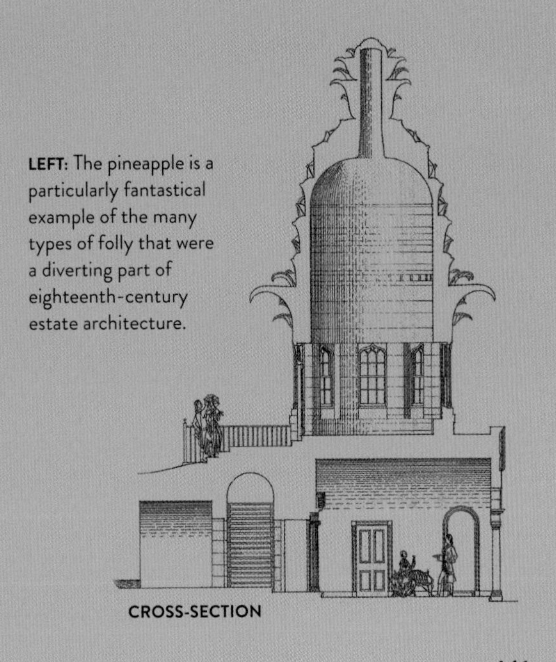

LEFT: The pineapple is a particularly fantastical example of the many types of folly that were a diverting part of eighteenth-century estate architecture.

FRAUNCES TAVERN

Manhattan, New York
1762

The New York inn that played a key role in the American Revolution.

In 1762, Samuel Fraunces opened the Queen's Head at 54 Pearl Street, in a house that in 1719 had been built for a wealthy merchant. Taverns were regular forums for social and political debate, and the Queen's Head quickly became popular. The first New York Chamber of Commerce was established at a meeting here in 1768, and many meetings for organizations—on both sides of the independence conflict in America—were also held here. By 1774, it was favored by the revolutionary side, hosting regular meetings of the Sons of Liberty.

At the end of the Revolutionary War, New York was the last city vacated by the British. Their defeat was celebrated with a large party at what was by now known as the Fraunces Tavern. On December 4, 1783, George Washington held a farewell dinner for his officers in the Long Room, before he returned home to Virginia.

Samuel Fraunces's connection with Washington wasn't over: Washington would use the tavern in 1789 to celebrate his inauguration as America's first president. In 1787, Fraunces sold the building and took up a new appointment as Washington's steward of the presidential household: first in New York, and subsequently in Philadelphia.

RIGHT: The tavern, like many others of its day, had started life as a private house.

BELOW: An artist's impression of Washington taking leave of his officers inside the Fraunces Tavern.

KNOWN FOR

- A popular meeting place for revolutionary groups in the 1770s
- The site of Washington's farewell speech to his officers at the end of the Revolutionary War
- Providing temporary offices for Washington's new government in the 1780s, during its short time in New York

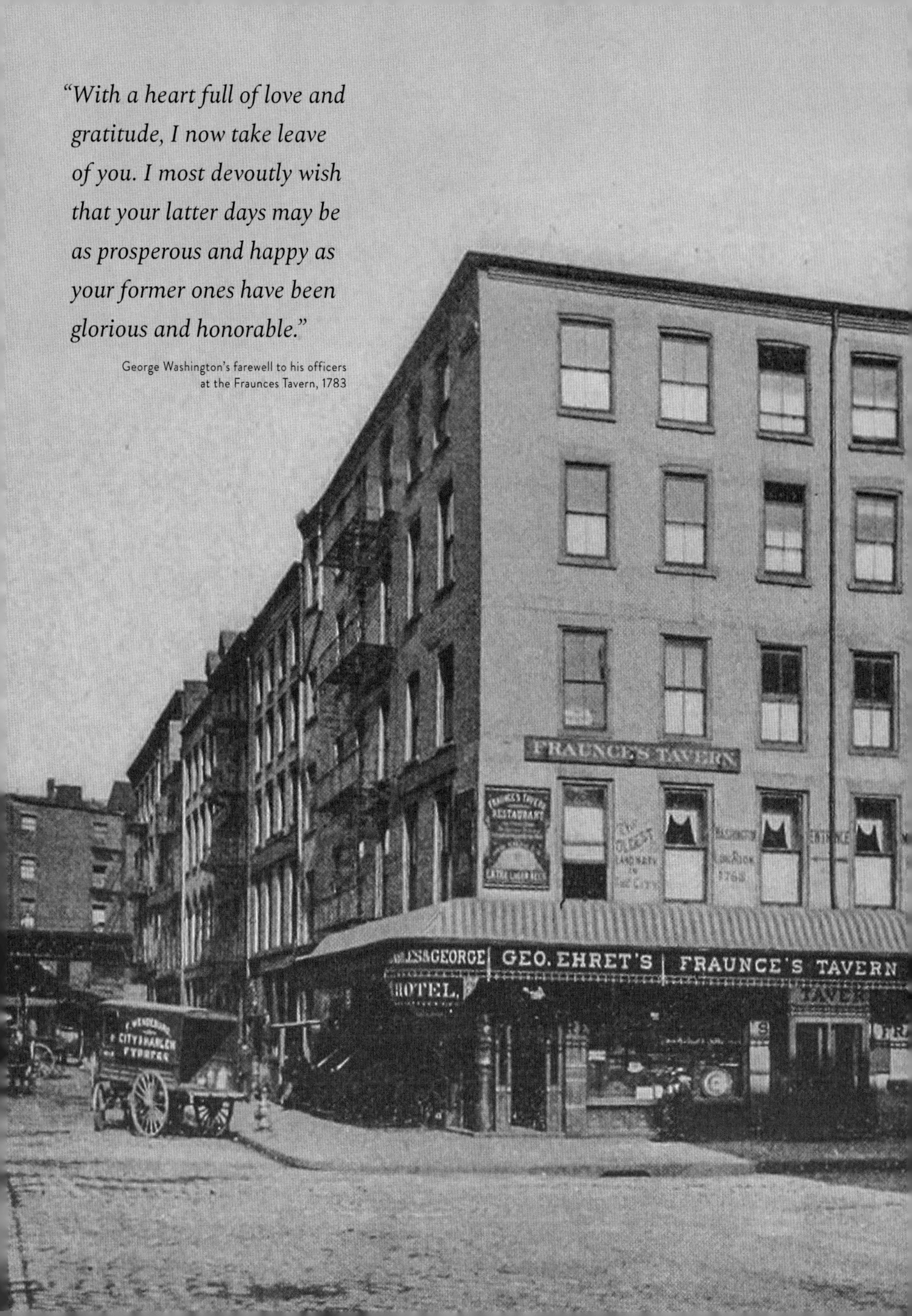

"With a heart full of love and gratitude, I now take leave of you. I most devoutly wish that your latter days may be as prosperous and happy as your former ones have been glorious and honorable."

George Washington's farewell to his officers at the Fraunces Tavern, 1783

196 RESIDENCE

ROYAL PALACE

Telavi, Georgia
1762

The only surviving royal palace of Georgia, remodeled under Heraclius II, shows the mix of Ottoman and Christian influences characteristic of the eastern part of this small country. Georgia often struggled to maintain its Christian identity in the face of territorial battles between the Islamic forces of the Ottomans and the Safavids. In 1783, Heraclius would finally succeed in placing his territory under the protection of Orthodox Christian Russia.

ABOVE: Some buildings in the compound resemble classic Roman basilicas.

197 PLACE OF WORK

WHITECHAPEL BELL FOUNDRY

London, England
c. 1770

The Liberty Bell, which cracked in transit

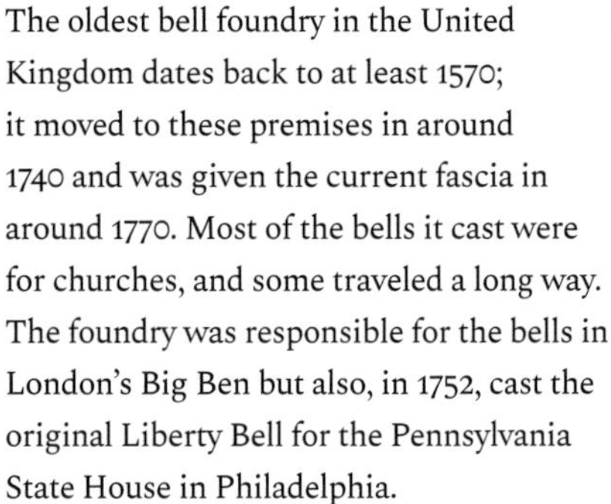

The oldest bell foundry in the United Kingdom dates back to at least 1570; it moved to these premises in around 1740 and was given the current fascia in around 1770. Most of the bells it cast were for churches, and some traveled a long way. The foundry was responsible for the bells in London's Big Ben but also, in 1752, cast the original Liberty Bell for the Pennsylvania State House in Philadelphia.

ABOVE: Today, the future of the foundry hangs in the balance.

198 INFRASTRUCTURE AND INNOVATION

CROMFORD MILL

Derbyshire, England

1771

The inventor Richard Arkwright built Cromford Mill to house his newly devised water-powered spinning machine, choosing the site because it had a supply of prewarmed water exiting a local lead mine. The mill employed 200 workers, mostly women and children, and was kept running 24 hours a day, with two 12-hour shifts. It was highly productive and would serve as a model for factory-run businesses as the industrial revolution gained traction.

ABOVE: Richard Arkwright was one of the first employers to provide accommodation for his workers.

199 RESIDENCE

MONTICELLO

Charlottesville, Virginia

1772

Neoclassical Monticello was designed by Thomas Jefferson, who remodeled the Virginia estate for over 40 years, dying deeply in debt. It remained a working plantation, reliant on the labor of enslaved people. While Jefferson was the main author of the Declaration of Independence, founded the University of Virginia, promoted religious freedom, and condemned slavery as a "moral depravity," he never resolved his own position.

200 ART AND CULTURE

WENJIN GE

Chengde, China

1773

Wenjin Ge was founded by the Quianlong Emperor in the Chengde Mountain Resort, where the Imperial Court spent their summer. The Imperial Library contained many books, in particular one of only seven copies of the *Siku Quanshu*, an encyclopedic collection of works in the disciplines of philosophy, history, classics, and literature—compiled under the authority of the literary emperor himself.

OLD SOUTH MEETING HOUSE

Boston, Massachusetts
1773

Site of the meeting that was the catalyst for the Boston Tea Party.

A handsome brick building, the Old South Meeting House was built in 1729 as a Puritan meeting place. It quickly became the location for Boston meetings that were too large for Faneuil Hall (see page 159). It was here, on December 16, 1773, that the political activist and leader Samuel Adams addressed a crowd of 5,000 men. He was speaking against the tea tax, which had been recently introduced by the British Parliament with the intention of forcing taxable tea from the East India Company on America, which hitherto had imported mostly tax-free Dutch tea. After the speech, Adams's "Sons of Liberty" marched to Griffin Wharf, boarded the tea ships, and emptied 342 chests of tea into the sea. The British Parliament promptly retaliated by passing the so-called Intolerable Acts, a raft of measures removing Massachusetts's right to self-governance, closing down trade in Boston, and in so doing, moving the situation one step closer to the Revolutionary War.

LEFT: Today, dwarfed by its surroundings, it's hard to believe that the Old South Meeting House was the largest building in colonial Boston in the early 1770s.

PENNSYLVANIA STATE HOUSE

Philadelphia, Pennsylvania
1776

The long conflict led to the signing of the Declaration of Independence.

The Pennsylvania State House was completed in 1753. It was here that the Second Continental Congress, made up of representatives from the 13 North American colonies, met to sign the Declaration of Independence on July 4, 1776. The building would become better known as Independence Hall, and the space outside—where the declaration was first read to an assembled crowd—as Independence Square.

Congress hadn't reached this point quickly. Established in 1775, it formed a Continental army, electing George Washington as its leader; it still hoped for a peaceful resolution with England. However, after a direct appeal to George III—known as the Olive Branch Petition—failed, the king declared that the colonies were in a state of revolt. When he then employed a group of German mercenaries to fight in America, Congress recognized that independence was their only possible route.

BELOW: On September 17, 1787, the United States Constitution was signed in the Pennsylvania State House.

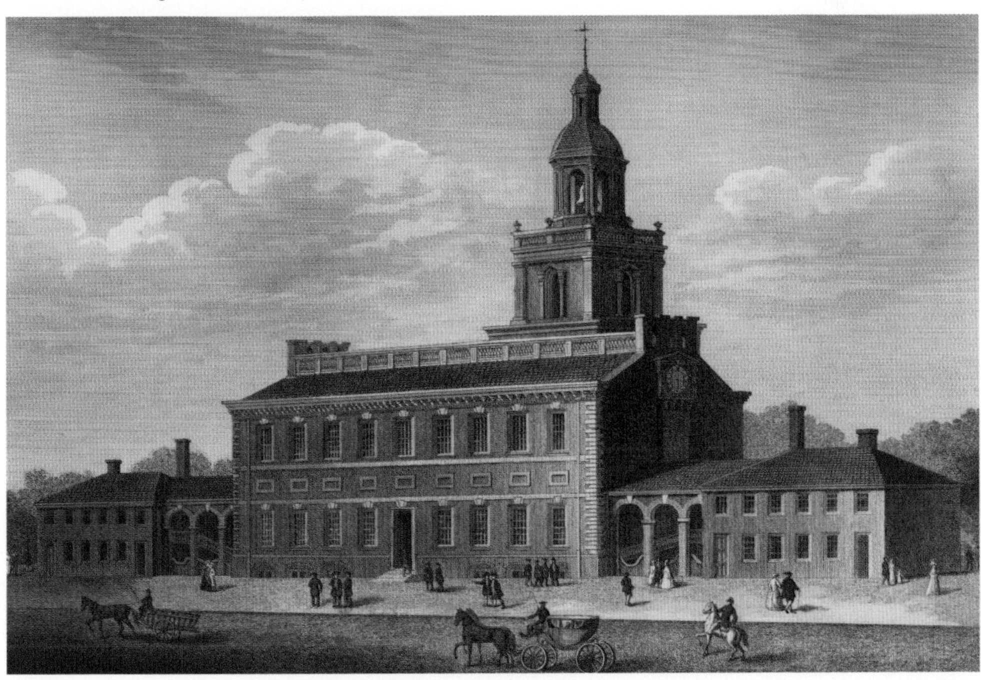

IRON BRIDGE

Shropshire, England
1779

An innovative use of iron which marked an important step in the industrial revolution.

In 1709, Abraham Derby of Coalbrookdale, a mining area in the west of England, mastered the art of smelting iron using coke rather than the more costly charcoal, a process that made it possible to produce iron in much larger quantities. The Coalbrookdale community was divided by a gorge through which the river Severn ran. Barges were the main method of transporting goods between the two sides, but the river was often too fierce to use in winter, and too shallow in summer, impeding trade.

In 1773, the Shrewsbury architect Thomas Pritchard had the idea of building a bridge made of iron to cross the gorge, both serving a practical purpose and acting as a public relations exercise for the local trade. Pritchard designed a single-span bridge, 100 feet long. He died suddenly in 1777, after which Abraham's grandson, Abraham Derby III, took over the project. Completed in 1779, the bridge opened to traffic two years later. It met with wide acclaim, gave its name to the community around it—which became known as Ironbridge—and ushered in a new era of building with iron. Just six years later, the first iron barge was launched on the Severn.

KNOWN FOR

- The first iron bridge in the world
- Opening up the possibilities of iron as a structural building material to a wider public
- Developing the iron-casting process for even larger structures

RIGHT: The use of iron produced a result that was stable and strong enough for the heavy traffic crossing the steep, heavily wooded gorge.

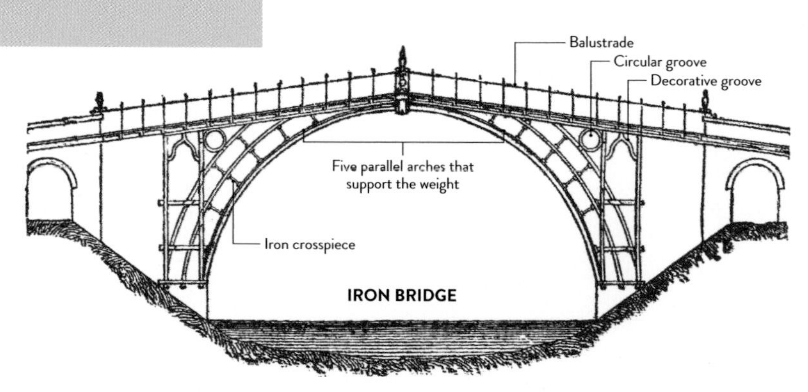

"It is one arch, a hundred feet broad, fifty-two high, and eighteen wide; all of cast-iron, weighing many hundred tons. I doubt whether the Colossus at Rhodes weighed much more."

John Wesley, theologian, 1779

HAMEAU DE LA REINE

MARIE ANTOINETTE

Versailles, France
1783

The fantasy hamlet built for the young queen of France.

In 1783, Marie Antoinette asked the court architect Richard Mique to build an idealized village in the grounds of the Petit Trianon, within the park of Versailles. The 13 buildings of the Hameau de la Reine, arranged along the bank of a small artificial lake, were completed in 1786. The queen's idea was not unique. There had been a fashion among the aristocracy for rustic entertainment, as there is a similar hameau at the Chateau de Chantilly. The royal version was used as an informal spot for hosting friends, and included a mill, cottages, and both working and "show" dairies. The working farm supplied fresh milk and cream, and was used to entertain the children of the royal household. In the lead-up to the French Revolution, the Hameau—Marie Antoinette's retreat from the rigid life at Versailles—was used to condemn her for playing at milkmaids while her people went hungry.

BELOW: The Hameau was a project of a sort not unusual among the owners of large estates, but it would label the queen as an incurably frivolous pleasure-seeker.

205 RESIDENCE/RELIGION AND MONUMENT

EJISU BESEASE

Kumasi, Ghana
c. 1780s

Between the early eighteenth and mid-nineteenth centuries, the Asante Empire was one of the most powerful in West Africa. Its traditional homes and shrine buildings took the same form: dwellings. Whether for deities or people, they had steeply pitched thatched roofs, and individual rooms around a central courtyard. Ejisu Besease is one of the last surviving Asante shrine buildings. Its earthen walls have been regularly remodeled and covered in deep-relief symbols from the Adinkra language used by the Asante.

206 RESIDENCE

DARIA DAULAT BAGH

Seringapatam, Karnataka, India
1784

Daria Daulat Bagh is one of seven palaces built for Tippu Sultan, the "Tiger of Mysore," a powerful local ruler who was implacably opposed to the English presence in India. The rectangular teak building contains murals showing his victory over the British East India Company at the Battle of Pollilur in 1780. Tippu Sultan was later killed fighting the British at the Siege of Seringapatam in 1799.

ABOVE: Like many Indian summer palaces Daria Daulat Bagh is largely open-air, with trellised walls ensuring both shade and ventilation in scorching weather.

207 RELIGION AND MONUMENT

CATACOMBS

Paris, France
1785

The subterranean burial ground that became a tourist attraction.

Between the fifteenth and eighteenth centuries, Paris grew so fast that its graveyards overfilled. Citizens started to complain that the cemeteries stank. The last straw came in 1780, when the boundary wall at the Holy Innocents' Cemetery gave way and bodies fell into the street.

The solution lay in the defunct limestone quarries under Paris, which had been abandoned since the fifteenth century. In 1785, an inspector was entrusted with organizing the miles of tunnels to store the bodies. Over 12 years, an estimated six million skeletons were moved—at night—and piled up in the passages of the newly christened Catacombs. During the French Revolution, between 1789 and 1799, many bodies were taken there directly.

In the early nineteenth century, the Catacombs became a visitor attraction. The first tourists were admitted in 1809; by then, the bones had been piled in decorative arrangements, lining the tunnels in elaborate patterns.

ABOVE: Before the Catacombs opened to the public in 1809, Inspector de Thury—who was in charge of their organization—had the bones arranged more appealingly, en masse.

THE BASTILLE

Paris, France
1789

The storming of a royal prison that marked the beginning of the French Revolution.

By the close of the eighteenth century, the Bastille was nearing the end of its useful life. A massive medieval fortress, it had been used to lock up opponents of the monarchy for hundreds of years. In the eyes of ordinary citizens, it represented the tyranny of the Bourbon regime. Despite the fact that in the summer of 1789 it held only seven obscure prisoners, its importance to the revolutionaries was twofold: it symbolized everything they opposed, and it was known to house a store of gunpowder. On July 14, Parisians who had already looted Les Invalides, the military hospital of Paris, seized a cache of muskets and a number of cannons, and surrounded the Bastille.

The governor of the prison tried to mediate, but the crowd scaled the walls and took over the building. The downfall of the Bastille would later be seen as the point at which the revolution began. Just three years later, the monarchy was abolished in France.

ABOVE: A contemporary engraving of the Bastille under siege, by Jean Louis Prieur the Younger.

BELOW: This historical reconstruction shows a view of the Bastille and Porte Saint-Antoine from the northeast. After the storming of the Bastille in 1789, the building was completely demolished. Today, the Place de la Bastille occupies its position.

BRANDENBURG GATE

Berlin, Germany
1791

A national landmark that has come to symbolize German identity.

Built by the king of Prussia, Brandenburg Gate was designed in the Greek Revival style with a double row of Doric columns, topped by a quadriga, or four-horse chariot. Used as a powerful symbol by different regimes, the quadriga was taken to Paris when Napoleon took Berlin (and returned on his defeat in 1814); later, the gate became a centerpiece for Nazi parades. In the postwar division of Berlin, it was contained in an exclusion zone, but since 1989 it has become a symbol of the reunification of Germany.

ABOVE: The quadriga traveled to France with Napoleon as the spoils of war, before returning in 1814.

BELOW: Noted for its strong, clean Neoclassical lines, the gate was a collaboration between the architect Carl Gotthard Langhans and the sculptor Johann Gottfried Schadow.

210 RESIDENCE

ELIZABETH FARM

New South Wales, Australia
1793

Built in 1793 by John Macarthur and named for his wife, Elizabeth Farm is the oldest European home surviving in Australia. Adapted to the local climate with a deep veranda, and enlarged numerous times, Elizabeth continued to live here and manage the land around it while John's life suffered ups and downs. He was involved in the local European community at Parramatta. He spent two long spells back in his native England, attempting to clear his name, the first after a duel, and the second after he tried to overthrow the colony's governor, William Bligh, in an armed revolt. After his return in 1817, he concentrated on successfully building Australia's new wool business, eventually becoming one of the richest men in New South Wales.

211 RESIDENCE

DOVE COTTAGE

Grasmere, England
1799

Dove Cottage, in the English Lake District, was rented by the 29-year-old Romantic poet William Wordsworth and his sister Dorothy in 1799. He had already co-authored *Lyrical Ballads* with Samuel Taylor Coleridge, and was becoming known for his fresh, simple style. The siblings stayed for nine years, during which time William, inspired by the landscape, wrote some of his best-known works, including *The Prelude*, "Ode to Duty," and many sonnets.

BELOW: The oldest European home in Australia, built by the man who organized the country's only military coup.

4 1800–1899

ABOVE: The south and north porticoes of the White House were added in the 1820s.

212 POLITICS AND NATIONAL DEFENSE

THE WHITE HOUSE

Washington, D.C.
1800

George Washington chose the location for the new capital of America, including the position and appearance of the White House—a fresh start in a city with no affiliations to any individual state. It was designed by the Irish-born architect James Hoban and built by a workforce that included enslaved people, local artisans, and immigrants. The Neoclassical mansion, at first simply known as President's House, was modeled on Ireland's parliament building, Leinster House, in Dublin.

213 RESIDENCE/PLACE OF WORK

THE HERMITAGE

Davidson County, Tennessee
1804

The cotton estate and mansion of the seventh American president.

Andrew Jackson was a lawyer, war hero, and the seventh president of the United States, serving from 1829 to 1837. He bought the 425-acre farm, which became known as the Hermitage, in 1804 after a disastrous business deal forced him to downsize from a larger estate to avoid bankruptcy. The first house on the site was a simple log cabin, which was replaced by a handsome brick house in the Federal style in 1821. During his presidency, it was converted once again into the Neoclassical mansion that can be seen today.

Over time, as more land was added, the estate became a profitable cotton plantation. In 1845, the year of Jackson's death, it had around 160 enslaved workers. Jackson was a fierce opponent of abolition, and to modern eyes the history of the Hermitage cannot be reconciled with the contemporary perception of his "liberal" values. In his time, this clash wasn't uncommon.

ABOVE: The well-appointed cottage belonged to Jane Austen's brother, Edward, who lived at Chawton House nearby.

CHAWTON COTTAGE

Hampshire, England
1809

Jane Austen spent her final—and most productive—years staying rent-free in this rambling house on one of her wealthy brother's estates. Living with her mother, sister Cassandra, and friend Martha Lloyd, she fitted her writing around menial household work. Over the eight years that she called this home, she saw *Sense and Sensibility* and *Pride and Prejudice* published, and also worked on *Mansfield Park*, *Emma*, and *Persuasion*. She left Chawton only during her final illness in 1817.

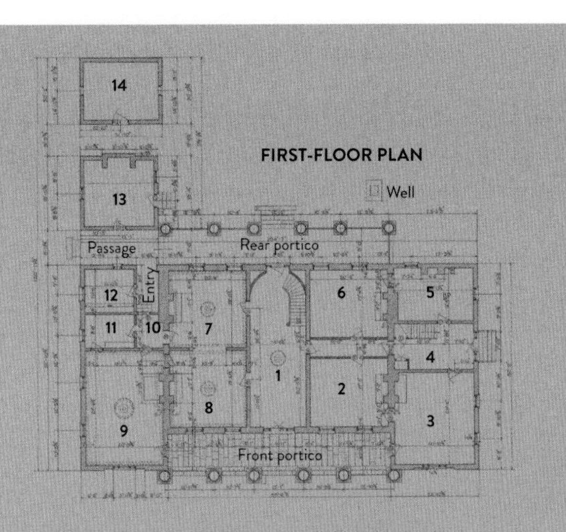

1 Entrance hall **2** General Jackson's room **3** General Jackson's library **4** Service hall **5** Steward's room **6** Andrew Jackson Jr.'s room **7** Back parlor **8** Front parlor **9** Dining room **10** Hall **11** Service pantry **12** Storage pantry **13** Kitchen **14** Smoke house

RIGHT: During the 1820s, the very basic house on the estate was gradually remodeled into a grander home, suitable to the needs of a president.

YASNAYA POLYANA ESTATE

Tula, Russia
1810

The Russian country estate that was both home and inspiration to Leo Tolstoy.

Yasnaya Polyana is around 120 miles south of Moscow. A typical nineteenth-century Russian country estate, Leo Tolstoy's grandfather built the main house in 1810 and the 4,000 acres of land around it were farmed by about 350 peasants. Tolstoy regarded the simple life as exemplifying the best of Russia. After fighting in the Crimean War, he returned to Yasnaya Polyana in 1851, married, and spent most of the next 48 years there, raising a large family with his wife Sonya, and writing. Both *War and Peace* (1869) and *Anna Karenina* (1877) were written here: Prince Volkonsky's estate and Levin and Kitty's estate that feature in the novels were both based on Yasnaya Polyana.

In older age, Tolstoy became more fixed in his beliefs, embracing pacifism and the importance of education, and rejecting conventional religion. On publication of his final novel, *Resurrection*, he was excommunicated by the Orthodox church. His extreme views led to a rift with his wife. At the time of his death in 1810, he had fled Yasnaya Polyana to try to escape what he perceived as the worldly life. He shortly succumbed to pneumonia, but his beliefs had made him influential to a wide number of freethinkers, notably Mahatma Gandhi. He is buried in woodland on the estate.

KNOWN FOR

- Typifying the Russian country life idealized by Tolstoy
- Featuring in two of the great Russian novels
- A rare, intact survival of a country estate from before the revolution

"Without my Yasnaya Polyana, I can hardly imagine Russia and my attitude toward it."

Leo Tolstoy

BELOW LEFT: Leo Tolstoy took a close interest in the extensive grounds at his estate: from the flower and vegetable gardens and orchards, to the birch forests around them.

BELOW: Of the numerous buildings at Yasnaya Polyana, Tolstoy made his home in the comparatively modest wing of an earlier, larger manor house.

216 RESIDENCE

CASA DE LA INDEPENDENCIA

Asunción, Paraguay
1811

The modest house that became a clandestine meeting place for Paraguay's revolutionaries.

Now a museum, the house is a small adobe building, a rare colonial survivor in Asunción. It would have been typical of homes of the early nineteenth century here. Antonio Saénz raised his family here. Two of his sons, Sebástian Antonio and Paolo Pablo, joined the growing revolutionary movement in Paraguay, and the house became a clandestine meeting place for those wanting to overthrow Spanish rule, imposed through the viceroyalty of Rio de la Plata (a huge area that took in most of present-day Uruguay, Bolivia, and Argentina, as well as Paraguay, then seen as a province of Argentina).

On May 14, 1811, a group of revolutionaries left the Casa de la Independencia and made their way to Governor Velasco's house nearby, where he was persuaded to resign peacefully. By June 17, a new political junta of five of the revolutionaries had taken power.

ABOVE: An artist's depiction of the revolutionaries demanding rights from Governor Velasco.

BELOW: A rare survival, the house would have been typical of the basic adobe homes in Asunción in the early 1800s.

217 ART AND CULTURE

LORD'S CRICKET GROUND

London, England
1814

The peripatetic beginnings of the world's most famous cricket ground.

Cricket clubs were becoming increasingly important to the game by the end of the eighteenth century. The White Conduit was named for the public fields on which the club played, but in 1787 some of the members—including the Duke of Richmond and the Earl of Winchelsea—asked Thomas Lord, a professional who had bowled for the club, to find a more private space.

Lord's first ground was on Dorset Fields in Marylebone. In 1809, it moved to a second site in Lisson Grove, but the building of Regent's Canal precipitated what was to be the final move to St. John's Wood. Lord's was bought by the Marylebone Cricket Club—the new identity of the original White Conduit Club—shortly after the move, although the ground retained its name. It has been regarded as "the home of cricket" ever since.

"A game which the English, not being a spiritual people, have invented in order to give themselves some conception of eternity."

Lord Mancroft,
Bees in Some Bonnets, 1979

ABOVE: The earliest building at the new grounds was a tavern for the refreshment of players and spectators. The pavilion was initially a basic addition; its current form was built in 1890.

218 ART AND CULTURE

VILLA DIODATI

Cologny, Lake Geneva, Switzerland
1816

During what was to be the coldest summer for 200 years, Lord Byron—fleeing scandal in England—with his doctor, John Polidori, rented Villa Diodati. It became the setting for a ghost-story writing competition between Byron, Polidori, the poet Percy Bysshe Shelley, and his wife Mary. It was to produce a literary milestone: here, Mary Shelley sketched the outline of *Frankenstein*, which was published in 1818.

219 RESIDENCE

LONGWOOD HOUSE

Saint Helena
1821

Napoleon's exile on Saint Helena, a remote island in the South Atlantic, began after his defeat at Waterloo and ended with his death in May 1821. Longwood House, the former farmhouse where he was confined, belonged to the East India Company and was far from grand. Many conspiracy theories grew up around his death—including that he had been killed by the arsenic in the house's wallpaper—but most likely he died of stomach cancer.

ABOVE: The exotic outline of the Royal Pavilion was considered outlandish when it was built in the fast-growing resort then known as Brighthelmston.

220 RESIDENCE

ROYAL PAVILION

Brighton, England
1823

A country retreat for the Prince of Wales (later King George IV), the Pavilion was built piecemeal over 30 years and completed by John Nash, later the architect of Buckingham Palace (see page 189), in 1823. An extreme expression of the Oriental style fashionable in England from the mid-eighteenth century, the Pavilion did a lot to help "exotic" styles—both architecture and interiors—filter down to a much wider audience through the rest of the nineteenth century.

ABOVE: The Petrovsky Theater burned down in 1853, but just two years later the Bolshoi Theater opened on the same site, in the form which exists today.

221 ART AND CULTURE

BOLSHOI THEATER

Moscow, Russia

1825

By the late eighteenth century, a number of private theater companies were working in Moscow, but they were often reliant on the aristocracy for performance space. In 1806, Tsar Alexander I established Moscow Imperial Theaters. However, the groups it covered—opera, ballet, and theater—still performed in a variety of different spaces. Opened in January 1825, the Bolshoi Petrovsky Theater (*bolshoi* means "great") gave them an appropriately imposing and modern performance space.

ABOVE: The fort originally consisted of a number of buildings for shelter and storage within a sturdy palisade with four watchtowers.

222 PLACE OF WORK

FORT LANGLEY

British Columbia, Canada

1826

In the early nineteenth century, the British-owned Hudson's Bay Company was trading in furs across a wide area of North America. Fort Langley, its headquarters, was situated on the south side of the Fraser River. At a time when the Canadian/American border was still under discussion, it was positioned on what was likely to be the Canadian side so that the company's trade could continue without being claimed by the American government.

ROUND STONE BARN

Hancock, Massachusetts
1826

An innovative design for easy, hygienic animal husbandry.

The Shakers—formally, the United Society of Believers in Christ's Second Appearing—were founded in 1747, a religious group known for their "shaking" during worship, their celibacy, egalitarianism, and simple, communal way of life. The elegant ease of their design has always been admired. The only round barn they ever built, at Hancock Village, expresses it as much as any of their furniture or household objects.

Round barns use less building material than rectangular ones, so were more economical. But the barn at Hancock also uses the curves: ramps outside allow horse-drawn wagons to reach the upper floor, unload, then carry on around the circle to the exit without having to turn. Plenty of windows keep the barn interior light and well ventilated. The lower floor has a hollow center, a ring to store hay, an outer ring with stalls for cattle, and trapdoors within the stalls so that dung can be shoveled down to the cellar and transported as needed to the garden. Despite its evident practicality, the barn remains unique, and something of a puzzle. Its design was never duplicated in other Shaker communities, and although other round barns were built in America, they don't share the extra features that make this one special.

RIGHT: The circular structure made loading and unloading easy, while numerous windows ensured the barn could be kept well ventilated. Although the original barn burned down in 1864, it was quickly reconstructed to the original design.

BELOW: Inside, the round stone barn was ideal for storing hay and milking cows.

KNOWN FOR

- A beautiful and progressive design for a practical building
- Demonstrating the Shakers' advanced agricultural practice
- The earliest, and most sophisticated, round stone barn built in North America

"Do your work as if you had a thousand years to live, and as if you were to die tomorrow."

Shaker proverb

224 ART AND CULTURE

ALTES MUSEUM

Berlin, Germany
1830

A magnificent Neoclassical building designed by Karl Friedrich Schinkel, the Altes Museum was built on the orders of Frederick William III of Prussia to give the royal art collection a home where it could be viewed by the public. Inaugurated in May 1830, it was an immediate success, and would form the centerpiece of a plan to dedicate the area—now called Museuminsel, or museum island—to the education of the public in the arts and sciences.

225 RELIGION AND MONUMENT

ALAMO MISSION

San Antonio, Texas
1836

The Alamo was originally a fortified Franciscan mission, but when the Texas Revolution against Mexican rule broke out in late 1835, it was being used as a military garrison. When Mexican forces arrived in San Antonio, Texan soldiers withdrew into the Alamo and a 13-day siege began. By the end of the long-delayed battle, the Texan defenders were dead. Despite this, fierce resistance continued, and it was only after two further battles that the status of Texas as a republic was finally agreed on April 22, 1836. The siege of the Alamo became a symbol of courage against impossible odds.

ABOVE: The remains of the fort that was the site of the Battle of the Alamo, which played a key part in the Texas Revolution.

BUCKINGHAM PALACE

London, England
1837

The London townhouse that became a palace.

Originally built in 1703 for the Duke of Buckingham, it was first known as Buckingham House. The palace was bought for Queen Charlotte by her husband, George III. Remodeled for George IV by the architects John Nash (see page 184) and Edward Blore, it only became the main London residence of British monarchs when Queen Victoria acceded in 1837. Queen Victoria moved in, choosing it over both St. James's Palace and Kensington Palace.

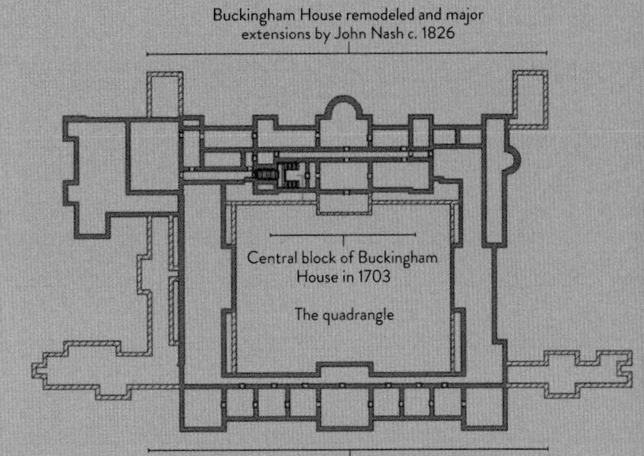

ABOVE: The ground plan of the palace shows the comparatively modest Buckingham House of 1703, the "garden" facade, and extensions added by John Nash in 1826. The East Front, the view most familiar today, was added in the mid-nineteenth century and augmented in the early twentieth century.

ABOVE: The East Front of the palace, facing the Mall, was remodeled in 1847, with a balcony added for the royal family's public appearances.

TREATY HOUSE

Waitangi, New Zealand
1840

The site of a signing of a controversial treaty between New Zealand's Maori chiefs and the British colonizers.

The home of James Busby, British resident minister in New Zealand from 1833, was a modest wooden house on land at Waitangi, overlooking the Bay of Islands on North Island. Busby had been appointed to his post after a number of Maori chiefs made a request to William IV for protection. They were concerned about the bad behavior of British settlers on their lands, and worried about possible French plans for colonization. The Waitangi Treaty was drafted by Busby and William Hobson, the newly appointed lieutenant governor.

A few days after Hobson's arrival, on February 6, 1840, the treaty was signed by a number of Maori chiefs in the grounds of Busby's house—subsequently known as Treaty House—then circulated around the country to be signed by others. Not all Maori leaders signed, and some aspects of the treaty's validity have been questioned ever since.

"He iwi tahi tatou"
(We are one people)

Lieutenant Governor William Hobson, on the signing of the Waitangi Treaty

BELOW: Treaty House has survived in much the same form as when it was built in the mid-nineteenth century.

228 RESIDENCE

KAIPING WATCHTOWERS

Guangdong, China
From c. 1840

The earliest watchtowers, or *dialou*, of Kaiping—a city in China's Pearl River Delta—were purely defensive. They had small windows and thick walls, allowing farmers to watch over their rice paddies and protect them when the fields flooded. But from the mid-nineteenth century, local people who had worked overseas began to style these practical buildings in ways they had seen abroad. Gothic and classical details started to appear in the dialou, reflecting the wider experience of their owners.

ABOVE: Over time, the traditional watchtowers gained details—inside and out—that reflected styles that their owners had seen abroad.

229 RELIGION AND MONUMENT

BUNKER HILL MONUMENT

Boston, Massachusetts
1843

The Battle of Bunker Hill on June 17, 1775, was the first pitched battle of the Revolutionary War. Despite being badly outnumbered, the Americans killed over 1,000 British soldiers, sustaining 100 dead themselves. The first monument, a wooden column dedicated to Dr. Joseph Warren, a hero on the American side, was erected in 1794; 49 years later, the permanent memorial, a granite obelisk, was opened in a ceremony attended by President John Tyler.

THOREAU'S HUT

Walden Pond, Massachusetts
1845

An experiment in basic living which produced a classic of Transcendental literature.

When Henry David Thoreau embarked on living in the woods for two years, he did so in a small wooden cabin that he had built himself; on land belonging to his friend and patron Ralph Waldo Emerson, he had a clear idea of what he was undertaking. Thoreau was 28 and, like Emerson, a devotee of the Transcendentalist movement. This was a loosely grouped set of writers and thinkers who emerged in the 1830s and who believed in imagination and intuition over intellectual philosophy. The Walden experiment was to see what would emerge if Thoreau relied on his individual experience in an isolated setting, surrounded by nature. The result, published in 1854, was *Walden; or, Life in the Woods*, a collection of 18 essays that not only became a classic of nature writing—probably its best-known aspect—but also addressed wider questions of the nature of individuality.

"I went to the woods because I wished to live deliberately, to front only the essential facts of life, and see if I could not learn what it had to teach, and not, when I came to die, discover that I had not lived . . ."

Henry David Thoreau, *Walden*, 1854

BELOW: Today a replica of Thoreau's hut, exact in all its simple detail, stands near to the site of the original in the Walden Park State Reservation.

REAL FABRICA DE TABACOS PARTAGÁS

Havana, Cuba
1845

A story of success in Havana's hugely profitable cigar trade.

One of the world's largest producers of tobacco, by the mid-nineteenth century not only were there 10,000 tobacco plantations on Cuba, but cigar factories were springing up all over the island. Jaime Partagás arrived in Cuba from Barcelona in 1831, aged just 14, one of a large number of Catalans coming to the Caribbean to seek their fortune. Partagás spent the next 14 years in the cigar business: he opened his first shop in 1838, built a warehouse by 1840, then in 1845 he opened his own factory, a grand rust-and-cream edifice on Industria Street, over the road from Havana's capitol building. Not just a businessman, Partagás was also an innovator, experimenting with new methods of blending tobaccos and improving the fermenting processes of the leaves.

Partagás was murdered in 1868, but his business continued to thrive, remaining successful after Fidel Castro's nationalization of the tobacco business in 1960.

BELOW: In 2013, Partagás's cigar production moved to a different factory, although the iconic building is still sporadically open as a museum.

232 PLACE OF WORK

THE ETHER DOME, MASSACHUSETTS GENERAL HOSPITAL

Boston, Massachusetts
1846

To commemorate the first publicly demonstrated administration of ether as an anesthetic, the hospital's surgical amphitheater would be named the Ether Dome. On October 16, 1846, in front of an audience, William T. G. Morton, a dentist, administered ether to a patient, rendering him unconscious, before a surgeon removed a tumor from his jaw.

ABOVE: To give surgeons as much natural light as possible, early operating theaters were built on the top floor of a building.

233 PLACE OF WORK/INFRASTRUCTURE AND INNOVATION

ROYAL ALBERT DOCK

Liverpool, England
1846

In the 1840s, Liverpool was one of the busiest ports in the world, handling an estimated 40 percent of global trade. When the Royal Albert Dock was opened, it represented a truly innovative development. Built entirely of stone, brick, and cast iron—eliminating wood—it hugely reduced the risk of fire. Two years later, it would introduce the world's first hydraulic cranes, halving the time it took to load cargo.

ABOVE: Made famous for being the first dock not to be built using any wood, the risk of fire was dramatically reduced, making it a far safer place to work.

234 RELIGION AND MONUMENT

KOLOBENG MISSION

Kolobeng, Botswana
1847

The mission at Kolobeng was the third and final built by the Scottish missionary David Livingstone. It was short-lived because when drought arrived in the region in 1848, Sechele I, leader of the local Bakwena people, held Livingstone responsible. He had dissuaded traditional rainmakers from practicing, recommending prayer and a new irrigation system instead. Four years later, Boer farmers declared war on the Bakwena, and Livingstone left the mission for good.

ABOVE: Of the church and mission buildings established by Livingstone, only the foundations remain today.

235 PLACE OF WORK

FREMANTLE PRISON

Fremantle, Western Australia
1850

Since 1787, British courts had been sentencing convicted prisoners to transportation to the east coast of Australia. When the *Scindian*, sailing from Portsmouth, and carrying 75 convicts plus staff, arrived in Fremantle, on the west coast, the jails were already full. The convicts were put to work building the Convict Establishment (renamed Fremantle Prison in 1867) themselves. By the time transportation to Australia stopped in 1868, nearly 10,000 prisoners had passed through its doors.

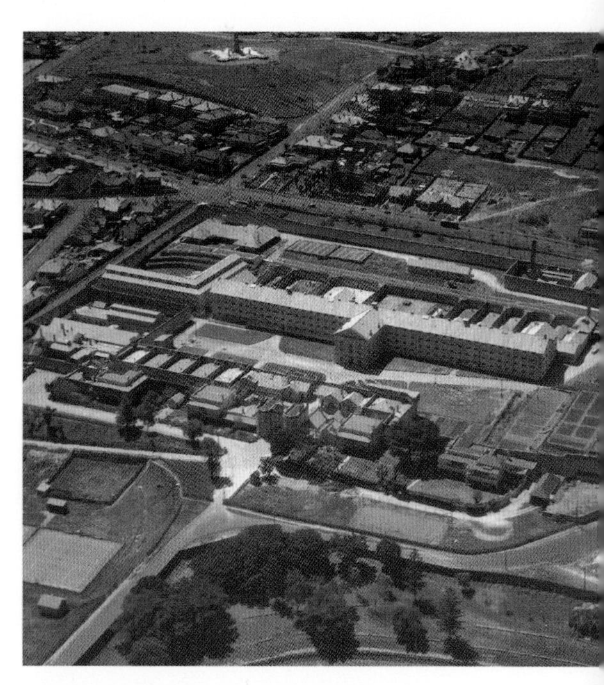

ABOVE: Long after transportation was stopped, Fremantle Prison was used as a high-security jail. It only closed in 1991.

236 PLACE OF WORK

GENERAL STORE, SOFALA

New South Wales, Australia
1851

A store built for the prospectors of Australia's short-lived gold rush.

In February 1851, a prospector, Edward Hargraves, found a few specks of gold in Lewis Ponds Creek, a deeply rural location about 143 miles northwest of Sydney. Within three months, a tent city of hopeful miners had arrived. By August, Sofala was declared a township. Shops, bars, and accommodation quickly sprung up for the ready-made clientele, and the newly christened general store opened later that same year. The gold rush was short-lived, however. Most prospectors moved on within a year or two, and Sofala's temporary population—at one point the town was famous for having 40 hotels—gradually diminished. Today, with a population of just a few hundred, it's a three-street village popular with tourists. The clapboard general store, with its false front, large windows, and picturesque ironwork balcony, is still open—one of 18 buildings that survive from Sofala's gold-rush days.

ABOVE: By the 1990s, gold rush–era buildings in Sofala were in a poor state of repair. Over the last decade, many have been refurbished and the tiny town has become a tourist stop.

CRYSTAL PALACE

Sydenham, London, England
1851

A popular success made possible by technical advances in modular construction.

The Crystal Palace was commissioned to house "The Great Exhibition of the Works of Industry of All Nations," on a site in Hyde Park, marking the start of the nineteenth-century love affair with world fairs. The organizing committee argued over the design, insisting it must be sensational, yet also affordable and temporary. The immense greenhouse proposed by Joseph Paxton, an architect and botanist, eventually won the architectural competition. He had worked on the Stove, a huge conservatory at Chatsworth, the Duke of Devonshire's estate, where he had experimented with an innovative "ridge-and-furrow" construction.

With the help of structural engineer Charles Fox, building the 1,848-foot-long behemoth took eight months. The iron skeleton was made in modules, joined on site, and then glazed with 293,000 panes. The result was hailed a masterpiece.

When the exhibition was over, the Crystal Palace was dismantled and re-erected at Sydenham Hill in south London. It burned down in 1936.

"That really was the birth of modern architecture, of pre-fabrication, of soaring spans of transparency. That was truly a seminal building."

Architect Norman Foster, *Dezeen*, 2019

BELOW: The innovative modular construction made it possible to build the Crystal Palace on site and to schedule.

LE BONNE MARCHÉ

Paris, France
1852

The first department store in Paris sees the start of shopping as entertainment.

In the mid-nineteenth century, although you could browse certain shops for particular goods, the idea of shopping as a leisure activity had not taken hold. When Aristide and Marguerite Boucicaut arrived to manage a medium-sized haberdashery and textile shop in Paris in 1852, they felt shopping could be made more exciting.

They introduced a greater variety of goods, all at fixed prices, made tighter margins to keep those prices competitive, and included returns, refunds, and seasonal sales, plus copious advertising and novelties—such as a reading room where customers could catch up on the newspapers. They also created a supportive environment for their staff, with health care, lectures, entertainments and, when the bigger store was built—particularly for the young female staff—on-site dormitories.

Le Bonne Marché (The Good Deal) enjoyed speedy success. By 1863, the Boucicauts had bought out the original owners, and by 1869 a new building had been designed with different departments covering every need. It was enlarged again in 1872 with the help of the design studios of Gustave Eiffel, who devised a structure that helped to keep the store interior light—another new departure. By the end of the nineteenth century, department stores could be found in most major cities, and Le Bonne Marché looked very much as it does today.

KNOWN FOR

- A very early "lifestyle" store
- A caring employer with an involvement in their employees' lives
- Introducing the first mail-order catalogs

LEFT: The store's eventual size made its boast that a shopper could find everything they wanted under one roof a real possibility.

RIGHT: By introducing more light to the interiors—and having goods openly on display—Le Bonne Marché was the first store to encourage impulse purchases.

THE PENITENTIARY

Port Arthur, Tasmania
1854

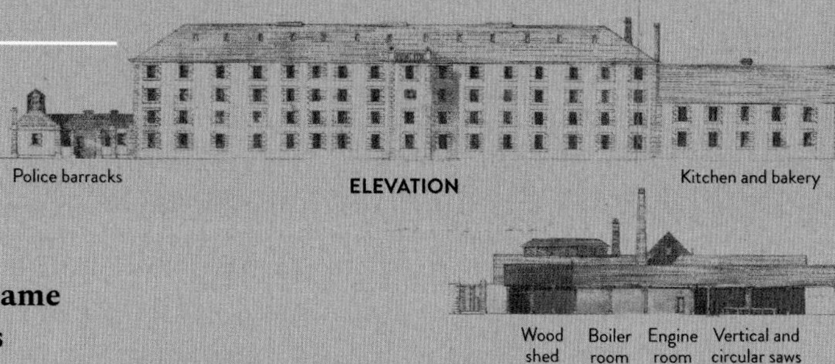

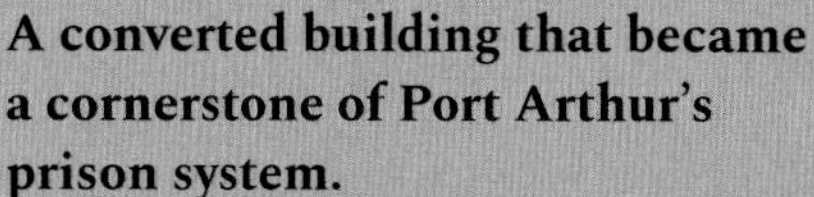

A converted building that became a cornerstone of Port Arthur's prison system.

Built as a flour mill, the Penitentiary failed as a business and was converted to a prison in 1854. Port Arthur, a penal settlement from the 1830s, was notorious for its cruelty. A remote site, 60 miles southeast of Hobart, it was believed to be impossible to escape from. The toughest regime was operated by the so-called Separate Prison, where all new prisoners served a spell before being reallocated elsewhere. The Penitentiary was less extreme, although 136 prisoners considered incorrigible had individual cells; an upstairs dormitory slept 348 more. Physical punishment was commonplace, and prisoners were often chained when working outside.

The use of transportation as a criminal punishment ended in 1853, and gradually the supply of convicts dwindled. As residents aged and became unable to work, they were moved elsewhere. Port Arthur finally closed as a penal settlement in 1877. It was gutted by fire in 1897, and survives today only as a ruined shell.

ABOVE: A former flour mill on a narrow-necked peninsula, the Penitentiary was believed to be impossible to escape from. All necessary facilities were on site, and groups of prisoners were employed to work nearby.

BELOW: Contemporaries admired the solidity of the stone construction at a time when many of Tasmania's buildings were still made of wood.

240 RESIDENCE

TYROL COT

St. Michael, Barbados
1854

Tyrol Cot names both the main house on the estate—which was built in 1854 by the Barbadian architect William Farnum—and the village around it, which consists of so-called chattel houses. These simple wooden homes, which house a museum today, were owned by plantation workers. Rather than being built on foundations, they were raised on blocks, so that they could easily be moved between locations as fieldwork required.

ABOVE: Chattel houses were simple and quick to dismantle and reassemble, so they could be moved around an estate to be near to where workers were needed.

241 POLITICS AND NATIONAL DEFENSE

EUREKA STOCKADE

Victoria, Australia
1854

The Eureka Stockade was a quickly constructed defense put together with timbers from the gold mine at Ballarat, Victoria. The miners, or "diggers," erected the structure when colonial soldiers were sent to break up a local rebellion against the punitive laws imposed on them. The ensuing clash on December 3, 1854, left a number of casualties, mostly on the diggers' side, but the conflict led to an improvement of their rights and, ultimately, to electoral reform.

ABOVE: Conflict at the stockade left an estimated 22 diggers dead, but the incident paved the way for a reform of the rights of miners in Australia.

NEW YORK TIMES BUILDING

Manhattan, New York
1857

Founded in 1851, the *New York Times* moved into custom-built headquarters at 41 Park Row in 1857, the first newspaper to do so. As other papers moved in nearby, Park Row became known as Newspaper Row. It was conveniently close to City Hall, source of much of the daily news. The building was considerably enlarged to house a growing staff until the *Times* moved to One Times Square in 1903.

BELOW: The *New York Times* lasted nearly five decades on Park Row, in the first purpose-built newspaper offices.

243 PLACE OF WORK/INFRASTRUCTURE AND INNOVATION

HARLAND & WOLFF SHIPYARD

Belfast, Northern Ireland
1858

Harland & Wolff was founded by two entrepreneurs: Edward Harland and Gustav Wolff. Harland started work for a small shipyard on Queen's Island in Belfast, owned by Robert Hickson. As a teenager, Wolff had come over from Hamburg, where he had strong shipbuilding ties, and ended up working as Harland's assistant. In 1858, Harland bought Hickson's yard; in 1860, Wolff was promoted from assistant to business partner; in 1861, Harland & Wolff was formed. Over the next three decades, the company grew extraordinarily fast: 100 employees in 1861 had become over 10,000 by the early 1890s. One of their most successful innovations was to use iron rather than wood for the upper decks of ships, which made their vessels substantially stronger. The yard became known for its liners—they built most of White Star Line's vessels, including the *Olympic*, the *Britannic*, and their ill-fated sister ship, the *Titanic*.

ABOVE: This innovative shipyard produced some of the greatest ocean liners of its era, including White Star Line's RMS *Titanic*.

NED KELLY'S BIRTHPLACE

Beveridge, Australia
1859

The Outback's famous outlaw, Ned Kelly, holds an important place in Australian folk history despite his short life and sad end: he was hanged in 1880. He appears in the paintings of Sidney Nolan wearing the home-welded armor in which he hoped to escape police. The armor is displayed in the National Library of Victoria. His birthplace, built by his father, John "Red" Kelly, is a poignant reminder of a hard life: the humblest three-room house, made from locally gathered timber.

RED HOUSE

Bexleyheath, Kent, England
1859

A house created as the embodiment—inside and out—of the Arts & Crafts movement.

The Red House was commissioned by William Morris from the architect Philip Webb in 1859. Morris, a key figure in the Arts & Crafts movement, envisaged his home as a center for a modern way of living that combined utility and beauty: a focus on craftsmanship and a distaste for mass production. Dante Gabriel Rossetti saw it as "more a poem than a house." Its warm, red brick and vaguely medieval air epitomized the Arts & Crafts spirit, and the interior—painted and furnished by such figures as Rossetti and Edward Burne-Jones—was equally satisfactory. It prompted the founding, in 1861, of "the Firm," a collaborative partnership which put the group's designs into commercial production. Ultimately, the dream proved too expensive, and Morris and his wife lived there only until 1866, but the ideals of the movement it spearheaded would become familiar all over Europe and America, and both its products and aspirations are still widely admired.

LEFT: Careful detailing and references to a romantic past—with dormer roofs, tall chimneys, and a tiled well—mark the Red House as typifying the ideals of William Morris.

HARRIET TUBMAN'S HOUSE

Auburn, New York
1859

The home of a tireless advocate for freedom, nicknamed the "Moses of her people."

Harriet Tubman was born into enslavement in Maryland. In 1849, she used the Underground Railroad to escape. Tubman became a prominent abolitionist and activist, freeing many others by the same means. In 1859, she bought a house and a seven-acre plot in Fleming—a village outside Auburn—from Frances Seaward, a fellow abolitionist. The deal was illegal. Property was not allowed to be sold to enslaved people who had liberated themselves, but Auburn was a liberal enclave and the sale was never exposed. Tubman lived here with her extended family, and in time she turned it into a productive and profitable farm. It was her base until her death in 1913.

She remained an activist. During the Civil War, as a scout for the Union side, she made many trips to the South. In later life, she established the "Harriet Tubman Home for Aged and Infirm Negroes" on her small estate.

ABOVE AND BELOW: Bought as the Civil War began to threaten, Harriet Tubman's home was used as a base by her extended family during her long absences.

247 RESIDENCE

THE LITTLE HOUSE IN THE BIG WOODS

Pepin, Wisconsin
1860

Laura Ingalls Wilder's accounts of her tough-but-resourceful pioneer childhood in the late nineteenth century have been popular for nearly a century. The Little House in the Big Woods, a log cabin near Pepin—the subject of the first book in the Little House series—was where she spent most of her first seven years. Although the original structure no longer stands, a replica has been re-created nearby.

248 MONUMENT

FORT WILLS

Queensland, Australia
1861

In the 1850s, a drive grew in Australia to explore the continent's interior, of which little was known—even by the Aboriginal peoples. In 1860, Robert Burke and William Wills led an expedition from Melbourne to chart a route north to the Gulf of Carpentaria. "Fort Wills" was the name given to the depot at Cooper Creek, at the last charted point heading north. The expedition was successful, but Burke and Wills died near Cooper Creek on the return journey after a series of misunderstandings resulted in no provisions being left for them.

BELOW: Although Robert Burke and William Wills were successful in finding a route north to the ocean, their support team gave up on them too early, and they starved to death.

THE TOMB OF NAPOLEON

Paris, France
1861

"It is my wish that my ashes may repose on the banks of the Seine, in the midst of the French people, whom I have loved so well."

From the will of Napoleon Bonaparte, April 16, 1821

When Napoleon died in 1821, he was buried on Saint Helena (see page 184). The restored Bourbon rulers in France were less than keen to bring him back to Paris, as was his dying wish. When Louis-Philippe, Duke of Orléans and nicknamed the "citizen king," inherited the throne in 1830, he felt that bringing Napoleon back might help reconcile two political factions: his own, the Orléanists, and the Bonapartists. In 1840, Napoleon's coffin was returned to Paris with great fanfare. However, it wasn't until 1861 that he was permanently buried, after a protracted process including a competition to design the tomb. The tomb incorporates rare stones for the sarcophagus, including quartzite from Karelia, which required a special permit from Tsar Nicholas of Russia.

By 1861, the rulers of France had changed again. Napoleon Bonaparte was seen to his resting place by his nephew, Napoleon III—France's new ruler—the Empress Eugenie, and a small gathering of officials.

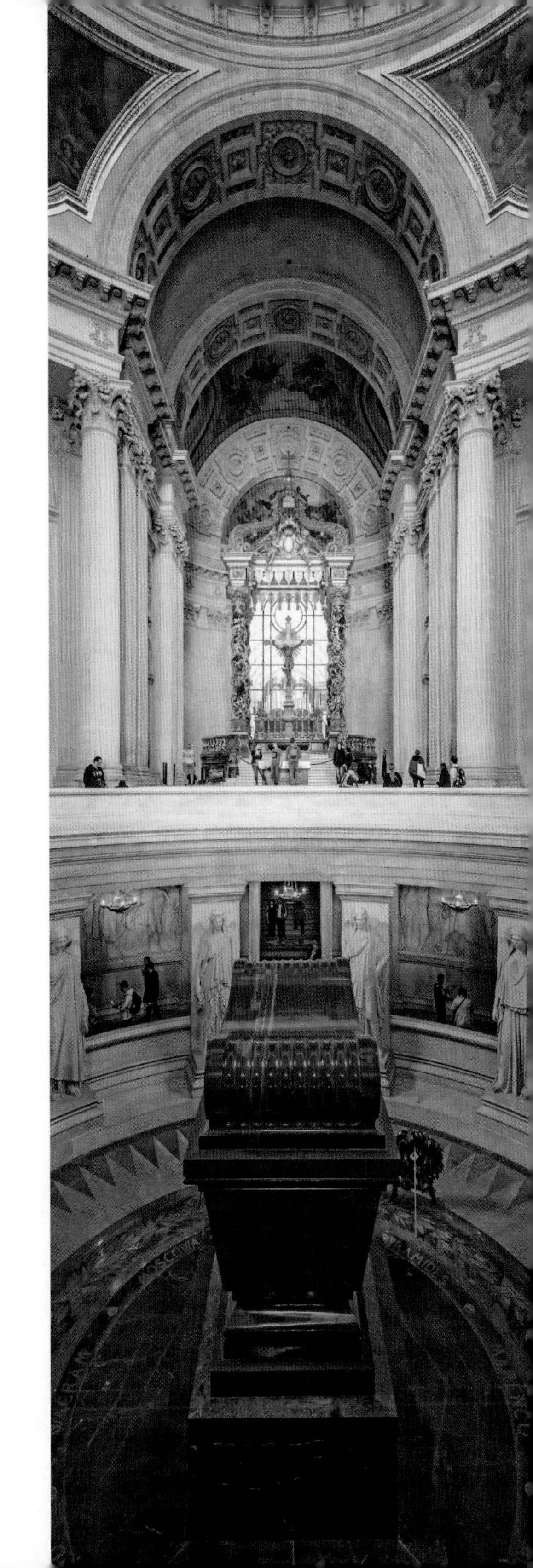

RIGHT: The grandiose sarcophagus, erected at Les Invalides in Paris, is surrounded by carved reliefs of twelve victories, each representing one of Napoleon's military triumphs.

250 RESIDENCE

JARRATT HOUSE

Petersburg, Virginia
1862

A simple brick Federal-style building, the house was originally built by a white merchant on Pocahontas Island in around 1820. Through the first half of the nineteenth century, the community had become a predominantly Black neighborhood. Even before the Civil War, the town of Petersburg had the largest number of free African Americans in the state, as well as strong connections with a number of Native American peoples. The history of the house's owners reflects the thriving community around it: in 1853, Lavinia Simpson—a Native American who may also have had African American heritage—bought half of the house, completing the purchase and becoming sole owner in 1862. In the 1870s, it was bought by an influential local Black family, the Jarratts. It stayed in their family until the 1990s.

251 RESIDENCE

IMPERIAL PALACE

Petropolis, Brazil
1862

The second—and last—emperor of Brazil, Pedro II, built the huge Neoclassical pink-and-white summer palace in the city named after him. Petropolis was founded just two decades earlier as an urban project, part of a movement for brand-new towns led by various commercial booms in South America. The presence of the palace, and the emperor, gave the town an immediate cachet, and it temporarily became capital of the state of Rio de Janeiro.

BELOW: Petropolis lasted as state capital until 1903, its cooler mountain climate making it a popular escape from the heat of Rio de Janeiro in the summer months.

252 RESIDENCE

GOVERNOR'S HOUSE

Obock, Djibouti
1862

In the mid-nineteenth century, the Afar Sultan of Ethiopia sold land for a new port town, Obock, to the French. It quickly became an early outpost of French colonialism, with an elegant house for its first French governor, Léonce Lagarde. Djibouti's position on the Red Sea made it particularly suitable for trade, especially after the construction of the Suez Canal in 1869 (see page 212).

253 ART AND CULTURE

TEMPERATE HOUSE, ROYAL BOTANIC GARDENS

Kew, Surrey, England
1863

Designed by Decimus Burton, who had already created the smaller Palm House at Kew, the Temperate House is the largest surviving greenhouse of its day. It serves as a reminder of the fashion for glass architecture—greenhouses and winter gardens—in the second half of the nineteenth century. Botanic gardens, which combined education with leisure, became particularly popular in this period, and sprang up in many major cities in Europe and beyond.

ABOVE: Although its first phase was completed in 1863, the Temperate House didn't reach its final form until 1899. It's the largest Victorian greenhouse in the world.

254 ART AND CULTURE

FORD'S THEATRE

Washington, D.C.
1865

Ford's Theatre, designed by local architect Charles Lessig, opened in 1863 and was already popular when Abraham Lincoln was assassinated there two years later. The murder finished it as a theater, and it was bought by the U.S. government to use as an office building. Between 1932 and 1968, it was home to the Lincoln Museum. In 1968, it was revived as a working theater, with historic tours on the side.

255 RESIDENCE

McLEAN HOUSE

Appomattox, Virginia
1865

On April 9, 1865, after almost four years and over 600,000 deaths, General Robert E. Lee of the Confederate Army surrendered to Union General Ulysses S. Grant in the parlor of McLean House, bringing an end to the American Civil War. The terms were not punitive; the Union side declared their intention to "bind up the nation's wounds." The house, a private home, would become known as Surrender House.

ABOVE: "The war is over; the rebels are our countrymen again," declared General Grant on signing the agreement that brought the Civil War to an end.

BUSSELTON JETTY

Busselton, Western Australia
1865

The remote town of Busselton was only 30 years old when the need for local cargo deliveries drove the construction of its first timber-piled jetty. Over time, it was used by larger ships needing deeper water. It was extended no fewer than nine times, finally reaching a record-breaking length of 1.1 miles by 1894. A railway was built along it to carry goods back to shore.

ABOVE: The Nautical Lady lighthouse, which overlooked the jetty, was converted into a waterslide in 1981; it was demolished in 2015.

BELOW: As the need for functional docking increased, Busselton simply extended its jetty farther and farther out to sea.

SUEZ CANAL

Egypt
1869

The waterway that transformed the pace of international shipping.

"The artery of prosperity for Egypt and the world . . ."

The canal described in a speech at its inauguration, November 17, 1869

The ambitious idea for a canal linking the Mediterranean with the Red Sea—cutting the arduous voyage around Africa—became a possibility in the 1850s. Entrepreneur Ferdinand de Lesseps signed two contracts with Sa'īd Pasha, viceroy of Egypt: to sell shares and initiate the project. At first, local labor was forcibly recruited to dig the waterway under terrible conditions, until the practice was stopped by Sa'īd Pasha's successor, Ismail Pasha, in 1863—although not before many thousands had died. The Suez Canal—120 miles long and 184 feet wide—was opened in 1869. After a shaky start commercially, the canal galvanized both local and international trade. In giving easier access to Asia and the east coast of Africa, it helped both to enable the rapid European colonialization of Africa and to consolidate British control over India.

ABOVE, LEFT, AND BELOW: The building of the canal was easier than that of the Panama Canal because, dug across level land, it required no locks. However, the sheer scale of the enterprise demanded an army of laborers, many of them compelled to work on the project.

258 RESIDENCE

KIRTI MANDIR

Porbandar, India
1869

Mahatma Gandhi was born to the chief minister, or *diwan*, of the then-princely territory of Porbandar, a small port city in the northwest of India, present-day Gujarat. His family home was a *haveli*, a three-story house around a courtyard, built by his great-grandfather. The household was strict and Gandhi's mother, Putlibal, was fiercely devout. She was influenced by Jainism, a faith with a central belief in nonviolence and the sanctity of life. She died—aged only 47—in the same house, which today is dwarfed by a memorial shrine to her son.

ABOVE: The home where Mahatma Gandhi was born is now a small museum, commemorating him and his wife.

259 PLACE OF WORK

SLAVE MARKET, STONE TOWN

Zanzibar, Tanzania
1873

Stone Town held the last open slave market in East Africa. Enslaved people were brought from the mainland, and stood in the town square to be appraised by potential buyers. Slavery was important to Zanzibar's economy: many enslaved people worked on its clove and coconut plantations. The British government eventually forced Sultan Barghash, ruler of Zanzibar, to close the trade on the island, and the market was shut down in 1873.

ABOVE: Five shackled figures standing in a pit form the Slave Market memorial, a grim reminder of Stone Town's past.

MARK TWAIN'S HOUSE

Hartford, Connecticut
1874

The fashionable family home of one of America's most famous writers.

"To us, our house was not unsentient matter—it had a heart, and a soul, and eyes to see us with."

Mark Twain, after the death of his daughter, writing to a friend in 1897

Samuel Clemens, better known as Mark Twain, and his wife, Livy, had the house designed by the architect Edward Tuckerman Potter. The American Gothic exterior was a riot of detail—balconies, verandas, and gables—and inside, 25 rooms were equipped with every modern convenience. They spent a happy 17 years there. Twain was productive, publishing *The Adventures of Tom Sawyer* (1876) and *Adventures of Huckleberry Finn* (1884), among others. In 1891, financially overstretched, they moved to Europe. In 1896, their daughter Susy died of meningitis in the house—while her parents were traveling. It proved too painful for them to live there again, so it was sold in 1903. Today, it houses the Mark Twain Museum.

CROSS-SECTION

ABOVE AND LEFT: The house has the elaborate woodwork that was fashionable in the last quarter of the nineteenth century, featuring shingles, fretwork, verandas, and a summerhouse.

DEPOT

Rorke's Drift, South Africa
1879

The propaganda victory that masked a much larger defeat.

In January 1879, British invading forces arrived in Zululand with the aim of subjugating its king, Cetshwayo, and colonizing his land. Their leader, an overconfident Lord Chelmsford, pressed on with the main force and met Cetshwayo's army at Isandlwana—a disaster for the British. Most of Chelmsford's 1,700 men were killed, and 4,000 Zulu warriors marched on the small depot at Rorke's Drift, where 50 British soldiers had set up a garrison and hospital. Over 12 hours, the soldiers fought off the Zulus. The heroism at Rorke's Drift offered a positive story to be recounted in Britain, against the much larger negative one of Isandlwana. Ultimately, even his major victory made little difference to Cetshwayo, or to colonial ambitions. The Zulus were finally defeated at the Battle of Ulundi in July, and by 1887 Zululand had been seized as a British territory.

"The stamina and valor of the English soldiery have not diminished."

Benjamin Disraeli, British prime minister, parliamentary speech praising the forces at Rorke's Drift, February 13, 1879

BELOW: A highly romanticized Victorian painting of the perceived David–Goliath struggle at Rorke's Drift. In reality, the story was used by the British to drown out the news of the Zulu triumph at Isandlwana.

262 ART AND CULTURE

FESTSPIELHAUS

Bayreuth, Bavaria
1876

The Festspielhaus was conceived by Richard Wagner, and designed for the performance of his own works. Today the center of the Bayreuth festival, the Festspielhaus has a number of unusual features, including a hidden orchestra pit and a single, shallow curve of seating. Although Ludwig II of Bavaria, an avid fan, contributed some funds, the effort of keeping the project financially solvent eventually broke Wagner. He died in 1883.

263 PLACE OF WORK

WRITERS' BUILDING

Kolkata, India
1879

Despite its name, Writers'—a frequent abbreviation—is actually one of the largest office buildings in the world, housing the staff of the administration of the city of Kolkata and the state of West Bengal. Built in 1777 for the clerks, or "writers," of the East India Company, it was repeatedly extended until it covered 13 blocks. The familiar red-and-cream facade fronting the square of B. B. D. Bagh was added in 1879.

264 RELIGION AND MONUMENT

LA PLATA CATHEDRAL

La Plata, Argentina
1880

La Plata was planned as an ambitious new provincial capital, distinct from nearby Buenos Aires, which had previously held the role but now served as the country's capital. The city was to be laid out on a rigid grid system, with a huge cathedral with Gothic towers at its heart. In reality, the plan didn't work. The cathedral wasn't completed until 1932, and its towers were only added in 1999.

BELOW: The vast cathedral took a century to complete and remains the largest church in Argentina.

ROYAL EXHIBITION BUILDING

Melbourne, Australia
1880

One of the earliest surviving international exhibition centers, meticulously restored.

One of a large number of buildings raised all over the world in the nineteenth-century heyday of international exhibitions, designed to showcase global ingenuity and design. The Melbourne building, built for the international exhibition of 1880, is an impressive mix of Renaissance, Byzantine, and Romanesque styles, with a grand Great Hall at its center. Carlton Gardens around it was designed as part of the overall scheme.

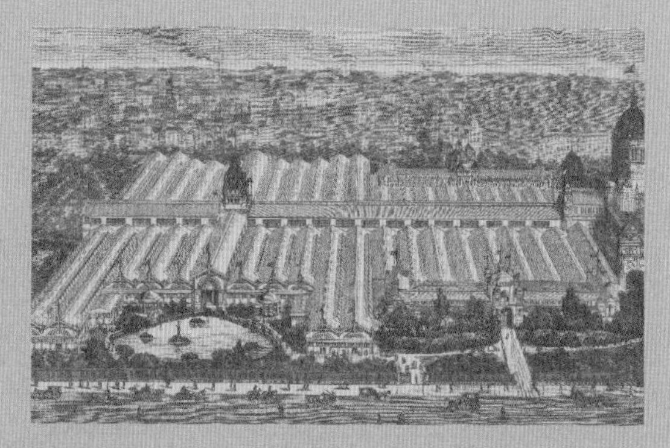

ABOVE AND BELOW: The lavish buildings were set in the equally impressive Carlton Gardens, laid out with formal parterres, mature trees, and two ornamental lakes—all designed specifically for the exhibition.

266 ART AND CULTURE

WHITE HORSE TAVERN

Manhattan, New York
1880

The White Horse Tavern started life in 1880. Located at the corner of Hudson Street and 11th Street, its first customers were the longshoremen who worked on the busy wharves of the Hudson River. Its Greenwich Village location would make it a popular spot for literary bohemians in the 1950s and 1960s—Jack Kerouac, James Baldwin, Anaïs Nin, and Norman Mailer, to name a few. Notoriously, it was here that Dylan Thomas, on his final visit to New York in 1953, drank his last whiskey before collapsing and dying from pneumonia (exacerbated by his alcoholism) a few days later. In 1955, it was also allegedly the birthplace of New York's countercultural weekly, the *Village Voice*.

ABOVE: The White Horse Tavern has retained most of its fittings, both outside and in. These days, it has a list of cocktails named after bohemian patrons of its past.

267 PLACE OF WORK

KENWYN HOUSE

Victoria, Seychelles
1880s

Built for a surgeon in 1855, this French Colonial-style house was bought by the Eastern Telegraphic Company in the 1880s to house its engineers. During the 1880s and 1890s, cables for telegraphic communication were being laid under oceans all around the world; the final connection for the Seychelles would be with Colombo, in present-day Sri Lanka, in 1922.

HUMBERSTONE SALTPETER WORKS

Pampas, Chile
1880

A major mineral mine in one of the most inhospitable landscapes on earth.

The Atacama Desert has huge natural deposits of saltpeter: a key ingredient in both the fertilizer sodium nitrate and the production of gunpowder. In the late 1870s, James "Santiago" Humberstone, a British engineer, imported a new system for extracting nitrate. By 1880, the former Peruvian Nitrate Works had been renamed after him. The Humberstone was just one of 200 scattered sites, staffed by thousands of miners from Chile, Bolivia, and Peru. They were linked by a railway that carried the nitrate to Iquique on the coast, from where it was shipped all over the world. In the 1930s, a process was invented for the artificial production of ammonia, and the need for sodium nitrate waned. By the 1960s, both the works and the towns were abandoned, losing both the industry and the culture that had grown up around it.

ABOVE AND BELOW: James Humberstone—nicknamed "Santiago"—was engineer and manager of the saltpeter works. He invented the so-called Shanks process for extracting nitrates from ore, after which the works—previously Oficina La Palma—were named.

269 INFRASTRUCTURE AND INNOVATION

DARJEELING HIMALAYAN RAILWAY

West Bengal, India
1881

Until the railway came to Darjeeling, the extremely steep and winding 55-mile route up from the plains could only be traveled by carts and pack animals. In 1878, Franklin Prestage—an agent of the Eastern Bengal Railway—suggested a small railway, tailored to the difficult landscape. Prestage's proposal was accepted, and in 1879 a company was formed to manage the construction. The narrow-gauge track, along a route built with zigzag reverses and loops to accommodate the terrain, was open and running by July 1881. Despite its toylike appearance, the Darjeeling railway was such a success that two other routes soon followed: the Nilgiri Mountain Railway, serving Tamil Nadu's hill stations, and the Kalka-Shimla Railway in the Himalayan foothills.

ABOVE: Famous for its intricate loops and switchbacks, the tiny "toy" train works impressively well.

270 ART AND CULTURE

METROPOLITAN MUSEUM OF ART

Manhattan, New York
1880

Founded by a group of philanthropists in 1870, the Metropolitan Museum was granted a plot of land between 79th and 84th Streets in Central Park. A modest Neo-Gothic building, designed by the architect Calvert Vaux, opened in 1880. It has since been entirely surrounded by the many extensions that have made the Met New York's largest museum. Today's familiar facade on Fifth Avenue was opened in 1926.

271 PLACE OF WORK

CANADIAN CANNERS

Picton, Ontario, Canada
1882

By the 1880s, canned food, originally devised to feed Napoleon's troops, was becoming a household convenience, but the industry hadn't traveled far north of New York City. When George Dunning, a businessman, teamed up with Wellington Boulter, a farmer, to found Canada's first canning factory, in Prince Edward County, their initiative quickly spread. Within three years, canneries were built all over the country and it became a center of the industry.

LA SAGRADA FAMÍLIA

Barcelona, Spain
1882

Barcelona's great expression of individuality: the Gaudí masterpiece that is yet to be completed.

La Sagrada Família, a Catholic cathedral for Barcelona, was funded by private donations. In 1883, Antoni Gaudí, architect and key figure in the nineteenth-century Catalan renaissance of arts and crafts, was appointed to lead the project. Since his death in 1926, building has continued—with only a few breaks—despite the loss of Gaudí's original plans and models in the Spanish Civil War.

Gaudí envisaged a vast building in his unique mixture of Catalan modernism and a sort of curvy, organic Gothic. It would have 18 spires: one for each of the apostles and evangelists, one for the Virgin Mary, and the last—and tallest—for Christ. Despite its unfinished state, in 2010 Pope Benedict XVI consecrated La Sagrada Família. On its completion, it's expected to be the tallest church in the world.

SITE PLAN

THE 18 SPIRES: **1** Virgin Mary **2** Jesus **3** Mark **4** Luke **5** Matthew **6** John **7** James the Lesser **8** Bartholomew **9** Thomas **10** Philip **11** Matthias **12** Jude **13** Simon **14** Barnabas **15** Andrew **16** Peter **17** Paul **18** James the Greater

KNOWN FOR

- An extraordinary, organic design; a building that seems to grow, rather than being built
- A completion schedule that has already taken well over a century
- A landmark that has come to symbolize Barcelona above any other

RIGHT: The foundation stone for the cathedral was laid in 1882.

"The straight line belongs to men. The curved one to God."

Antoni Gaudí

BROOKLYN BRIDGE

Brooklyn, New York
1883

A link that created New York City's fifth borough.

Begun in 1869 and completed in 1883, the Brooklyn Bridge spans the East River and connects Manhattan Island to Brooklyn. The bridge transformed Brooklyn into a borough of New York City, enabling the safe transportation of goods and labor between the two metropolitan areas. It has a span of 1,595 feet, a fifth longer than any built previously. About 140,000 vehicles cross the bridge every day.

"When it comes to planning, one mind can in a few hours think out enough work to keep a thousand men employed for years."

Washington Roebling, engineer

The Brooklyn Bridge was designed by civil engineer John Augustus Roebling, who died in an accident on-site in 1869, and was succeeded by his son Washington.

It was regarded as an impressive feat of engineering at the time. For the first time, dynamite was used in excavating the foundations. The innovative use of steel cables replaced the rigid rods linked with chains used in earlier suspension bridges, and the use of caissons and anchorages to secure them allowed it to be both bigger and stronger.

The bridge has become an icon of New York City, featuring in the films *Saturday Night Fever* (1977) and *Vanilla Sky* (2001). "If you believe that, I have a bridge to sell you" has even entered into idiomatic use to describe gullibility, after con man George C. Parker attempted to "sell" the bridge several times in the early 1900s.

ABOVE AND BELOW: At either end of the bridge, a huge wood and steel box—or caisson—was sunk into the river and pressurized, to keep the water out and the air in while the workers dug. When they reached solid rock, the caissons were filled with concrete and brickwork, giving the towers a solid foundation.

MONET'S HOUSE

Giverny, France
1883

The home and garden of the great Impressionist, which would become familiar through his art.

In 1883, when the painter Claude Monet arrived at his new home in Normandy, the house and garden were simple and very rustic. Over time, the house was enlarged for his family. The barn was converted to make a studio. Monet became a keen gardener, influenced by his friends, the artist Gustave Caillebotte and the writer Octave Mirbeau, both enthusiastic horticulturalists. His new water garden was largely inspired by his interest in Japanese art, which was fashionable at the time. A small pond was gradually extended and enhanced by a humpbacked Japanese bridge; it was planted with water lilies that he was to paint around 250 times over his last three decades. The water lily paintings, full of shifting light and reflections, are widely considered to be his greatest works.

"I perhaps owe having become a painter to flowers."

Claude Monet

LEFT AND ABOVE: Monet's home—and particularly his garden—became the most frequent subject of his art.

HOME INSURANCE BUILDING

Chicago, Illinois
1885

The first skyscraper with a frame made of iron and steel.

Following the Great Chicago Fire of 1871, a construction boom revitalized the city's economy and transformed the Chicago skyline. Rather than wood, buildings were made of stone, iron, and a new material: steel. Architect William Le Baron Jenney designed the world's first skyscraper. The 10-story building was 138 feet high and took advantage of technological advances, incorporating four new Otis elevators. It was the first building to have a fireproof internal iron-and-steel frame that was clad in masonry, rather than load-bearing walls. It was also the first to incorporate steel as a structural material. As the price of land rose, Jenney's innovations made it possible for cities to grow upward instead of out.

ABOVE: Building on the project was halted at points to ensure that such a tall building wouldn't simply collapse.

BELOW: Partial plan of the first skeleton steel-frame construction.

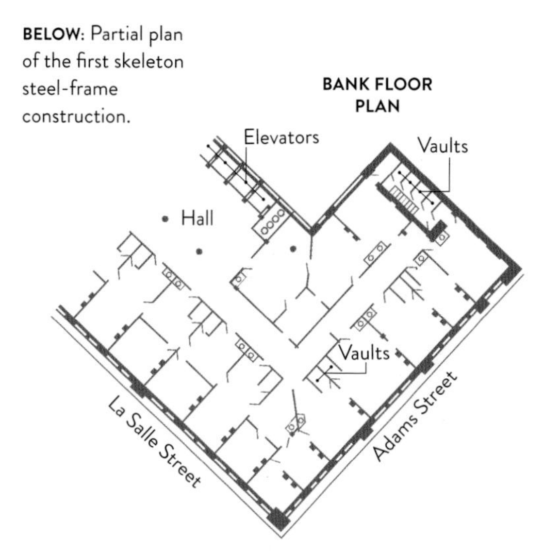

276 RESIDENCE

PALACE OF MANDALAY

Burma
1885

The invasion that saw the end of a Burmese royal dynasty.

On November 28, 1885, a flotilla of British gunships reached Mandalay, the capital of Burma. Filled with Indian troops, the ships had crossed the Bay of Bengal and sailed up the Irawaddy River without encountering opposition. When Colonel Sladen of the Burma Commission entered the gilded wooden palace to tell King Thibaw that he had been deposed, it marked the end of a long game of competing influences. Britain had worried about other powers in Burma monopolizing trade and gaining a back door into China. Eventually, when a number of concessions were granted to the French, the British issued an ultimatum they knew was unlikely to be met, and set sail for Mandalay. Following the annexation of Upper Burma, Thibaw, the last of the Konbaung dynasty, spent the rest of his life in exile in India.

TOP AND ABOVE: At the time of King Thibaw's overthrow, the teakwood palace complex was only about 30 years old. The original was destroyed during World War II, and today's replica is largely built of concrete.

277 RESIDENCE

16 TITE STREET

London, England
1885

When the Irish writer Oscar Wilde and his wife moved into Number 16 (now 34), this was a fashionable new street in bohemian Chelsea. Surrounded by modish aesthetic decor, Wilde wrote some of his great successes here, including *The Importance of Being Earnest* (1895). Exposed as a homosexual, he left to serve a jail term for gross indecency in 1895. The house's contents were auctioned to pay his creditors.

ABOVE: Tite Street was fashionable among creatives; artists James McNeill Whistler and John Singer Sargent also lived here.

RIGHT: Neuschwanstein was built with modern conveniences such as plumbing, as well as a lot of completely nonfunctional, faux-medieval turrets.

278 RESIDENCE

NEUSCHWANSTEIN

Bavaria, Germany
1886

Ludwig II of Bavaria was a troubled, opera- and architecture-loving eccentric. The hyper-romantic style of the palace at Neuschwanstein was one of a number of grandiose buildings commissioned by the king, and inspired by his love of Wagner's operas and medieval legends. It took ten years to build. Shortly after its completion, Ludwig—by then deposed—was found drowned. Neuschwanstein is often cited as Walt Disney's inspiration for Sleeping Beauty's castle.

STATUE OF LIBERTY

Liberty Island, New York
1886

The iconic statue that came to symbolize the freedoms of America.

The French sculptor Frédéric-Auguste Bartholdi first proposed a massive figure holding a torch for a lighthouse at the entrance to the Suez Canal. It was rejected, but the idea—which originated with Bartholdi's friend, the academic Edouard de Laboulaye—remained. On a visit to America, Bartholdi proposed a similarly huge statue as a gift from France, celebrating the centenary of American independence. Raising the money in France was undertaken jointly by de Laboulaye and Bartholdi, while the American side agreed to build the pedestal. The site, Bedloe's Island in New York Harbor, was agreed upon. The statue, *Liberty Enlightening the World*, was made from copper sheet, raised on an iron skeleton designed by Gustave Eiffel, then dismantled for its voyage to America in 1885—where it was met by an incomplete pedestal. It was finally unveiled to great acclaim on October 28, 1886.

"I can only say I am enchanted. This thing will live to eternity, when we shall have passed away."

Frédéric-Auguste Bartholdi, on the statue's inauguration

RIGHT: "Lady Liberty" was an emigrant to America, conceived and built entirely in France.

280 RESIDENCE

TE WAIROA

North Island, New Zealand
1886

The missionary's model village was destroyed by a volcanic eruption.

Te Wairoa was founded in 1848 by the Reverend Seymour Spencer, an American missionary who, with his wife, set out to create a European-style village from which to convert the local Maori population to Christianity. An unusual mix of Maori and European-style buildings, the village was entirely buried and around 100 people were killed by the eruption of the nearby volcano, Mount Tarawera, on June 10, 1886. The so-called Buried Village is of archaeological interest because of the rarity of intact missionary settlements—excavated buildings include the community's simple hotel, Maori whares and pataka (houses and storehouses), and a huge range of contemporary artifacts, from canoes to furniture and cooking utensils.

ABOVE: The majority of the settlement's buildings were flattened in the eruption and it was left completely abandoned.

281 INFRASTRUCTURE AND INNOVATION

VICTORIA RAILWAY TERMINUS

Mumbai, India
1887

Named to commemorate Queen Victoria's Jubilee, the station took almost ten years to build. The headquarters of the Great Indian Peninsula Railway, it is also one of the busiest stations in India. The facade, designed by architect Frederick Steven, is an elaborate mashup of Indo-Saracenic-Gothic-Revival style, abiding by government policy that new buildings should blend Indian and Western traditions. It was renamed Chhatrapati Shivaji Maharaj Terminus in 2017.

282 ART AND CULTURE

221B BAKER STREET

London, England
1887

At the time of its first literary appearance, the home of Sherlock Holmes was fictional: *A Study in Scarlet* (1887) gave the great detective an address that didn't yet exist. The popularity of Conan Doyle's character—and the volume of fan mail and visitors—eventually led to the Sherlock Holmes Museum being gifted the 221B address, despite the true location, slotted between 237 and 241 Baker Street.

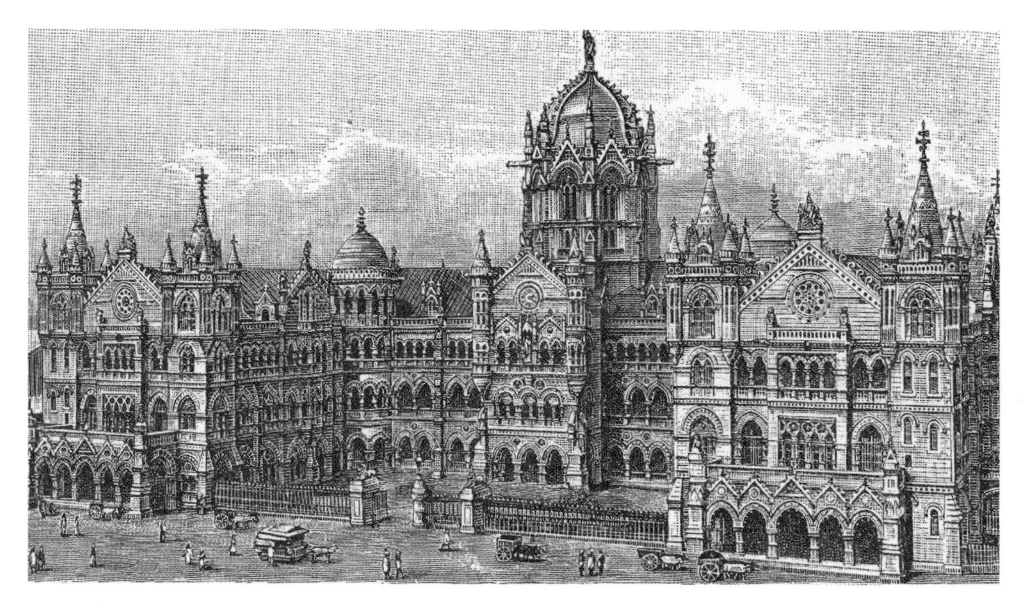

ABOVE: The entrance gates of the vast new station were finished with a lion and a tiger—representing Britain and India respectively.

283 PLACE OF WORK

BANFF SPRING HOTEL

Banff, Canada
1888

The Canadian Pacific Railway was built to connect the east and west coasts of Canada, both to enable trade and to make it possible for workers to get around the country. But the company that owned it also had interests in tourism. In building destination hotels along its route, they virtually guaranteed their own success. The Banff Spring Hotel, picturesquely sited in the Rocky Mountains, was just one of these.

"If we can't export the scenery, we'll import the tourists."

William Van Horne,
Chairman of the Canadian Pacific Railway

284 RESIDENCE/ART AND CULTURE

FRANK LLOYD WRIGHT HOME AND STUDIO

Oak Park, Illinois
1889

Architect Frank Lloyd Wright was just 22 years old when he borrowed $5,000 from his employer, Louis Sullivan, to build his family home. This was the first building that Wright had complete control over, and he altered it many times to develop his aesthetic of open living spaces, natural materials, and geometric forms. He also installed electricity and a telephone, both cutting-edge technology at the time.

ABOVE: Frank Lloyd Wright's own home had the horizontal lines so characteristic of his later work.

LEFT: An early example of a railway hotel in Canada—over 30 similarly grand projects were built between the 1880s and the 1930s.

ABOVE: Painted by Vincent van Gogh in 1889, this picture shows the asylum where the artist was a voluntary patient for a year, until May 1890.

ABOVE RIGHT: The suburban music hall that attracted a wide audience.

285 ART AND CULTURE

ST. PAUL DE MAUSOLE ASYLUM

Saint-Rémy de Provence, France
1889

On May 8, 1889, Vincent van Gogh, aged 36, was admitted to St. Paul de Mausole Asylum. After a severe breakdown, his friends felt he needed professional care, and he stayed there for just over a year. He had three serious mental episodes while in the asylum, but also experienced an outburst of creativity, painting many of his most acclaimed works, including *Starry Night*, *Self-Portrait with Bandaged Ear*, and *Wheatfield with Cypresses*.

286 ART AND CULTURE

MOULIN ROUGE

Paris, France
1889

Charles Zidler and Joseph Oller, the businessmen who founded the Moulin Rouge, didn't pick a particularly fashionable spot for their new music hall. Montmartre, in the 18th arrondissement, was then on the extreme outskirts of Paris. They knew what attractions to offer: the entrance, topped by the red windmill, made it easy to spot, while inside, mirrored walls and chandeliers ensured the whole place glittered. There was plenty of dancing—notably the daring cancan—along with a variety of other music hall acts. Launched on October 6, 1889, the Moulin Rouge enjoyed near-immediate success. It attracted both out-of-towners and Parisians who preferred to take their pleasures a little distance from home. The artist Henri Toulouse-Lautrec kept a visual record of it all for posterity.

287 ART AND CULTURE

EIFFEL TOWER

Paris, France
1889

The tower was a centerpiece for the Exposition Universelle, a world fair held in Paris in 1889. Gustave Eiffel, an engineer whose workshops specialized in metal viaducts and bridges, won the commission. The iron units that made up the tower were put together in the Eiffel workshops, then assembled on site. It took over two years to build, and was the tallest built structure in the world until the Chrysler Building (see page 275) outstripped it in 1930. Originally given an expected life span of 20 years, it gained a reprieve when it proved useful for wireless experiments, and soon it had become a beloved landmark in the city.

RIGHT: The "temporary" structure that has become an enduring symbol of Paris.

288 RELIGION AND MONUMENT

SAN SEBASTIAN BASILICA

Manila, Philippines
1891

By the late nineteenth century, there was a large Catholic population in Manila needing a sufficiently large space in which to worship. After a series of churches either burned down or were destroyed by earthquakes, the fireproof answer was found in a steel-framed church. Despite its Neo-Gothic style, it was an entirely modern structure made from segments prefabricated in Belgium, with stained-glass windows imported from Germany.

BRADBURY BUILDING

Los Angeles, California
1893

Commissioned by Lewis Bradbury, a mining millionaire, the Bradbury Building was designed by Sumner Hunt. It was completed, with numerous modifications, by his draftsman, George Wyman. The oldest commercial survivor in downtown Los Angeles, it was considered startlingly innovative. The plain exterior opens into a glass-roofed atrium rising to 50 feet, complete with marble staircases with art nouveau balustrades and open-cage elevators—which were then a novelty—arranged around the outer walls.

BELOW: The Bradbury Building was notable for its extraordinarily fine detailing, as well as its technical innovation.

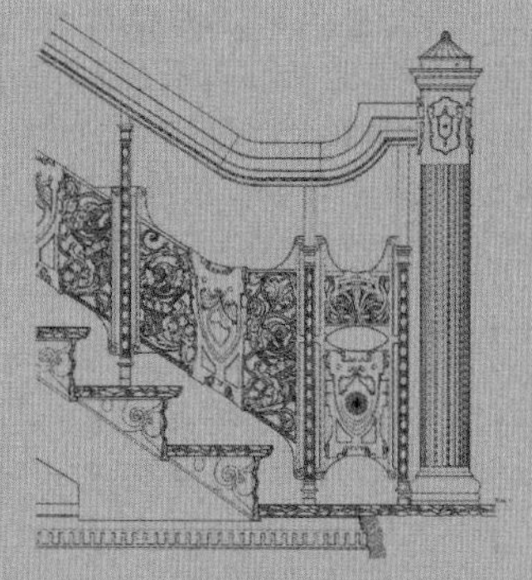

STAIR DETAIL

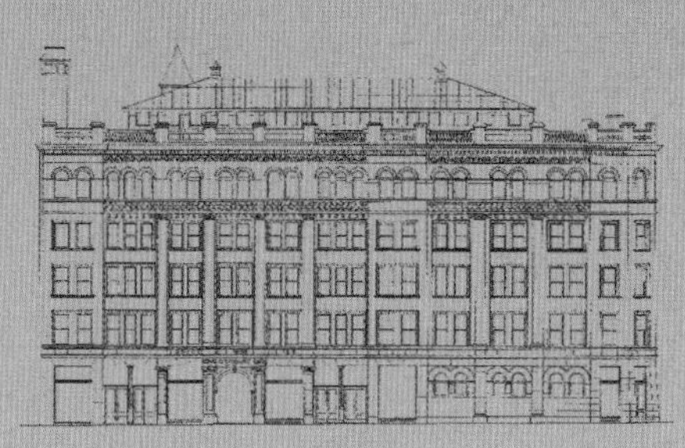

ELEVATION

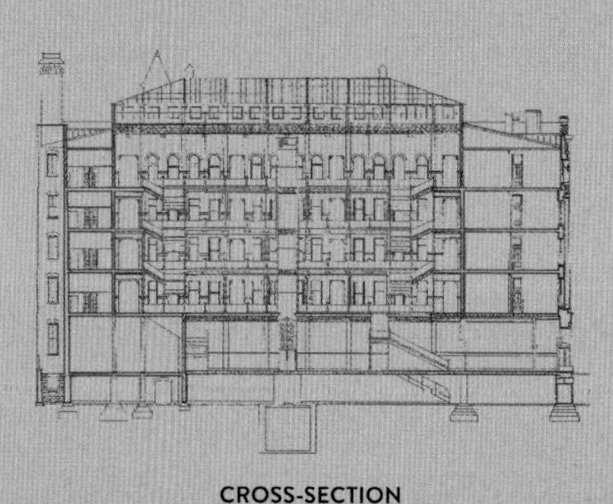

CROSS-SECTION

290 RESIDENCE

BOGD KHAN PALACE MUSEUM

Ulaanbaatar, Mongolia
1893

Built between 1893 and 1903, the complex houses the winter and summer palaces of the Bogd Khan—the spiritual leader of Outer Mongolia. They are rare survivors of the country's Communist rule when most similar buildings were destroyed. Ranking only below the Dalai and Panchen Lamas, the eighth Bogd Khan came under the control of the Mongolian Communist party, which seized power in 1922, two years before his death.

291 PLACE OF WORK

AVENIDA DE MAYO

Buenos Aires, Argentina
1894

Buenos Aires became Argentina's capital in 1880, and its first mayor, Torcuato de Alvear, longed to turn it into a sophisticated city—more like Paris—with wide boulevards. Avenida de Mayo, inaugurated in 1894, was one result. Named after the May Revolution—which had marked Argentina's independence—it runs from the presidential palace to the parliament building, and was soon lined with Belle Epoque apartment buildings, theaters, and cafés.

292 ART AND CULTURE

SECESSION BUILDING

Vienna, Austria
1896

A breakaway group of artists in Vienna, led by Gustav Klimt, the Secession movement was formed in reaction to staid, Academy-influenced art. The Secession building—an exhibition venue built over two years by the young architect Joseph Maria Olbrich—opened in 1898, and was its public face. Topped with a globe of gilded laurel leaves, its blocky white facade had the intended look of a temple to contemporary art.

RIGHT: The gilded-iron leaves of the building's open-worked dome haven't always been admired; locals have nicknamed it the "Golden cabbage."

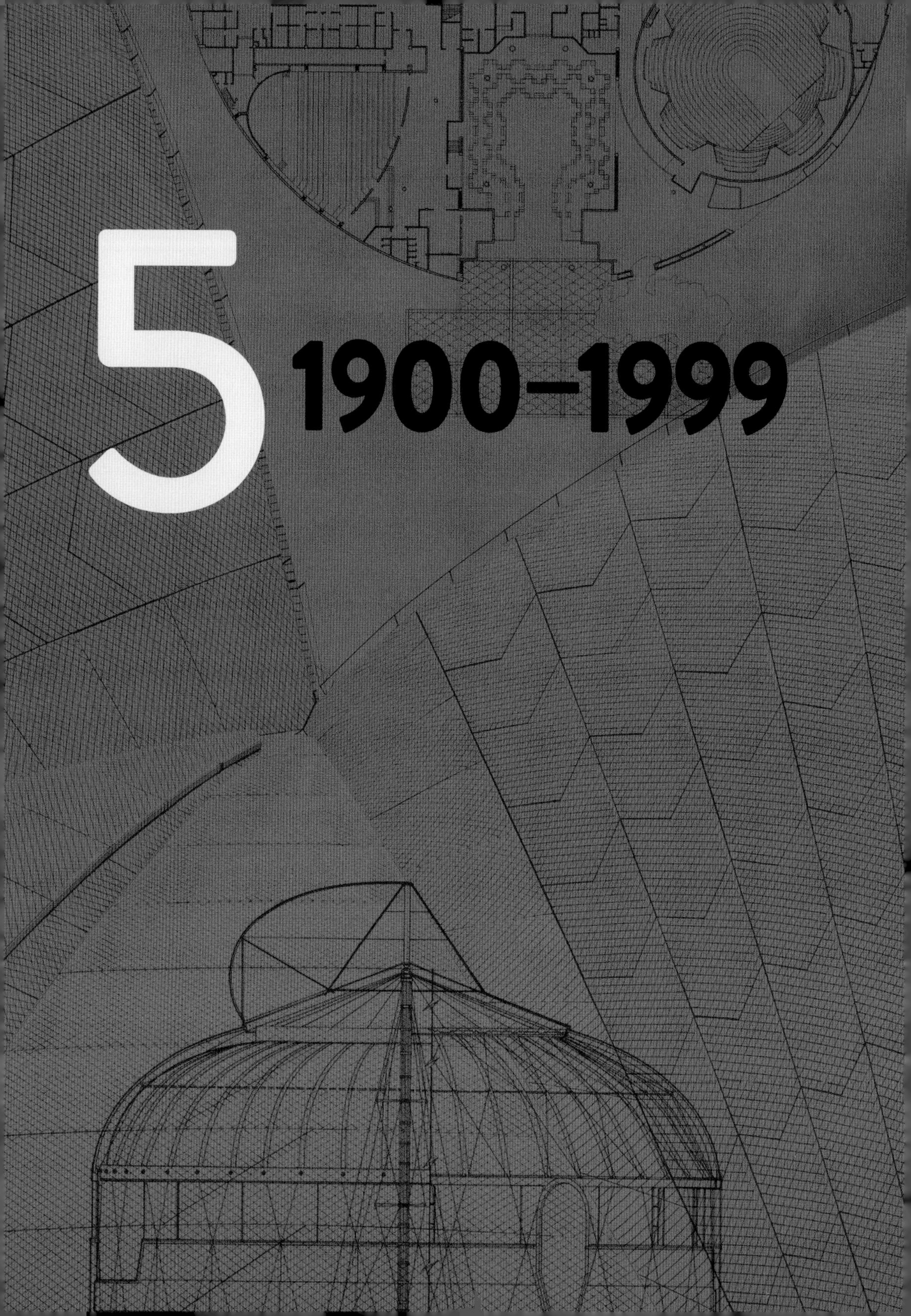

5 1900–1999

293 RELIGION AND MONUMENT

SPIRIT HOUSES

East Sepik, Papua New Guinea
c. 1900

Along the Sepik River, the Abelam people of Papua New Guinea use these traditional triangular buildings for meetings, initiation ceremonies, and storytelling. Up to 100 feet tall, and held together with ropes made from lianas, they are decorated and redecorated with traditional symbols and patterns—particularly patterns associated with yams, the Abelam's survival crop. The oldest date back over a century, but are constantly updated and remodeled.

ABOVE: The Sepik land is home to a number of different peoples. Each has a distinctive style for the construction and decoration of their spirit houses.

294 RESIDENCE

HOUSE OF TAN TENG NIAH

Singapore
c. 1900

Notable as the only surviving Chinese merchant house in the Little India district of Singapore, the villa is a reminder of the many small Chinese factories and businesses that operated in the area in the early twentieth century—since completely redeveloped. It belonged to the owner of a candy factory and is in its original arrangement, with a covered gallery around the outside of the first floor.

CABOT TOWER

St. John's, Newfoundland, Canada
1901

The reception site of the world's first transatlantic wireless signal.

Cabot Tower was named after Giovanni Cabot, an Italian explorer who was the first European to arrive in Newfoundland in the late fifteenth century. It is a castellated structure on Signal Hill, built in 1897 to celebrate the twin anniversaries of Queen Victoria's Diamond Jubilee and the fourth centenary of Cabot's voyages. Four years later, on December 12, 1901, the site would become internationally famous when Guglielmo Marconi flew a kite bearing an antenna here. It successfully received the first transatlantic wireless signal (the letter "S" in Morse code: dot-dot-dot), sent from Poldhu in Cornwall, England. The experiment defied the predictions of contemporary scientists that the curvature of the earth would make it impossible for radio waves to travel.

BELOW: Cabot Tower saw one of the most exciting scientific developments of the early 1900s when Guglielmo Marconi took the first step toward transatlantic communications nearby.

296 ART AND CULTURE

AU LAPIN AGILE

Paris, France
1902

Au Lapin Agile was an established, if seedy, bar and cabaret in Montmartre when it was bought by Aristide Bruant, a cabaret performer and entrepreneur. It became especially popular with artists, many of whom lived in cheap studios nearby—Pablo Picasso, Amedeo Modigliani, and Maurice Utrillo among them. Picasso's *Au Lapin Agile*, a famous early work, shows the artist as a morose harlequin, standing at the bar.

297 PLACE OF WORK

PACKARD AUTOMOTIVE PLANT

Detroit, Michigan
1903

At the time it was built, the Packard Automotive Plant was considered the most advanced automobile factory in the world. It was the first building to use concrete reinforced with steel, developed and patented by the engineer Julius Kahn, and incorporated by his brother Albert, the plant's architect. The additional strength of reinforced concrete enabled larger open spaces in buildings, as well as bigger windows, uninterrupted by supports.

BELOW: Reinforced concrete made large-scale production lines more achievable because it enabled the creation of uncluttered working spaces with more natural light.

FLATIRON BUILDING

Manhattan, New York
1903

An early skyscraper on one of the most challenging lots in New York City.

Named for its distinctive shape (it was originally named the Fuller Building, but its nickname stuck), the Flatiron is built on a sharply triangular site between Fifth Avenue and Broadway. It was commissioned by the Fuller Company, a major contractor based in Chicago, who chose the prestigious Chicago architect Daniel Burnham to design it. Despite the then-modern construction—22 stories around a steel frame, with plenty of elevators—the building's look was pure Beaux Arts: the Renaissance-inspired style so popular in late nineteenth-century Europe and America.

It wasn't immediately popular, and its extreme proportions—only 6.5 feet wide at its narrowest point—led to public fears that it would be unstable. Over time, the Flatiron Building became a popular landmark of a new, mid-Manhattan commercial district. Within 30 years, most skyscrapers would be needle-shaped. Today, it is an unusual survivor of early twentieth-century style.

BELOW AND RIGHT: Despite its striking and elegantly detailed exterior, the Flatiron Building's unusual footprint meant that much of the office space inside was cramped and awkwardly shaped.

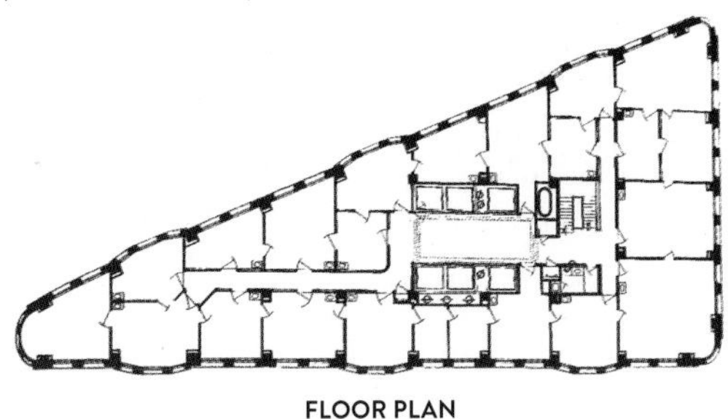

FLOOR PLAN

299 RESIDENCE/INFRASTRUCTURE AND INNOVATION

LETCHWORTH GARDEN CITY

Hertfordshire, England
1903

The first garden city, Letchworth, was a pioneering project implementing the ideas of social reformer Ebenezer Howard. Howard envisaged a network of small cities, each with a "garden" center incorporating public amenities, surrounded by spacious suburbs and ringed with farmland, creating pleasant living conditions in largely self-sufficient communities. The concept proved too expensive for large-scale implementation, although some elements have become standard practice in town planning.

ABOVE: "Town and country must be married," wrote Ebenezer Howard, an early believer in the importance of integrated green space for city dwellers.

300 PLACE OF WORK

WHALING STATION

Grytviken, South Georgia, Antarctica
1904

Built by the Norwegian explorer and sea captain Carl Anton Larsen, the station was the first in the area, taking advantage of the large number of whales that spent the summer in Antarctic seas. The station processed whale meat and blubber. Eight years later, there were six other stations nearby, all making good profits. It remained open for 60 years, finally closing its doors in 1965.

BELOW: Whales were soon overfished in the South Atlantic; by the 1960s the whaling stations had become commercially unviable.

301 RESIDENCE/ART AND CULTURE

LA CASA AZUL

Mexico City, Mexico
1904

The birthplace of one of Mexico's most famous artists—and a feminist icon.

Three years before his daughter Frida was born, Guillermo Kahlo built La Casa Azul in the suburb of Coyoacán as a family home. Even after Frida Kahlo had grown up, much of her adult life was spent here. First came a long convalescence after a terrible streetcar accident when she was 18; forced to lie flat, she learned to paint in her childhood bedroom.

Although Kahlo left the house during her first marriage to the Mexican muralist Diego Rivera, she returned in 1939 after their divorce. When they remarried, the previously white house was painted a brilliant cobalt and became La Casa Azul—they lived here until her death in 1954.

Now a museum, La Casa Azul reflects Frida Kahlo's personality. It houses her studio, much of her art, her collections of pre-Columbian sculpture and Mexican folk art, and her eclectic wardrobe.

ABOVE LEFT: Although the house is now a museum, it is still arranged very much as it was during Kahlo's lifetime.

ABOVE RIGHT: Frida Kahlo is a diminutive figure as she walks arm-in-arm with her tall, bulky husband, Diego Rivera. Their stormy union was cuttingly described by her mother as a marriage "between an elephant and a dove."

GREAT MOSQUE

Djenné, Mali
1907

The largest mud structure in sub-Saharan Africa, maintained in an annual town ritual.

Although the latest incarnation—it's the town's third—was completed in the early twentieth century, there has been a Great Mosque on this site since the late thirteenth century, when the local ruler, Sultan Koi Konboro, converted to Islam. This was the first version to use vernacular materials and design. The current prayer hall is big enough for 3,000 worshippers, alongside a walled courtyard, all made from mud brick mortared with more mud mixed in with baobab leaves, shea butter, and palm husks. The prayer wall, or *qibla*, features three large minarets facing east toward Mecca, each topped with an ostrich egg, symbolic of both purity and fertility in Mali. Holes in the hall's roof, covered during the day, are left open overnight, helping to keep the interior cool.

Djenné sits on the Niger and Bani Rivers, between the arid Sahara and the temperate Sahel region. It has a significant rainy season which "melts" earthen buildings, so the mosque needs annual replastering, accomplished in a day's festival—*crépissage*—which is organized by the community under the guidance of master masons. The supports extending from the walls—made from the dried stems of local rodier palms, called *toron*—are both decorative and practical, serving as scaffolding during the plastering process.

RIGHT: Mali's mud masons learn their skills over years. Too much mud—or the wrong mix—and the building's outline "melts," losing its distinct shape.

BELOW: An early photograph of the Great Mosque, showing its huge scale and crisp outlines when newly completed.

KNOWN FOR

- The largest earthen building in sub-Saharan Africa
- An outstanding example of vernacular Sahel-Saharan architecture
- A traditional focus for a working celebration for the community

303 PLACE OF WORK

FORT PIQUETTE AVENUE PLANT

Detroit, Michigan
1908

Ford Motor Company's first purpose-built factory, a modest redbrick plant, housed the production line of the world's first truly affordable car: the Model T. Over 12,000 cars were made here, but in 1911 Ford moved to larger premises at Highland Park, selling the building to Studebaker. This next manufacturer produced cars in the plant until 1933.

LEFT: A Model N drives down Piquette Avenue in 1906, two years before the introduction of the Model T, which would become Ford's runaway success.

ABOVE: Today, Kolmanskop's well-appointed bourgeois houses have been completely reclaimed by the desert.

304 PLACE OF WORK

KOLMANSKOP

Namibia, Africa
1908

Built for the community that grew up around a short-lived diamond rush in a German colony of southwestern Africa, Kolmanskop resembled a provincial German town. Briefly prosperous, with its own diamond market, it lasted only 20 years before diamonds were found in Oranjemund, to the south. The town was gradually abandoned to the Namib Desert, which filled its houses with sand.

305 ART AND CULTURE

GLASGOW SCHOOL OF ART

Glasgow, Scotland
1909

Begun in 1898 and completed in 1909, the Glasgow School of Art is an early masterpiece of the architect Charles Rennie Mackintosh. When the firm that the 28-year-old draftsman worked for, Honeyman & Keppie, was commissioned to produce the building, Mackintosh's designs drew from influences as broad as Art Nouveau, Scottish Baronial, and Japonisme. The result is a dramatically eclectic building that has proved influential internationally.

ABOVE: The school's main facade has tall windows, embellished with the decorative wrought iron particularly characteristic of Charles Rennie Mackintosh's work.

306 PLACE OF WORK

CHANEL ATELIER, 21 RUE CAMBON

Paris, France
1910

Coco Chanel opened her first Parisian business, Chanel Modes, selling hats at 21 Rue Cambon. It was a small shop, but in a fashionable part of town. Her flair for business and fashion allowed her to open a larger store at No. 31 in the same street, in 1918. She ran a new kind of business—with hats, accessories, and later clothes and scent—all under one roof.

307 PLACE OF WORK

SCOTT'S HUT

Cape Evans, Antarctica
1911

The prefabricated hut provided the base from which Captain Robert Scott led his Terra Nova expedition to the South Pole. The idea of a "race to the pole" was typical of the late Imperial era; the Norwegian explorer Roald Amundsen got there first; Scott and his British party reached the pole but died on the way back. The hut sheltered expedition members over two winters. Its frozen surroundings have kept it in a remarkable state of preservation.

ADZIOGOL LIGHTHOUSE

Kherson, Ukraine
1911

A new design that could be used in all kinds of practical structures.

The delicate-looking, 210-foot-high Adziogol Lighthouse is highly functional. Its position on the Dnipro Estuary is famously difficult for ships to navigate. The design, a particular speciality of its Russian engineer and architect, Vladimir Shukhov, is a diagrid tower: a crisscrossed lattice of steel rods. After the Russian Revolution, diagrids, or "Shukhov towers"—light, strong, and inexpensive—would be used for everything from water towers to radio masts.

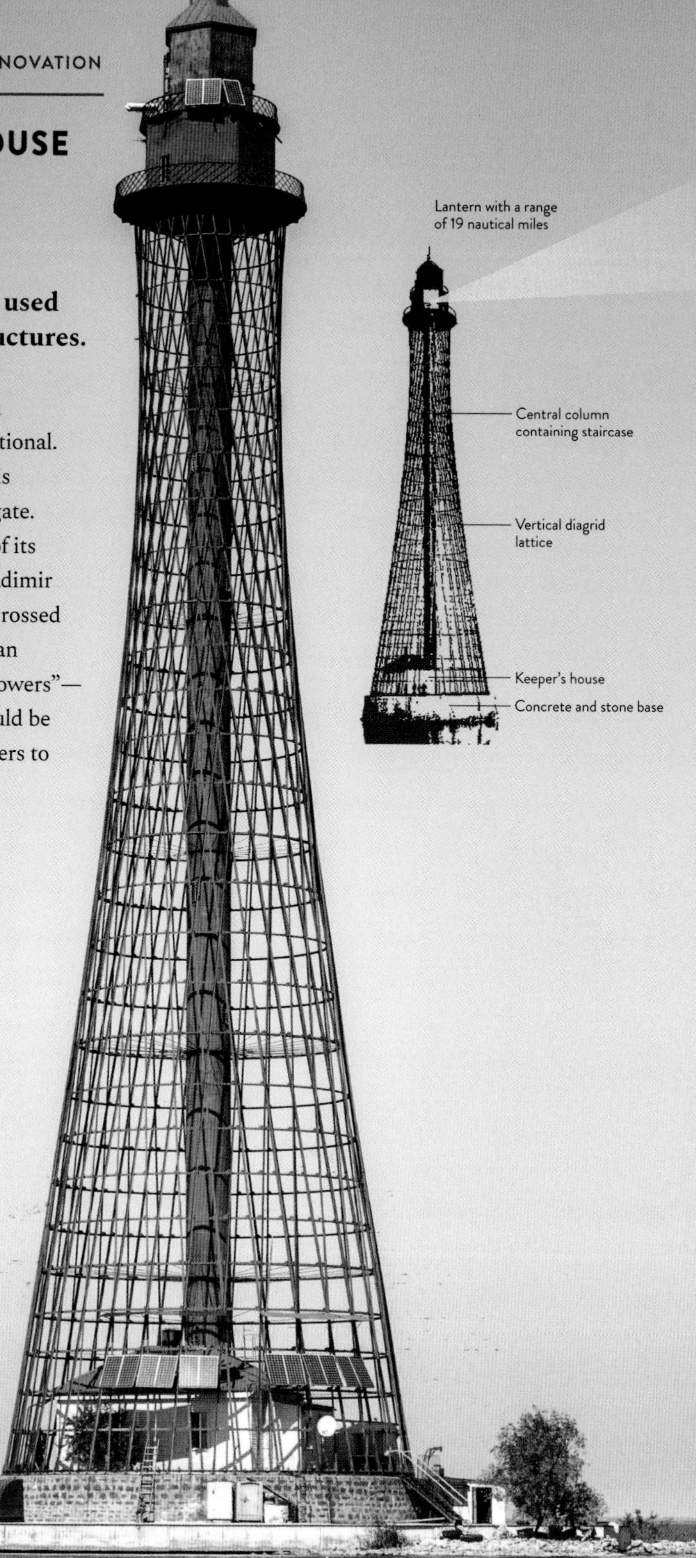

RIGHT: Vladimir Shukhov's lattice, arranged vertically on horizontal hoops, had the twin virtues of being both light and very strong.

AMBA VILAS PALACE

Mysore, India
1912

A vast Indo-Saracenic palace built for an ancient dynasty.

Locally known as the "Palace of Electricity," 98,260 bulbs are needed to illuminate the huge building. It is an opulent three-story palace, topped by pink domes, and set in 97 acres. It was commissioned by Krishnaraja IV of the Wodeyar Dynasty, rulers of Mysore since 1399. It is one of the grandest Indian buildings of the early twentieth century. Many of the royal families in India retained huge personal wealth, even as their hold over their territories weakened and ultimately came to an end with Indian independence in 1947.

The palace was designed by the architect Henry Irwin, who specialized in the Indo-Saracenic style. His other buildings include the Gaiety Theatre in Shimla, and the Madras High Court. The palace is now part museum and part royal residence—the current Wodeyar Raja still lives there.

BELOW: The palace was constructed with the finest artisan workmanship available in every medium, from stained glass to gilding and wooden latticework.

AMERICAN ACADEMY IN ROME

Rome, Italy
1913

The classical building that gave a home to American ideas and creativity in Europe.

The idea of an American-funded school based in Europe, a center where artists could work and research, was first discussed by a group working on the World's Columbian Exposition in 1893.

The well-known Chicago architect Charles McKim pursued the idea vigorously and, despite many subsequent problems with funding and location, the academy opened in its first incarnation, the American School of Architecture, in 1894. The second incarnation, the American Academy in Rome, opened in 1912 in two parts: as a school of classical studies and a school of fine arts.

Shortly before his death in 1913, the financier and philanthropist J. P. Morgan donated land and funds, and McKim's company—McKim, Mead & White—designed the dedicated Academy Building, a grand classical villa—the company's only project in Europe—which opened in 1915.

BELOW: Charles McKim designed a building in the Renaissance style and incorporated a gallery, library, and other public rooms, as well as studios and living quarters for the scholars.

311 PLACE OF WORK

GARDEN OF ALLAH

Los Angeles, California
1913

Built by developer William Hay, the house on Sunset Boulevard was later converted into a louche bohemian hotel, with chalets in the garden added by a subsequent owner, the silent-film star Alla Nazimova, who named it after herself. For two decades, it hosted a range of stars—including Humphrey Bogart and Ginger Rogers—and many Hollywood screenwriters—among them Dorothy Parker, Robert Benchley, and F. Scott Fitzgerald.

312 INFRASTRUCTURE AND INNOVATION

GRAND CENTRAL TERMINAL

Manhattan, New York
1913

Often mistakenly called Grand Central Station, it is in fact a terminal, being the final stop for three major railroads. It was the largest construction project undertaken in New York. Reed & Stem, the architects, delivered a glamorous Beaux Arts–style building that conquered technical obstacles in style. The vast, vaulted concourse roof was painted with a mural of stars. It was lit entirely by electric chandeliers, and ramps were introduced to make it easier to move between levels.

ABOVE: At the time of its opening, Grand Central Terminal was considered a magnificent new landmark for New York, as well as a technical triumph. It was one of the first major public buildings to offer plenty of access to motor traffic.

PANAMA CANAL

Panama
1914

An American—technical and economic—triumph that transformed the face of global trade.

In 1869, President Ulysses S. Grant ordered a feasibility report on cutting a canal through the Central American isthmus. He came to believe it was impossible. A French attempt, made by the Panama Canal Company, ended in failure after almost a decade when the company went bankrupt in 1893.

In 1902, President Theodore Roosevelt began negotiations with Colombia for a route through Panama (then Colombian territory). When its financial offer was rejected, the United States sent gunships to the area. Panama promptly declared independence, and in 1904 its new government granted the United States land for the canal in return for a payment of $10 million, an annual usage fee, and a guarantee of continued support. This time, the canal was built.

A program to eliminate mosquitoes in the area was undertaken by Dr. William Gorgas, who identified them as the source of most on-site diseases. Of the 5,000 people who died during construction, the majority of deaths were a result of industrial accidents rather than mosquitoes.

Three locks along, the 50-mile route balanced the different water levels and the canal finally opened on August 15, 1915. The new shortcut played a vital part in growing global trade in the early decades of the twentieth century.

RIGHT: Work on the canal was notoriously punishing. Frequent landslides during construction caused many injuries and deaths.

KNOWN FOR

- When built, the largest engineering project ever undertaken
- The first time that health precautions—mosquito elimination—were used to keep the labor force healthy
- A crucial shipping shortcut: 1,000 vessels used it in its first year of operation

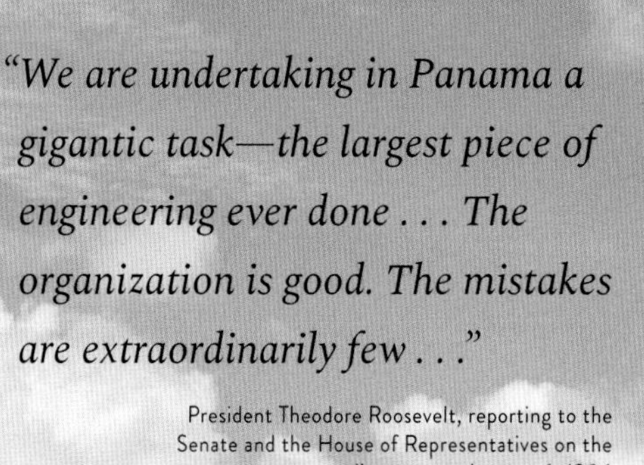

"We are undertaking in Panama a gigantic task—the largest piece of engineering ever done . . . The organization is good. The mistakes are extraordinarily few . . ."

President Theodore Roosevelt, reporting to the Senate and the House of Representatives on the canal's progress, January 6, 1906

BELOW: At the time of its completion, the Panama Canal—linking the Atlantic and Pacific Oceans—was the most expensive construction project in U.S. history, having cost an estimated $375 million.

PARK GÜELL

Barcelona, Spain
1914

The failed housing project that became one of Barcelona's best-loved public spaces.

Park Güell was conceived by Eusebi Güell, an early patron of Antoni Gaudí. Inspired by the English idea of a garden city (see page 244), it sits on a hill at the edge of Barcelona. The original plan was to build 60 houses in lavish grounds for the town's wealthiest citizens.

The idea never took off—the plots failed to sell—although from 1906, Gaudí himself lived in one of the houses on site (now the Gaudí Museum). The concept was officially abandoned in 1914. Gaudí, and to a much lesser extent his contemporaries, transformed the park into a fantastic landscape full of Catalan Modernist structures—including the undulating main terrace, benches, and fountains—vividly mosaiced, and the Hypostyle Hall, with treelike columns, originally intended as the community marketplace.

After Güell's death in 1918, his family offered the park to the city. It was opened to the public in 1926.

BELOW: The undulating benches and balcony around the Placa de la Natura (Nature Square) are covered with the mosaic work typical of Antoni Gaudí's constructions in the park.

315 ART AND CULTURE

WRIGLEY FIELD

Chicago, Illinois
1914

Christened Weeghman Park, the stadium was built for the Chicago Whales of the short-lived Federal League. Built in two months, it had a single-deck grandstand but was subsequently extended. When that league folded, Charles Weeghman purchased the Chicago Cubs of the National League, and it became their home stadium. William Wrigley took over in 1920; by 1926, the ballpark was known as Wrigley Field, which has been hugely popular in Chicago ever since.

ABOVE: The stadium could seat 14,000 people when it opened; it can accommodate over 41,000 today.

316 INFRASTRUCTURE AND INNOVATION

FUNICULAR SYSTEM

Valparaiso, Chile
1915

Valparaiso, with its deep bay, was a lively commercial hub, the most important port on the Pacific coast in the mid-nineteenth century. Wealthy neighborhoods grew up on the steep hills of the city. The sites were difficult to access, so a system of *ascensores*, or funiculars, was built to serve the different districts. Cable cars were winched up steep tracks, counterbalanced by one on the opposite track; by 1915, there were 31.

When the Panama Canal opened in 1914, ships generally found that route easier than the Valparaiso–Magellan Strait, and many of the wealthier residents took their business elsewhere.

ABOVE: A unique transport system, providing access to a precipitously hilly port town.

ABOVE: The siting of the church—within the canyon—was extraordinarily demanding structurally.

317 RELIGION AND MONUMENT

SANTUARIA DE LAS LAJAS

Ipiales, Colombia
1916

Built to mark a popular pilgrimage site, the church was constructed between 1916 and 1949 on a canyon of the Guaitara River. The commission required the Ecuadorian team of architect Lucindo Espinosa and engineer Gualberto Perez to not only bridge the ravine but also to enclose an earlier church within a neo-Gothic shell. Completed after more than 30 years, the church was as much a triumph of engineering as of architecture.

ABOVE: The lifestyle of the Bloomsbury creatives who lived here was much less traditional than the farmhouse's pretty facade.

318 RESIDENCE

CHARLESTON FARMHOUSE

Sussex, England
1917

During World War I, artist Vanessa Bell, sister of Virginia Woolf and a key member of the Bloomsbury Group, took a lease on this Sussex farmhouse and moved in with her children, her lover—the painter Duncan Grant—and Grant's lover, the writer David Garnett. The farmhouse quickly became an out-of-London center for the wider group, a place where they were free to experiment with art, philosophy, and unconventional relationships.

THE WINTER PALACE

St. Petersburg, Russia
1917

The key event of the October Revolution, restaged as powerful propaganda.

The storming of the Winter Palace on October 26, 1917, would come to be regarded as a pivotal event of the October Revolution. The latter saw Lenin's Bolsheviks seize power from the provisional government that had been in charge of Russia since the tsar's abdication in March 1917. In reality, it was more of a takeover than a "storming": Bolshevik soldiers quickly overcame the small force guarding the palace, and any government ministers who hadn't already fled were arrested.

The scenes at the Winter Palace took on their heroic iconography three years later, when a huge reenactment was staged to celebrate the anniversary of the revolution. There were over 2,500 participants and an estimated 100,000 spectators. Scenes were stage-managed by Nikolai Evreinov, a Soviet dramatist, while screens in the windows of the palace showed silhouetted "conflict" inside. Footage of the event would form an important piece of Soviet propaganda for decades.

"The Winter Palace itself has been included as a performing actor, as an immense character with a body language and inner emotions of its own."

Nikolai Evreinov, 1920

ABOVE AND BELOW: With its immense courtyard, the palace offered the perfect vistas for a grand, cinematic re-creation, even though the original "storming" had been undramatic.

IPATIEV HOUSE

Yekaterinburg, Russia
1918

The last lodgings of the last tsar of Russia and his family.

After Tsar Nicholas II's abdication in 1917, the imperial family was moved to a series of increasingly remote locations. Their final destination, Ipatiev House, at the eastern edge of the Ural Mountains, had been requisitioned from a local engineer, and was ominously referred to by their Bolshevik guards as the House of Special Purpose.

In the small hours of July 17, 1918, the family, with their doctor and three servants, were ordered to ready themselves for another move. Instead, they were shot and bayoneted to death in the Ipatiev basement. Their bodies were burned, partially dismembered, and disposed of in a nearby forest. Details of the assassinations were kept secret—the Soviet regime was fearful that the Romanovs might be resurrected as martyrs. Today, the Church on Blood, consecrated in 2003 and dedicated to the memory of the newly canonized family, stands on the Ipatiev site.

"If this was not the detested imperial family . . . one could have considered them as simple and not arrogant persons . . ."

Yakov Yurovsky, member of the Ural Regional Soviet, in charge of the assassination squad, 1922

BELOW LEFT: The imperial family photographed in 1913, before the abdication.

BELOW: During the imperial family's stay at Ipatiev House in the 1920s, its windows were whitewashed and a high fence was built around it.

321 PLACE OF WORK

OLD BEIJING STOCK EXCHANGE

Beijing, China
1918

Set behind Tiananmen Square, this two-story brick building with a pitched wooden roof, an internal gallery, and a double-height central court finished with elegant traditional wooden carving, was built to house the Beijing Stock Exchange. It opened on June 5, 1918. It was the first in the country to be run by—and for—the Chinese.

A marker of China's move toward modernity, it survived a period of conflict, but closed in 1949, after the Communists gained ascendency and Mao Zedong established the People's Republic of China. Beijing wouldn't have its own stock exchange again until 2021, when President Xi Jinping opened a new establishment.

322 RESIDENCE

HEARST CASTLE

San Simeon, California
1919

Hearst Castle is the centerpiece of the vast estate at San Simeon, owned by the press baron William Randolph Hearst. The Spanish Revival castle—with its cathedral-like facade—was commissioned from the architect Julia Morgan in 1919. Constantly remodeled over the next 30 years, it became famous for the huge parties Hearst held there with his mistress, actress Marion Davies. Hearst Castle inspired the estate in Orson Welles's movie *Citizen Kane*.

ABOVE: The classically inspired Neptune Pool, one of several at the castle, was enlarged three times.

323 RESIDENCE

PICKFAIR

Los Angeles, California
1920

The portmanteau name was put together by the house's owners, Douglas Fairbanks and Mary Pickford, two of the biggest silent-movie stars of the 1920s. Pioneers in the art of managed publicity, they were one of the earliest Hollywood couples to use their house as a press background for their lifestyle—from playing tennis to swimsuit shots in the first private pool in Los Angeles.

324 ART AND CULTURE

JIYU GAKUEN GIRLS' SCHOOL

Tokyo, Japan
1921

Frank Lloyd Wright's colleague Arata Endo introduced him to the Hanis, a freethinking couple who were opening a school in Tokyo. Finding himself in sympathy with their ideas, he offered to build it. Designed quickly, on a budget, the result is nonetheless recognizable as his work, particularly the way the buildings extend horizontally, characteristic of both traditional Japanese style and the Prairie style for which Wright became known.

ABOVE: Frank Lloyd Wright designed innovative geometric window frames for the school's chapel, to replace the more traditional—and costly—stained glass.

CENTRE COURT

Wimbledon, London, England
1922

By 1919, largely thanks to the glamorous young French champion Suzanne Lenglen, spectators had begun flocking to tennis matches. The All England Lawn Tennis and Croquet Club needed a larger court. Architect Stanley Peach took eight months to build a modern stadium to accommodate over 13,500 spectators on a new site at Church Road; it opened in time for the 1922 season, and Lenglen won three Wimbledon titles at Centre Court.

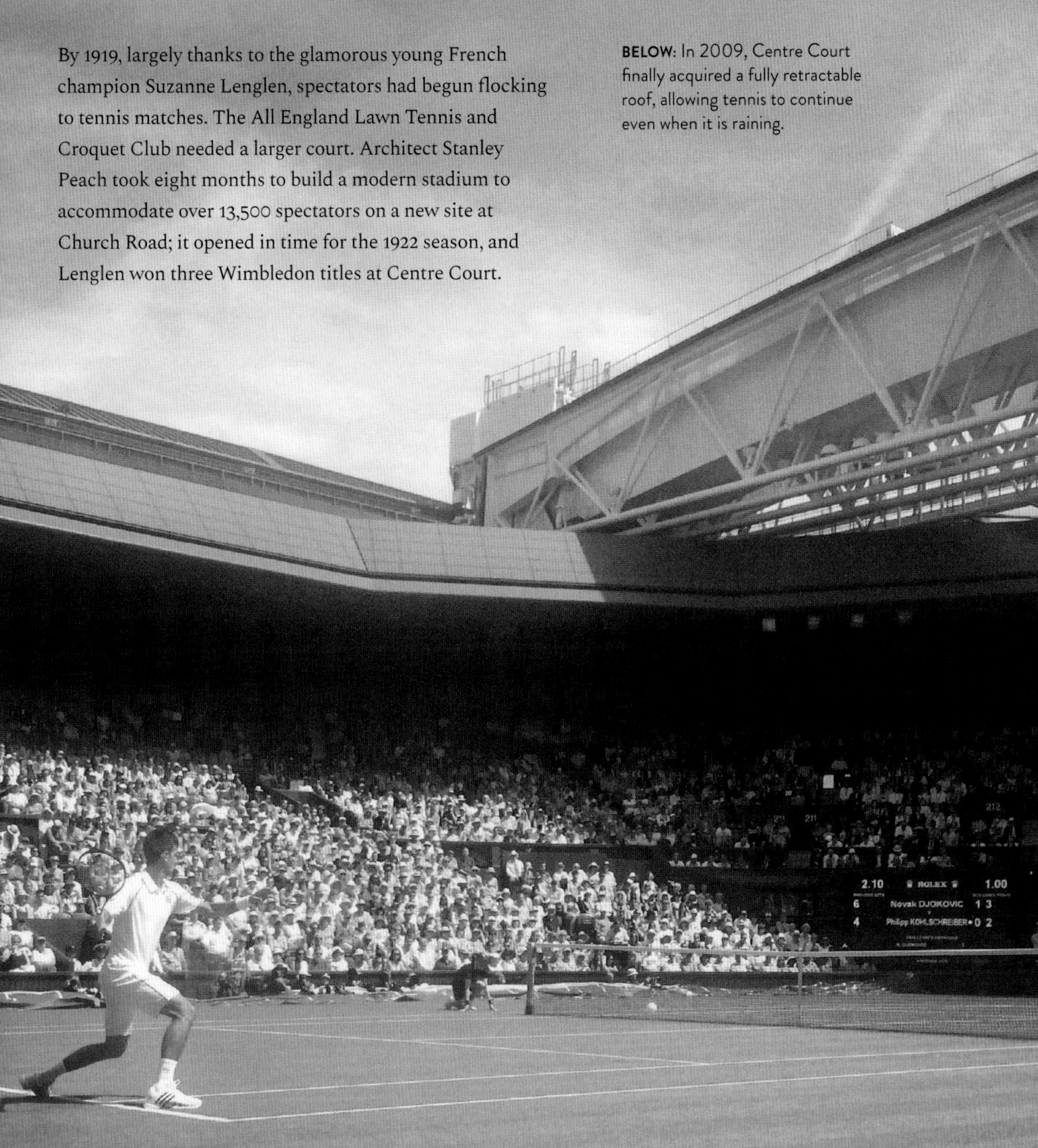

BELOW: In 2009, Centre Court finally acquired a fully retractable roof, allowing tennis to continue even when it is raining.

FIAT LINGOTTO FACTORY

Turin, Italy
1923

The novel production line where spare parts emerged as completed cars—five stories up.

When Giovanni Agnelli, founder of Fiat, visited the Ford Highland Park Factory in Detroit in the early 1920s, he was inspired to create a modern new production plant for Fiat. Charged with its design, the engineer Giacomo Matté Trucco created a huge building of reinforced concrete in which raw materials were delivered at ground level, and cars were built on a production line with ramps rising upward, a different construction stage on each floor.

Emerging on an oval track at roof level, the cars were test-driven before being returned to ground level down a long spiral ramp.

Highly admired by modernists, the Lingotto factory dated fast. What had been cutting-edge in the 1920s was considered slow by the early 1930s. It finally closed in 1982. It was repurposed as a mixed-function complex by the architect Renzo Piano, reopening in 1989.

BELOW: Le Corbusier visited the factory in 1923; he wrote admiringly that "atop the building the test track is like a king's crown."

327 ART AND CULTURE

EMPIRE STADIUM

London, England
1923

The suburban stadium conceived to support a concept of empire.

Empire Stadium was planned as a key element in the British Empire Exhibition of 1924, a time when the empire was at its greatest extent but also faced a number of threats. In particular, there was a growing movement for Indian independence. The exhibition was intended both to celebrate empire and to strengthen its bonds.

Located in a remote suburb of London, Wembley offered a spacious site. The stadium was completed in time to host the first Football Association final on April 28, 1923. It was built of reinforced concrete; the two towers flanking the central gate were in a loosely "Mughal" style, referencing India, while 37 huge arches around the outer walls were reminiscent of the ancient Roman Colosseum. Ultimately, the exhibition was a financial flop, but the stadium, renamed Wembley Stadium, became a hugely popular venue. It was demolished in 2003.

ABOVE: Empire Stadium was scheduled to be demolished when the British Empire Exhibition closed; instead, it remained a much-loved national sports venue for another 80 years.

RENAISSANCE BALLROOM AND CASINO

Harlem, New York
1923

The cultural center that gave its name to the Harlem Renaissance of the 1920s.

An important social and civic center for Harlem's thriving African American community, the Renaissance was the focus of the movement that celebrated and promoted the arts of the Black community from the early 1920s. It was built by members of Marcus Garvey's Universal Negro Improvement Association, a group of African American businesses. Concerts held here featured artists such as Count Basie and Duke Ellington; it was a center for new Black theater, and it also hosted political fundraisers and important community events as well as being the crucible for many modern social dancing styles.

The grand theater was the first building here, designed by the architect Henry Creighton Ingalls, with elaborate tiled facades. By 1923, the complex included a dance hall, a casino, a billiard parlor, and a restaurant. The dance hall doubled as a basketball court, home to the famous Black Fives team, colloquially known as the Harlem Rens.

The establishment closed in the 1970s. By the 1990s it had decayed enough to feature as the crack den in Spike Lee's movie *Jungle Fever*. After a long debate with successive owners about granting it landmark status, it was finally demolished in 2015.

RIGHT: So substantial was the Renaissance Ballroom complex that it spanned the whole frontage of Adam Clayton Powell Jr. Boulevard, between 137th and 138th Streets.

BELOW: Cootie Williams playing trumpet with Duke Ellington's band in the Renaissance Ballroom in the 1930s.

KNOWN FOR

- Its role as "the heart and soul" of 1920s and 1930s Harlem
- Operating exclusively for Harlem's Black community
- Combining multiple roles as a social, artistic, sporting, and political center

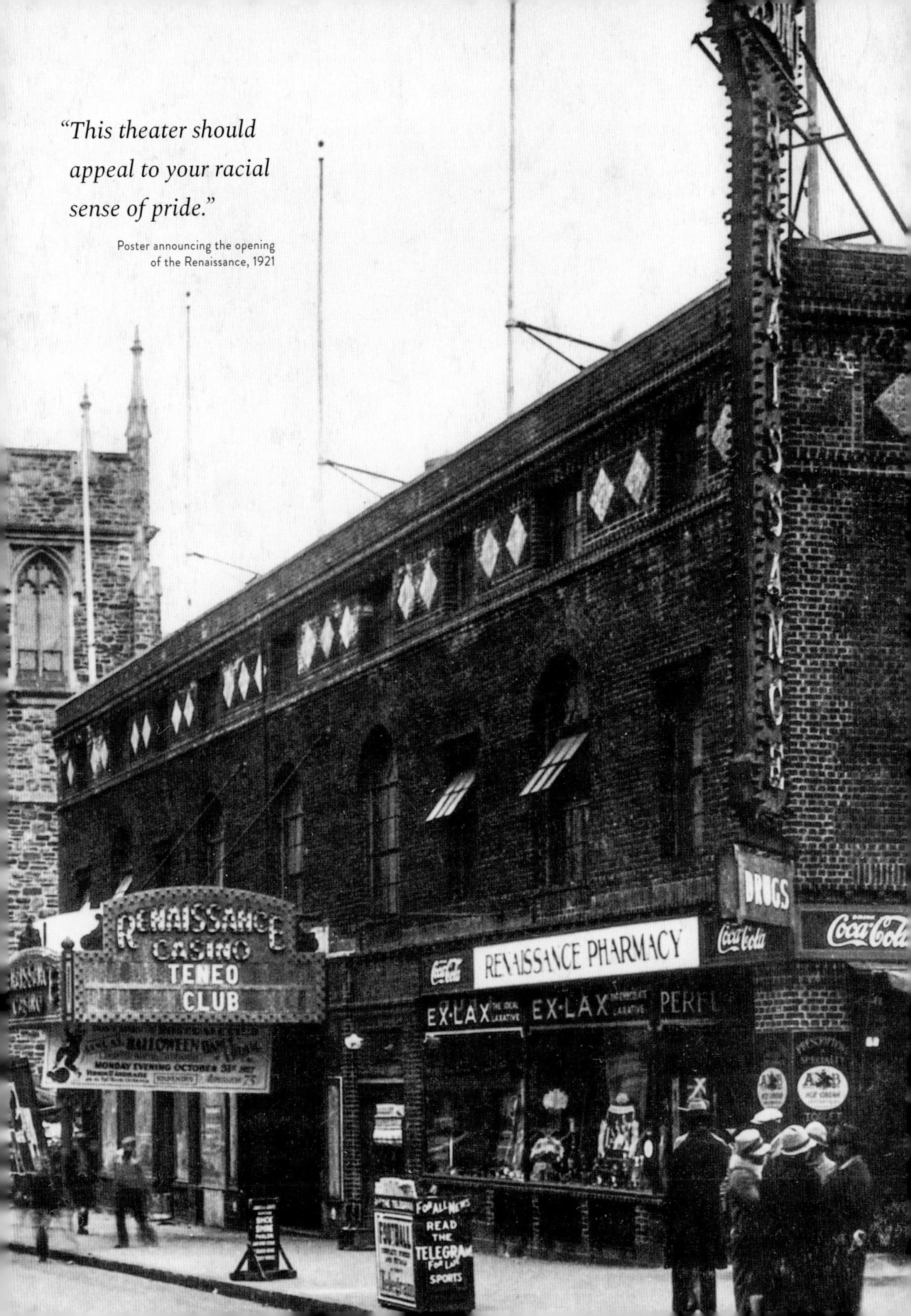

"This theater should appeal to your racial sense of pride."

Poster announcing the opening of the Renaissance, 1921

UNION STATION

Chicago, Illinois
1925

The station that played a key part in a plan for a rapidly enlarging Chicago.

After the Great Fire destroyed a large part of Chicago in 1871, the idea of a holistic urban scheme took root. In 1909, the architects Daniel Burnham and Edward Burnett published the Chicago Plan, laying out concepts for every aspect of the growing metropolis. Rail transport was a key element. Until his death in 1912, Burnham was the architect and planner of Union Station, a new central hub for Chicago, where four different railroads combined.

The station took several years to plan and a decade to build; it was completed by the successor to Burnham's firm, Graham, Anderson, Probst & White. It has a classical facade, and the Great Hall is roofed with a glazed barrel vault and overseen by two statues of Night and Day—referencing an age of 24-hour travel. It was an impressive dressing for a practical, modern building that managed the heaviest traffic of any station outside New York City.

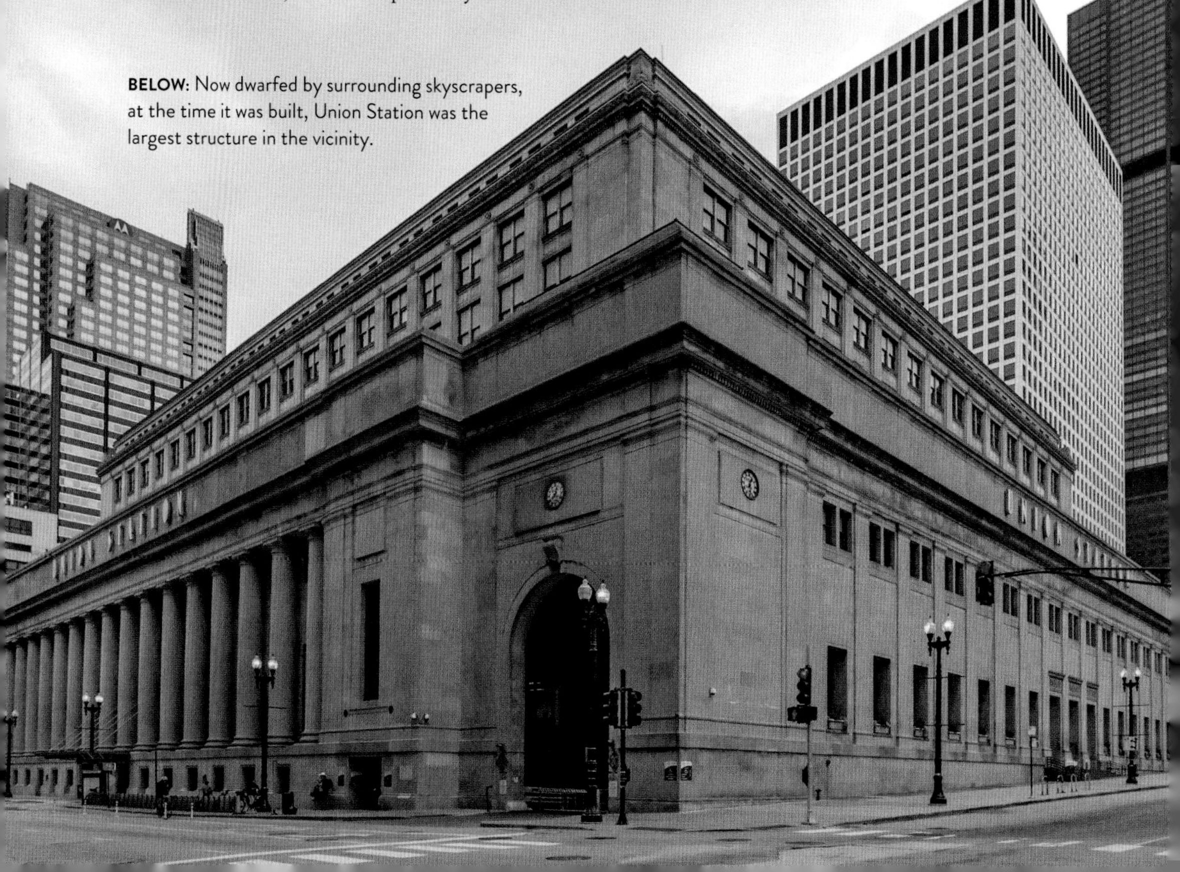

BELOW: Now dwarfed by surrounding skyscrapers, at the time it was built, Union Station was the largest structure in the vicinity.

PLEČNIK HOUSE

Ljubljana, Czech Republic
1925

The Slovenian architect Jože Plečnik, who studied under Otto Wagner in Vienna, set a strong personal stamp on the architecture of Ljubljana, his country's capital. His influence there has been compared to Gaudí's on Barcelona. His home, now a museum, reflects his esoteric style: a unique mixture of Art Nouveau and Classical. He operated under a waste-not, want-not policy, integrating elements left over from other projects in his own house.

ABOVE: Architect Jože Plečnik lived in the house he designed until his death in 1957. He called it a "testing hotbed" for his new ideas.

HAVERSTRAW HOUSE

Haverstraw, New York
1925

Built in 1885, the Victorian Gothic house sits on Route 9W in Haverstraw, New York. Passers-by are often gripped by a strong feeling of familiarity, recognizing it either as the subject of one of Edward Hopper's famous early works, *The House by the Railroad* (1925), or as the eerie Bates House that the painting inspired, which appeared to chilling effect in Alfred Hitchcock's 1960 masterpiece, *Psycho*.

ABOVE: The Edward Hopper painting inspired by Haverstraw House.

BAUHAUS BUILDING

Dessau, Germany
1926

A short-lived design movement with long-lasting global influence.

Bauhaus began in Weimar in 1919, where, in the aftermath of World War I, its founder, the architect Walter Gropius, produced the Bauhaus Manifesto, conceiving a movement that would enable students to develop their creative potential and apply it to improving everyday design. In 1925, increasing hostility from the conservative government of Weimar's state, Thuringia, forced Gropius to move to Dessau, where the city commissioned him to design new buildings for the school and supplied the land on which to build them.

The school opened in 1926. It incorporated workshop and studio wings, a separate vocational school, and houses for the masters and director. Their look was strongly modern for the time, based on clean, interlocking white shapes with subtle details. The lineup of tutors was distinguished, and included the painter Paul Klee, the textile designer Anni Albers, and the architect and furniture designer Marcel Breuer.

During its six years in Dessau, the Bauhaus flourished; those who worked there would spread its philosophy all over the world. Locally, it had political problems. When the Nazis attained a majority in Dessau, the Bauhaus moved briefly to Berlin, before closing for good in 1933.

KNOWN FOR

- Its effect on the design of everyday objects, from buildings to furniture and wallpaper
- Its lasting, worldwide influence on art and design philosophy
- Embracing mass production as a part of good design

BELOW: The workshop and studio wings are linked by a two-story bridge, which also housed the Bauhaus's administrative offices.

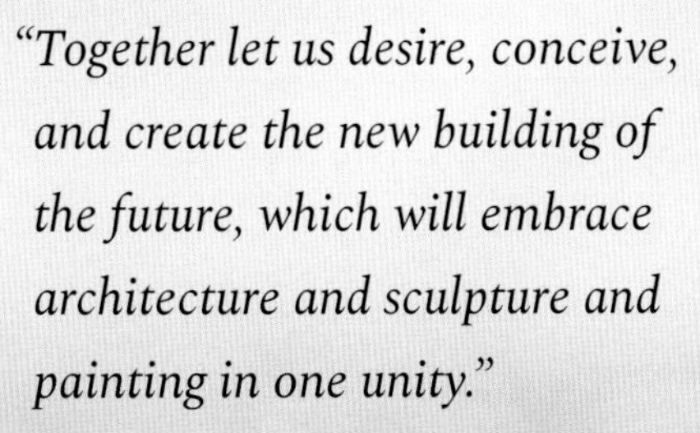

"Together let us desire, conceive, and create the new building of the future, which will embrace architecture and sculpture and painting in one unity."

Walter Gropius, *Bauhaus Manifesto*, 1919

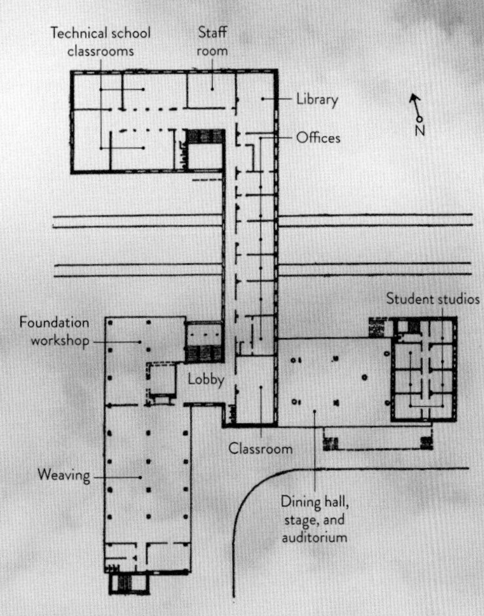

FIRST FLOOR SITE PLAN

RIGHT: The goal of the floor plan was to have the correct use of incidental light, short time-saving routes, clear separation of the various divisions, with the possibility of varying the sequence of rooms to respond to additional changes by means of axial division.

BELOW: The flat-roofed blocks have no immediately identifiable "main" facade. Walter Gropius was determined that they should be defined by their function.

333 RESIDENCE

PALACIO PORTALES

Cochabamba, Bolivia
1927

This astoundingly lavish mansion in the French Renaissance style was built for Simon Patino, known as the "Andean Rockefeller," a tin baron and well-known philanthropist whose foundries were at one time processing more than half the tin in the world. He never actually lived here. After a heart attack in the mid-1920s, doctors warned him that he couldn't risk living at the high altitude of his home country.

ABOVE: Simon Patino imported almost all the building materials and furnishings for Palacio Portales from Europe—no expense was spared.

334 ART AND CULTURE

GRAUMAN'S CHINESE THEATRE

Los Angeles, California
1927

The Chinese Theatre was the most famous of the themed movie theaters popular in the 1920s. Its instigator, Sid Grauman, had built the nearby Egyptian Theatre five years earlier, and his new enterprise—styled with a pagoda and much authentic Chinese art—opened with the premiere of Cecil B. DeMille's *King of Kings.* It would also become celebrated for the handprints of major stars set in cement in its forecourt.

ABOVE: In search of authenticity, Sid Grauman imported many Chinese works of art to decorate his new project.

335 PLACE OF WORK

ST. MARY'S HOSPITAL

London, England
1928

St. Mary's teaching hospital opened in West London in 1851. It was already notable for its research department by the time that Alexander Fleming, a young bacteriologist, found that the mold that had accidentally contaminated a petri dish of staphylococcus bacteria had stopped the bacteria from spreading. His observation led to the discovery of antibiotics, which were marketed commercially from the 1930s, revolutionizing the treatment of infections.

336 RESIDENCE/ART AND CULTURE

MELNIKOV HOUSE

Moscow, Russia
1929

Formed from two linked cylinders, pierced with regular hexagonal windows, and topped by a flat roof, Melnikov House was built by the artist and architect Konstantin Melnikov as his family home and studio—and as a prototype for future homes. A major star of post-revolutionary Russia, he fell drastically from favor under Stalin, but his reputation was rehabilitated after his death in 1974. The house is now a museum.

TOP: Founded in the mid-nineteenth century, St. Mary's was the first institution to be conceived as a teaching hospital, with a medical school attached.

ABOVE: After the revolution, the best way to create successful communal housing preoccupied many Russian architects; Konstantin Melnikov planned his own house for potential mass duplication.

E-1027 VILLA

Roquebrune-Cap-Martin, France
1929

Built by the Irish designer Eileen Gray for her lover Jean Badovici, this elegant white box was designed complete with interiors and furniture. In 1938, the architect Le Corbusier, a temporary lodger, painted energetic murals in the stark interior, unasked. Gray was horrified, comparing the result to a rape. The murals remain *in situ*, and the villa has recently been restored from a near-derelict state and opened to visitors.

BELOW: Eileen Gray is now best known for her furniture designs, but E-1027 is admired by many contemporary architects as a Modernist masterpiece.

SALVADOR DALÍ HOUSE

Portlligat, Spain
1930

In 1929, the young Surrealist artist Salvador Dalí was thrown out of his well-to-do family's home, and the following year he bought a tiny cabin in the fishing village of Portlligat. This would become his home and center for his creativity for the next 40 years. As his success grew, Dalí gradually bought up additional land, augmenting his ever-enlarging house with characteristically fantastical sculptures and *objets trouvés*.

ABOVE: Among many memorable details is the characteristically eccentric dovecote tower at Salvador Dalí's house, studded with pitchforks and topped with a giant egg.

339 PLACE OF WORK

CHRYSLER BUILDING

Manhattan, New York
1930

Walter Chrysler, the automobile magnate, acquired the lease to build the Chrysler Building in 1928. The architect William Van Alen incorporated plenty of automobile motifs, and finished the building with a seven-layer Art Deco tower. Gleaming with chromium, it was finished by a 185-foot spire, sealing its status as the world's tallest building—it was outgrown by the Empire State Building (see page 276) just a year later.

ABOVE: An aerial view shows the way in which the newly completed Chrysler Building dominated the city blocks around it.

340 RELIGION AND MONUMENT

LENIN'S MAUSOLEUM

Moscow, Russia
1930

When Lenin died in 1924, the cult of the leader of the Russian Revolution went into overdrive. Commissioned to design a mausoleum, the architect Alexey Shchusev created a temporary stepped wooden structure in Red Square, inspired by the pyramids of ancient Egypt. The fourth and final version was built in red and black granite in 1930.

The stepped structure recalled ancient memorial architecture. It was topped with a platform from which party officials could give speeches.

ABOVE: Lenin's tomb was topped with a stepped structure from which party officials could give speeches or view parades on Red Square—giving it the dual functions of mausoleum and podium.

EMPIRE STATE BUILDING

Manhattan, New York
1931

The iconic Art Deco skyscraper prompted by a 1930s race to the top.

Conceived to surpass the height of the Chrysler Building (see page 275), the Empire State Building was the first building to exceed 100 stories. It was the idea of General Motors executives and a former New York governor, Al Smith. Designed by Shreve, Lamb & Harmon, construction began on March 17, 1930, on Fifth Avenue, employing 3,400 workers a day—welcome in the initial bite of the Great Depression. The building was raised at the rate of four and a half stories every week.

Inaugurated on May 1, 1931, the Empire State Building was initially only 25 percent occupied, despite plenty of tourists and a guest appearance in the blockbuster movie *King Kong* (1933). It eventually became profitable in the 1940s. It remained the tallest building in the world until the first tower of the World Trade Center was completed in 1970.

RIGHT: The spire on top of the Empire State Building added an extra 200 feet to its height.

342 ART AND CULTURE

VILLA MAJORELLE

Marrakech, Morocco
1931

Both the villa and its famous garden, strongly linked with their late owner Yves St. Laurent, were the creation of Jacques Majorelle, a French artist and botanist. By 1931, he was laying out an exotic garden around his new Cubist-style villa, using plants collected from all over the world. He also painted the villa the strong cobalt, named "Bleu Outremer," which is still a feature of the site.

ABOVE: The exotic gardens of the villa were well established by the time Yves St. Laurent, its most famous owner, took possession in 1980.

343 PLACE OF WORK

MASONIC HOTEL

Napier, New Zealand
1932

In 1931, the town of Napier was flattened by the Hawke's Bay earthquake. It was quickly rebuilt with fashionable new Art Deco buildings. The Masonic Hotel—low, cream-stuccoed, with a pink colonnade—was built by the Wellington architect W. J. Prowse and is one of the most notable examples. The design incorporates Maori motifs along with all the streamlined curves and angles characteristic of the style.

ABOVE: With its scarlet stained-glass signage, the hotel's facade is quintessentially Art Deco.

344 PLACE OF WORK

REICHSTAG

Berlin, Germany
1933

On February 27, 1933, a month after Adolf Hitler became chancellor of Germany, an arson attack destroyed the debating chamber of the German parliament building, the Reichstag. It was a flashpoint; claiming the fire was part of a Communist plot, Hitler enabled the passing of a decree abolishing many freedoms. The detention of 81 elected Communist deputies left few to speak up about the National Socialist power grab.

ABOVE: The Reichstag fire gave Hitler's National Socialists an excuse to condemn rival political parties.

345 PLACE OF WORK

HOTEL NACIONAL DE CUBA

Havana, Cuba
1933

The hotel was besieged in what became known as the Battle of the Hotel Nacional. The conflict was between opposing army factions: officers in the hotel, and lower-ranking soldiers outside, under their leader, Fulgencio Batista—who, in the 1940s and 1950s, would become the president and much-feared dictator of Cuba. The officers eventually surrendered. Forty combatants were killed; the bullet holes in the hotel walls can still be seen.

ABOVE: Now Cuba's most famous "heritage" hotel, the Nacional is a key landmark on the Malecón, Havana's seafront promenade.

346 PLACE OF WORK

RESEARCH LABORATORY

Arcueil, France
1933

When the work of the great scientist Marie Curie grew too extensive for her original lab, the University of Paris built her a new one in Arcueil, south of Paris, in 1933. Her work, involving the extraction of radium, was extremely toxic. She died of its effects a year after the lab opened. Although the building closed in 1978, the site remains a radioactive hot spot, locally nicknamed "Chernobyl sur Seine."

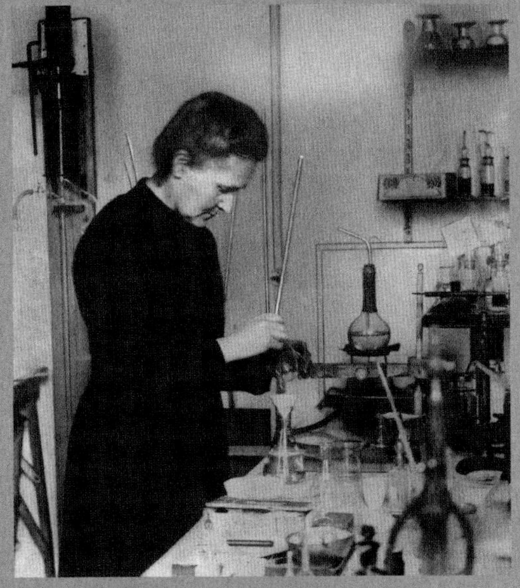

TOP: Opened in 1919, the Radium Institute in Paris, of which the Arcueil lab was an offshoot, became a leading center for the study of radioactivity under Curie's management.

ABOVE: Curie died of aplastic anemia in 1934, probably contracted as a result of her research.

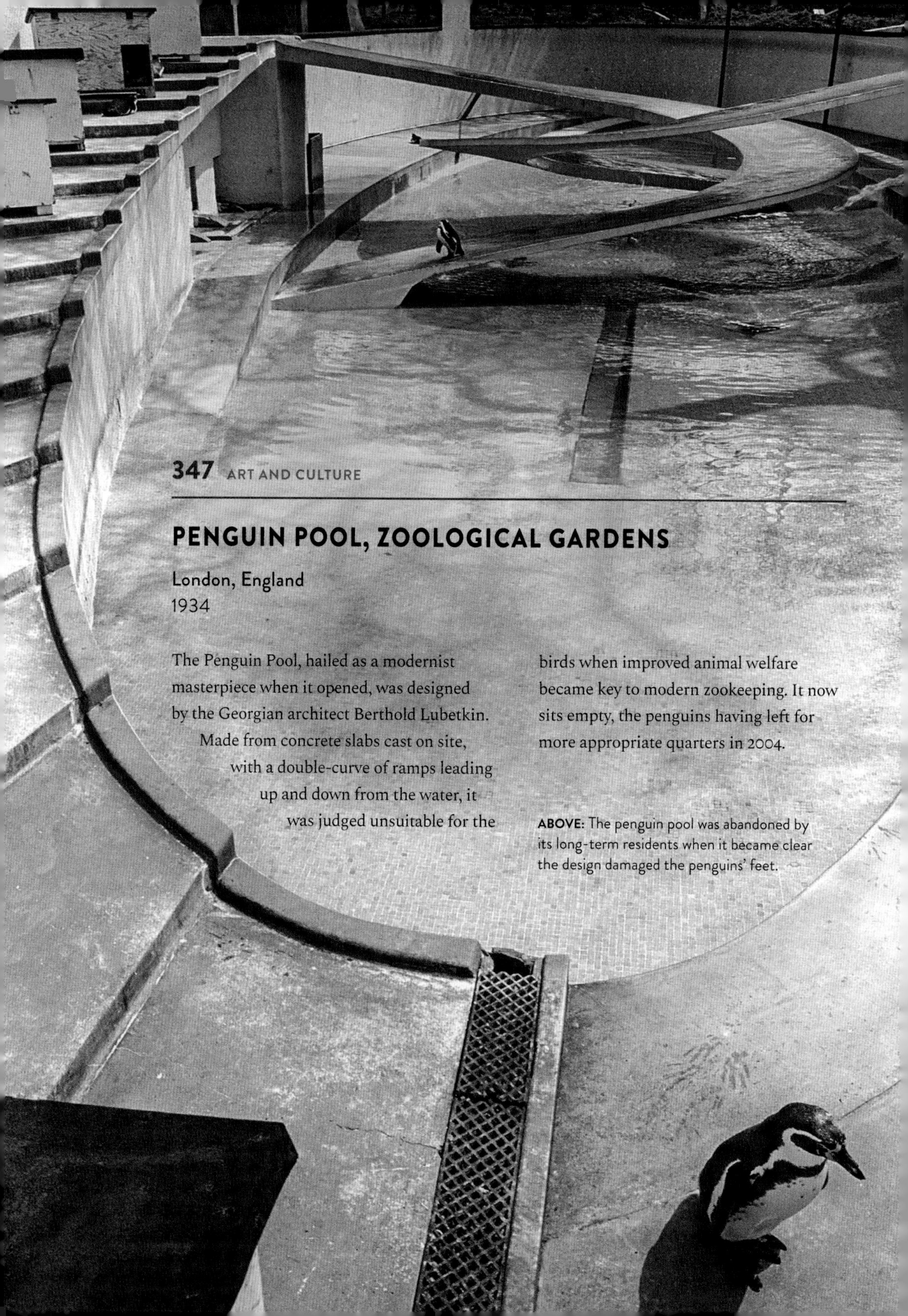

PENGUIN POOL, ZOOLOGICAL GARDENS

London, England
1934

The Penguin Pool, hailed as a modernist masterpiece when it opened, was designed by the Georgian architect Berthold Lubetkin. Made from concrete slabs cast on site, with a double-curve of ramps leading up and down from the water, it was judged unsuitable for the birds when improved animal welfare became key to modern zookeeping. It now sits empty, the penguins having left for more appropriate quarters in 2004.

ABOVE: The penguin pool was abandoned by its long-term residents when it became clear the design damaged the penguins' feet.

348 ART AND CULTURE

BOMBAY TALKIES STUDIO

Mumbai, India
1934

Himanshu Rai became involved in the movies while studying for the bar in London. He married Devika Rani, a distinguished Indian actress. Together they founded Bombay Talkies in Malad, then a dowdy suburb of Bombay, in 1934. The first major Hindi studio, it produced a string of successful films over the following decade.

349 PLACE OF WORK

PIMA COUNTY COURTHOUSE

Tucson, Arizona
1934

John Dillinger was a Depression-era gangster so notorious that "Public Enemy No. 1" was coined to describe him. By the time he was arrested, he had carried out 24 bank raids, ten murders, and staged three jailbreaks. Courthouse guards sold tickets to the public so that people could gawk at him in his cell.

350 ART AND CULTURE

PALACIO DE BELLAS ARTES

Mexico City, Mexico
1934

Originally commissioned by then-president Porfirio Diaz in 1904, the Palacio had taken almost 30 years to build by the time of its inauguration. In a single building, it incorporates aspects of both pre- and post-revolutionary Mexico, with an imposing Beaux Arts exterior, Art Deco interiors, a concert hall, and works by all three of the great revolutionary muralists: José Clemente Orozco, David Siqueiros and, most famous of all, Diego Rivera.

RIGHT: Construction of the Palacio was suspended numerous times; it was finally completed in 1934.

MOSKVA HOTEL

Moscow, Russia
1935

One of Stalin's favored hotels, with an important place in 1930s Moscow society.

Alexey Shchusev was the architect of Lenin's mausoleum (see page 275). After Stalin came to power in 1927, Shchusev became one of Stalin's favorites, so he was the natural choice to design a prestigious new hotel. The result was imposing, blocky—and asymmetric. The best explanation, though probably apocryphal, for this eccentric design sums up the tensions of the times. Stalin, presented with two options for the facade within one drawing, signed the whole thing off. Those around him were too frightened to ask his preference, so the hotel was built exactly as drawn.

The Moskva Hotel opened in 1935 and was much loved in Soviet society. Stalin held his birthday parties there, Yuri Gagarin stayed when he returned from his first space mission, and many distinguished foreigners were put up there, too—all under the observation of the KGB. Even by Soviet standards, the hotel was famous for being heavily bugged.

The Moskva's story has an odd postscript. Deemed old-fashioned and impractical, it was demolished in 2003. An exact facsimile, complete with mismatched facade—but incorporating modern luxuries—opened in 2014, operating under the Four Seasons chain.

RIGHT: In the 1930s and 1940s the Moskva was one of the city's most popular hotels. Celebrities and dignitaries stayed, dined, and danced there.

KNOWN FOR

- An early example of Stalinist modernism
- A popular venue for the elite of 1930s and 1940s Moscow
- Surviving in facsimile when much of the mid-twentieth-century architecture has been demolished

"Despite the fact that the Moskva was a new hotel and the largest, nothing in it worked as it should . . . it was cold, the faucets leaked, and the bathtubs . . . flooded the floor."

Milovan Djilas, member of the Yugoslavian Politburo, recalling Moscow stays in the 1940s, *Conversations with Stalin*, 1961

ЛЕНИНИЗМ - НАШЕ ЗНАМЯ!

352 INFRASTRUCTURE AND INNOVATION

HOOVER DAM

Colorado River, Nevada
1935

With the population of the American southwest growing and the area of farmed land on the rise, the need to manage large-scale irrigation and water supply became increasingly urgent; damming the Colorado River seemed to be the answer. Plans for what became the Hoover Dam were ongoing from 1922, when Secretary of Commerce Herbert Hoover negotiated an agreement over water distribution between the seven states affected. Even after a dam was authorized by President Calvin Coolidge in 1928, the technical challenge remained immense. When construction started, Depression-era America saw thousands flock to work on it.

The Hoover Dam opened seven years later. On completion, it was the world's tallest, and one of the most impressive engineered structures of its day. It created Lake Mead, America's largest reservoir, and not only met its irrigation aims but also produced hydroelectric power.

353 ART AND CULTURE

VIIPURI LIBRARY

Viborg, Russia
1935

The design of the Viipuri Library, commissioned from the Finnish Modernist Alvar Aalto, was sophisticated and new: built across many levels, with interiors full of natural light from conical skylights. It was a hallmark of Aalto's style and became a model for mid-century library design. Viborg was ceded to Russia in 1930, during its construction, and many of its neighboring buildings were destroyed in World War II. The dilapidated library was fully restored in 2020.

TOP LEFT: The dam was a towering feat of engineering, achieved in the teeth of the Great Depression.

ABOVE: The light-flooded interiors of Viipuri made it the prototype for much late-twentieth-century library design.

OLYMPIASTADION

Berlin, Germany
1936

Hitler became chancellor of Germany in 1933. When Berlin was chosen to host the 1936 Olympic Games, he built a new stadium—large enough to seat 110,000 people—to impress visitors with the achievements of the Third Reich. Designed by Walter Marchas, the Olympiastadion was a Colosseum-inspired structure, with an entrance flanked by two vast towers, the Olympic rings suspended between them.

ABOVE: Directly inspired by the Colosseum in Rome, the new stadium was intended to show off the power of the Third Reich.

RIGHT: Located in deep water, the south tower of the bridge had to be set in the bedrock, requiring a skilled diving team.

GOLDEN GATE BRIDGE

San Francisco, California
1937

As the city grew rapidly in the early twentieth century, public demand for a bridge linking San Francisco with Marin County, to the north, became pressing. The longest, tallest suspension bridge of its time, together with its picturesque setting, gave it immediate iconic status when it opened in 1937. Like the Hoover Dam (see page 284), the project offered valuable employment to many during the Great Depression.

356 RESIDENCE

XIMENG HOUSE

Shanghai, China
1938

Built for a merchant in a hybrid of Chinese and European styles, characteristic of Shanghai architecture in the early 1930s, the Ximeng family home would be converted to a so-called comfort house before the end of the decade.

After the outbreak of the Second Sino-Japanese War in 1937, Japan invaded Shanghai in November, and the notorious Massacre of Nanking—in which thousands of civilians were raped and murdered—took place in December. One result was that Emperor Hirohito ordered more comfort houses—brothels in which enslaved women were used as prostitutes by Japanese soldiers—to be created to try to curb the troops' excesses. The owner of Xinmeng House fled, and by the beginning of 1938 it had become a comfort house. An estimated 90 percent of mainly Chinese, Korean, and Filippina "comfort women" did not survive the war; their existence, and that of comfort houses, were only formally acknowledged in the 1990s.

357 RESIDENCE

FALLINGWATER

Mill Run, Pennsylvania
1938

Built by Frank Lloyd Wright for his friend Edgar Kaufmann, on a site straddling a waterfall in the Bear Run Nature Reserve, the house is designed in cantilevered horizontal "layers" over the water, maximizing its dramatic surroundings and blending completely with the landscape around it. Wright also designed the interiors and furnishings, creating a perfectly integrated whole. Critical admiration for the building rekindled interest in Wright's late career.

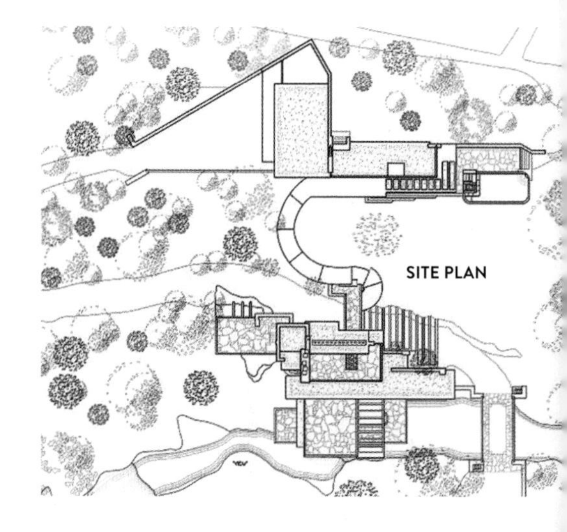

RIGHT: Edgar Kaufmann, Frank Lloyd Wright's friend and client, believed that the architect had set himself an impossible feat. "Nature cantilevered those boulders out over the fall [and] I can cantilever the house over the boulders," was Wright's response.

ESTADIO NACIONAL JULIO MARTINEZ PRADANOS

Santiago, Chile
1938

The sports stadium that oversaw the worst horrors of the Pinochet regime.

Santiago's national stadium was modeled on the one built for the Berlin Olympics in 1936. After the socialist president Salvador Allende was ousted in a violent coup in 1973, the new military junta—led by General Augusto Pinochet—used it as a detention center for anyone opposed to the new regime. More than 40,000 people were held here in the autumn of 1973. Many were tortured and executed; thousands—the *Desaparecidos*—disappeared. The stadium was cleared and the prisoners hidden in advance of a soccer match between Chile and the USSR but, alerted to the atrocities going on, the Russian team failed to turn up. The Chilean team carried out the farce of a one-sided game, scoring in 30 seconds and then leaving the field.

The stadium has been largely rebuilt, but a section of the old wooden bleachers—Escotilla 8—has been retained as a memorial to those who were held here.

"For moral considerations [the] Soviets cannot at this time play in the Stadium of Santiago, splashed with the blood of the Chilean patriots . . ."

Letter sent to FIFA by the Russian team's managers, 1973

BELOW: "A people without memory is a people without a future" reads the slogan above Escotilla 8, a memorial to Augusto Pinochet's victims held in the stadium.

UN PUEBLO SIN MEMORIA ES UN PUEBLO SIN FUTURO
8

GREAT HALL, MONTSALVAT ARTISTS' COLONY

Eltham, Melbourne, Australia
1938

The most ambitious creation of the earliest artists' colony in Australia.

Justus Jorgensen, an architect-turned-painter, designed a studio for fellow artist Percy Leason in Eltham, a suburb of Melbourne. He then decided he wanted one for himself. Thus began the creation of the artists' community that would become Montsalvat. Word spread, more artists gathered, and over the next decade a colony sprang up with a collection of buildings ranging from houses and studios to stables and workshops.

Unusually for the 1930s, the artists used a lot of repurposed materials, many of them pressed into service from the Victorian buildings that were being demolished in the center of Melbourne. The community's Great Hall, started in 1938, was perhaps its most notable achievement, with an impressively baronial interior, and windows and stone balconies salvaged from Melbourne's recently demolished Royal Insurance Building. It incorporates whimsical and grotesque gargoyles, carved by the artist/builders themselves.

ABOVE RIGHT: The Gothic-style windows of the Great Hall were salvaged from the recently demolished Royal Insurance Building in Melbourne.

RIGHT: Inside the hall, a mezzanine designed as a musicians' gallery emphasizes the building's medieval inspiration.

360 PLACE OF WORK

FIAT TAGLIERO STATION

Asmara, Eritrea
1938

Eritrea became an Italian colony in 1882, prompting a number of Italian settlers to move to its capital. Asmara underwent a building spree in the 1920s and 1930s, earning the city the nickname "la piccolo Roma"—Little Rome. Resembling an aircraft in flight, this service station, by the architect Giuseppe Pettagi, is just one of the Futurist designs built in anticipation of Mussolini's planned new empire in Africa.

361 PLACE OF WORK

ROYAL FLYING DOCTOR BASE

Alice Springs, Australia
1939

The Flying Doctor service was founded in 1928 to provide a medical service for the remote communities of the Australian Outback. By 1939, most states had opened their own bases to cover the vast areas involved. The independent South Australian base in Alice Springs was the sixth in Australia, financed by the women of the Pioneer Women's Memorial Trust.

BELOW: One of the most remote settlements in Australia, Alice Springs was an obvious candidate for a Flying Doctor service base.

PORTMEIRION

Gwynned, Wales
1939

An Italianate village created in a very Welsh setting.

The resort village of Portmeirion was built around an existing mansion by the eccentric architect Clough Williams-Ellis, who lived nearby. He bought the site in 1925, converted the house into a hotel, and made Portmeirion his life's work. It was constructed over two periods—the first stage was completed by 1939, the second between 1954 and 1975, by which time Williams-Ellis was well into his nineties. The village's romantic Mediterranean appearance led to comparisons with Portofino, Italy, although Williams-Ellis never gave away his inspiration, simply referring visitors to its beauty.

Unsurprisingly, Portmeirion remains one of Wales's most popular tourist attractions and has starred in numerous films and advertisements, notably the 1960s British cult serial *The Prisoner*.

BELOW: Overlooking the Dwyryd Estuary in northwest Wales, the multicolored buildings of Portmeirion make an exotic and unexpected impact.

363 RELIGION AND MONUMENT

VALLE DE LOS CAIDOS

San Lorenzo de El Escorial, Spain
1940

Built under the Spanish dictator Francisco Franco, the Valle de los Caidos (Valley of the Fallen), in the mountains south of Madrid, memorializes the Nationalist casualties of the Spanish Civil War. Franco himself was buried there in 1975, although he was later disinterred. Republican soldiers were forced to build the massive basilica under gruesome conditions; the cross above it was added later. It remains a controversial site in Spain.

ABOVE: At over 500 feet, the granite cross towering over the controversial monument is the tallest in the world.

364 RESIDENCE

SECRET ANNEX

Westermarkt, Amsterdam, Netherlands
1942

After the Nazi invasion, the "annex" became the hiding place for the Jewish businessman Otto Frank and his family. It was here that his daughter Anne wrote her diary. They were discovered and transported to concentration camps in 1944. Anne's father, the only one to survive, published *The Diary of a Young Girl* in 1947, and it became one of the most widely read personal testaments of World War II.

ABOVE: Throughout the two years the Frank family hid in the cramped annex, Anne faithfully kept her diary.

365 POLITICS AND NATIONAL DEFENSE

AUSCHWITZ-BIRKENAU

Poland
1942

The Polish camp that was a key part of the Nazis' "Final Solution."

The decision to build a concentration camp at Auschwitz was taken in 1940. The following year, Heinrich Himmler, head of the SS, ordered an enlarged camp to house prisoners who would work as forced labor in nearby factories. Auschwitz become a sprawling site that included accommodation for laborers in Auschwitz I, and a couple of miles away, Auschwitz II (or Auschwitz-Birkenau), the camp's main killing center. By the end of the war, it was estimated that 1.1 million people, the majority of them Jews, had been murdered here. The Nazis continually aimed to enlarge the killing capacity of the camp—between the first large-scale gassings with Zyklon B in 1942 and the last, late in 1944, the camp's efficiency was constantly reviewed.

Auschwitz was liberated by Soviet troops on January 27, 1945. Its horrors, and those of the other concentration camps, were first publicized by the Allies in April of that year.

ABOVE: On arrival at Auschwitz, travelers were sorted into those who were fit for forced labor, and those who would be sent straight to their deaths.

RAILWAY BRIDGE 277

Kanchanaburi, Thailand
1943

A real bridge that became part of the mythology around World War II.

The story of *The Bridge on the River Kwai*, the 1957 film that won six Oscars, was only very loosely based on historic fact. Japanese forces invaded Siam (now Thailand) in 1941, intending to use it as a stepping-stone to take Burma and Malaya (now Malaysia), which at the time were both British colonies. To achieve this, they needed good transportation links. Construction began on the so-called Death Railway, built with thousands of slave laborers: a mixture of Southeast Asian civilians and captured Allied soldiers. It is estimated that over 100,000 people died during the construction, with many of them forced to work 18-hour days in terrible conditions.

Unlike the bridge in the film, the real bridge, Railway Bridge 277, still stands. Survivors of the railway's construction criticized the film for not reflecting their terrible experience in a plot that largely revolved around questions of nationality and honor.

"The Japanese will carry out their schedule and do not mind if the line is dotted with crosses."

Brigadier Arthur Varley, on the savage working conditions on the Burma-Siam railway

BELOW: A tourist train schedules regular trips across Bridge 277 for visitors, well aware of its terrible history.

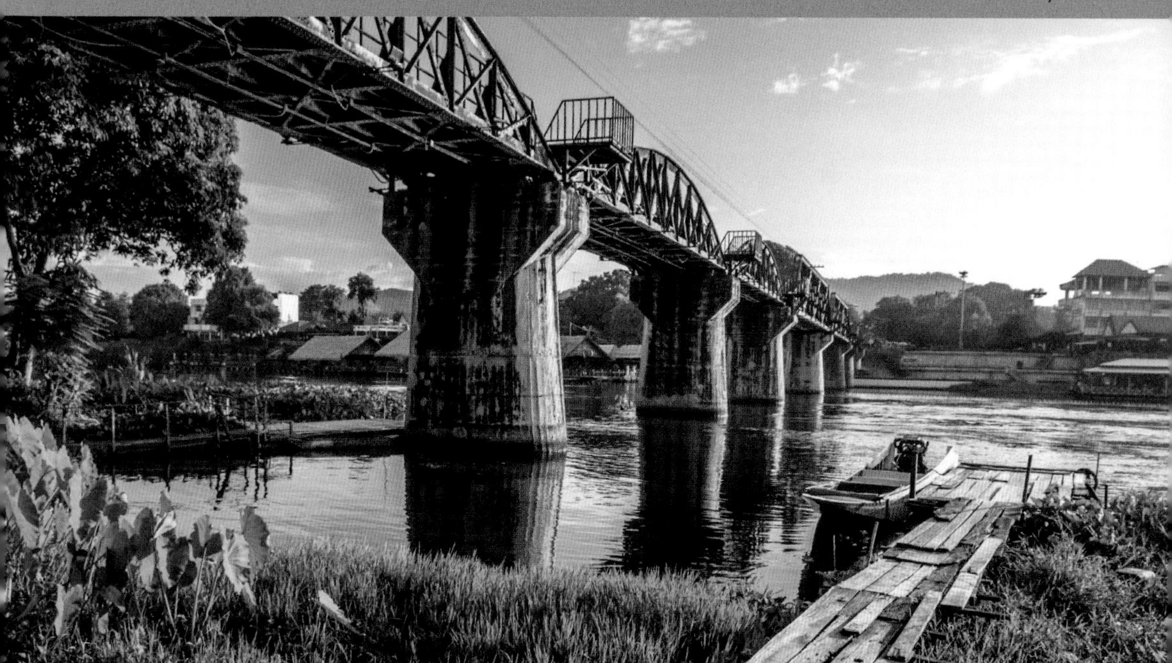

367 PLACE OF WORK

THE PENTAGON

Washington, D.C.
1943

In the 1930s, a shortage of office space in Washington meant that key personnel of the War Department were scattered around the city. At the beginning of World War II, the increasing threat of armed conflict led to plans for a single-story site to house senior staff of the Army, Air Force, Navy, and Marine Corps in one place. The five-sided design was low-rise, with five floors above ground, and two below. Built from steel and reinforced concrete, it could accommodate 33,000 people. Ground was broken on September 11, 1941; less than three months later, following the bombing of Pearl Harbor, America entered the war. Pentagon staff moved in even before the building was officially finished in January 1943.

368 RESIDENCE/ART AND CULTURE

ALBERT NAMATJIRA'S HOUSE

Northern Territory, Australia
1944

An Aboriginal artist of the Aranda people, Albert Namatjira's atmospheric landscapes of central Australia were widely admired. He built this simple whitewashed cottage with the help of friends after the success of an exhibition of his work in Melbourne. He lived in the house for five years, but when one of his children died there, he and his wife abandoned it.

ABOVE: A deserted memorial of an artist whose life fell between two cultures; today Albert Namatjira's house is locked up and abandoned.

369 ART AND CULTURE

COLETTE'S APARTMENT

9 Rue de Beaujolais, Paris, France
1944

During the German occupation, the author Colette, who turned 70 in 1942, remained in her apartment in the 1st arrondissement. Ill and often bedridden, she used the time to write the novella *Gigi*, the story of an ingenue in training to be a courtesan. It was to be one of her last, yet best-loved, works. Published in the same year as the liberation of Paris, it offered light relief to a nation worn out by war.

ABOVE: One of France's most celebrated authors, Colette continued to write throughout the Germans' occupation of France.

370 PLACE OF WORK

JOHNSON WAX BUILDING

Racine, Wisconsin
1944

A late work by Frank Lloyd Wright, this building—headquarters for a cleaning company, sited in an unglamorous industrial park—included an early example of a completely open-plan office. Despite numerous technical problems in construction, the end result was airy, featuring clear skylights made from Pyrex tubes, and narrow-based columns that terminate in wide, canopy-like discs at the top, giving the impression of an indoor forest.

ABOVE: "You catch no sense of enclosure whatever at any angle . . ." was Frank Lloyd Wright's claim for this new sort of office building.

GEORGIA O'KEEFFE'S HOUSE

Abiquiú, New Mexico
1944

The New Mexican home that was both background and inspiration for O'Keeffe's mature work.

Georgia O'Keeffe was one of the first women to be recognized for her significant contribution to American modernist art. Much of her work was inspired by the desert landscapes of New Mexico, where she spent long periods from 1930. The remote Ghost Ranch in the New Mexican desert was her summer home, but she needed a larger, warmer house for the cold desert winters. In the small town of Abiquiú, she bought an old adobe courtyard ruin a few months after seeing it. It was restored, and by 1949 it was an ascetic but beautiful home and studio which mirrored the style of her work. Today it forms part of the Georgia O'Keeffe Museum.

ABOVE: Both Ghost Ranch, above, and the Abiquiú house were notable for the refined, spare interiors favored by O'Keeffe.

"As I climbed in and walked about in the ruin I found a patio . . . with a long wall with a door on one side. That wall with a door in it was something I had to have . . ."

Georgia O'Keeffe, on first seeing the Abiquiú house

HIROSHIMA PREFECTURAL INDUSTRIAL PROMOTION HALL

Hiroshima, Japan
1945

The commercial building that an atomic attack transformed into a memorial for peace.

Between 1915 and 1945, the Promotion Hall, a European-style building topped with a copper dome, was used as a display center, where products made locally were displayed and sold. In a city still largely composed of low-rise wooden buildings, it was a noticeable landmark. On August 6, 1945, when the first atomic bomb was dropped on Hiroshima, the three-story building was very near the epicenter—ground zero—of the blast. The near-vertical force meant that it remained standing but was blasted to a shell. The people inside were killed instantly, and its dome stripped to a skeleton.

After the blast, the remains of Promotion Hall became a landmark, but of a much darker kind. As the city was gradually rebuilt, a debate arose over whether to demolish the shell or to preserve its ruins as a memorial of the bombing and the horror it represented. In 1966, the city council voted to preserve what was by then known as the "A-Bomb Dome." It has since been renamed the Hiroshima Peace Memorial and stands in the new Peace Memorial Park in the city.

RIGHT: The Promotion Hall's skeletal ruin survives as a powerful memorial in a fully rebuilt Hiroshima.

BELOW: An aerial view of the city taken shortly after the explosion shows Hiroshima utterly destroyed.

KNOWN FOR

- The only building left standing in the area directly below where the atomic bomb fell
- A monument for peace in the city where at least 70,000 people were killed by a single blast
- A long-term reminder of the destruction of war

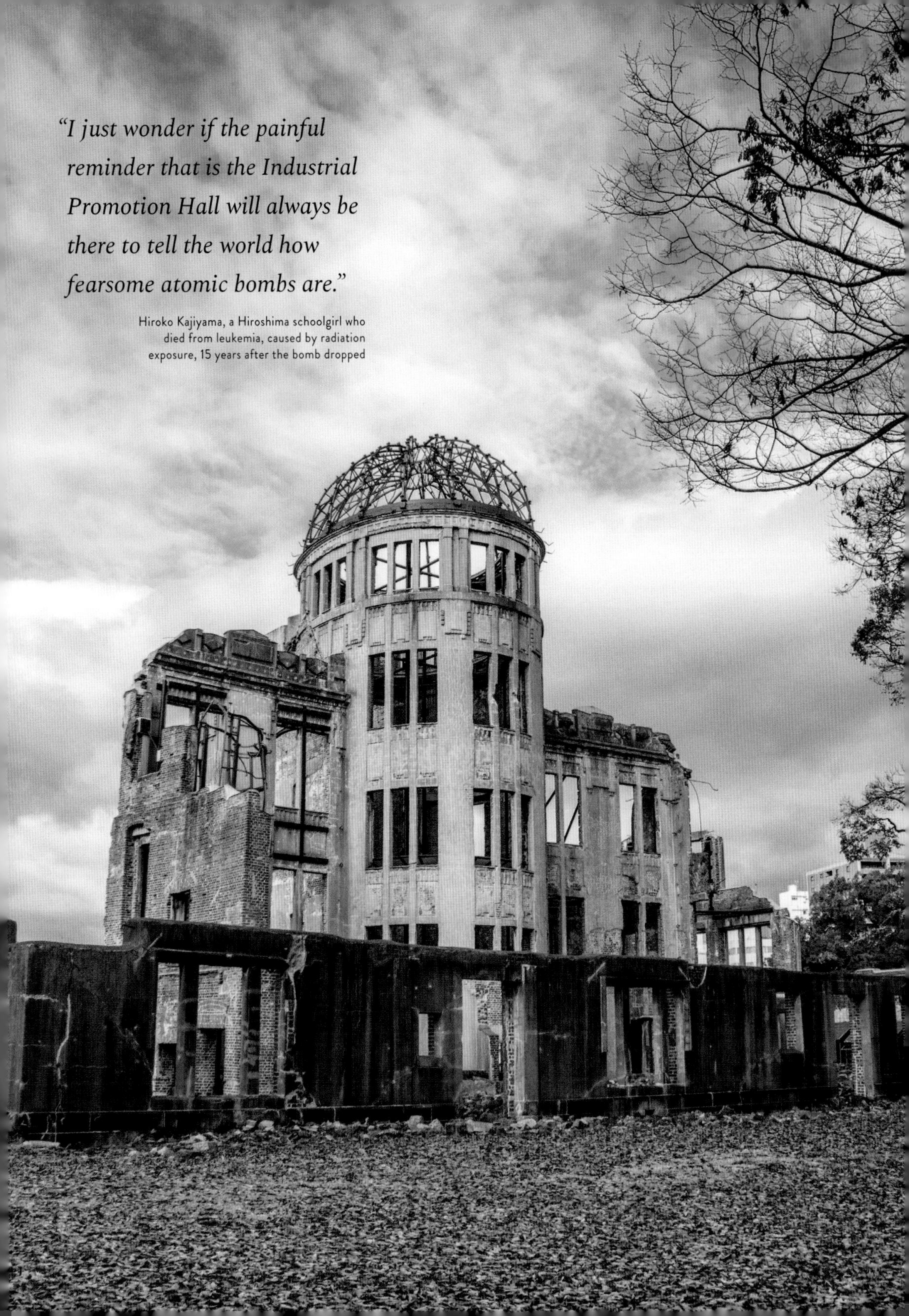

"I just wonder if the painful reminder that is the Industrial Promotion Hall will always be there to tell the world how fearsome atomic bombs are."

Hiroko Kajiyama, a Hiroshima schoolgirl who died from leukemia, caused by radiation exposure, 15 years after the bomb dropped

COURTROOM 600, PALACE OF JUSTICE

Nuremburg, Germany
1945

Site of the trials of major figures of the Nazi regime.

Between 1945 and 1949, the Nuremburg Trials took place in Courtroom 600 of the Palace of Justice. The location was chosen for its large size, its proximity to Nuremburg Prison, and the many surrounding rooms that could be used as offices and for meetings. It still had to undergo alterations: neon lights were installed to make filming easier, and the back wall was removed to make space for additional seating.

The first stage of the trials began in November 1945 and lasted nine months; twelve more trials took place between 1946 and 1949. They were held before an International Military Tribunal, with representatives from the Allied nations; the accused included key Nazi figures, mostly military or political leaders such as Hermann Göring and Rudolf Hess, but also prominent doctors, judges, and industrialists who had supported the regime.

In 2008, Courtroom 600 became the museum it is today.

BELOW: Ernst Biberstein, SS officer in charge of the Einsatzgruppen killing squads, went on trial in Courtroom 600 on September 29, 1947.

374 RESIDENCE/ART AND CULTURE

STUDIO BARN, KRASNER-POLLOCK HOUSE

Springs, New York
1945

In November 1945, Jackson Pollock and his wife, Lee Krasner, both painters, moved from the pressures of life in Greenwich Village to a quiet clapboard house at Springs, on Long Island. Pollock, using the barn on the property as a studio, developed the drip painting technique: flinging and splattering paint onto the canvas from above. The resulting paintings would see him recognized as a leading artist in the abstract expressionist movement.

375 ART AND CULTURE

BARNHILL FARMHOUSE

Isle of Jura, Scotland
1946

George Orwell lived in this remote farmhouse from 1946, writing here while convalescing from an episode of tuberculosis. The apocalyptic novel *1984*, a warning about authoritarianism, was completed at Barnhill. Many of the terms in the novel, since translated into 65 languages—"Big Brother," "thoughtcrime," "Room 101"—have passed into everyday speech. The struggle to finish it contributed to Orwell's decline; he died in 1950, aged only 46.

RIGHT: Barnhill offered George Orwell a peaceful base, where he could tend the garden and write uninterrupted.

376 RESIDENCE

CASA LUIS BARRAGÁN

Mexico City, Mexico
1948

The great Mexican Modernist Luis Barragán built his own home and workshop in Tacubaya, an old, working-class suburb of Mexico City. Although he created no works outside Mexico, Barragán's style is familiar to many who might never have heard of him: plain, unfinished materials—stucco, cement, wood—painted in bright, saturated colors, an aspect of his work that became widely imitated internationally.

ABOVE: Luis Barragán used bright colors, mixes of rough and smooth textures, and ingenious plays of light and shade to create maximum impact in his own home.

377 RESIDENCE

LUNUGANGA

Bentota, Sri Lanka
1948

Geoffrey Bawa, one of South Asia's most influential postcolonial architects, bought this lakeside estate in 1948, just before Sri Lanka was declared independent. He created his home—a complex of indoor and outdoor spaces—here, as he gently revolutionized architecture in Sri Lanka with elegant, distinctive buildings designed in sympathy with the landscapes around them. This was a clear departure from the relatively straitlaced colonial styles.

ABOVE: Admirers came up with the term "Tropical Modernism" to describe Geoffrey Bawa's use of local materials and careful, meticulous style.

THE GLASS HOUSE

New Canaan, Connecticut
1949

One of 14 structures that the Modernist architect Philip Johnson built on his 47-acre estate at Canaan, the Glass House was his response to the landscape that surrounded it, creating a sea of reflections both outside and in. Widely admired by other architects, it featured in various residencies by different artists, even undergoing a red spotty phase as part of a visit by the Japanese artist Yayoi Kusama.

RIGHT: Johnson built a range of other buildings around the house for various uses—essential given the very public nature of the Glass House itself.

BELOW: Philip Johnson at his desk, sharing the living space of the Glass House with the work *Two Circus Women* by the sculptor Elie Nadelman.

"I found a great oak tree and I hung the whole design on the oak tree and the knoll because of this place."

Philip Johnson

EAMES HOUSE

Los Angeles, California
1949

The architectural challenge that saw Charles and Ray Eames become their own clients.

Originally designed for the Case Study House Program, in which *Art & Architecture* magazine sponsored houses, designed by U.S. architects, which made use of new materials and methods developed in the course of World War II. The Eames House was first known as Case Study House No. 8. Designed by the architects and industrial designers Charles and Ray Eames, the house became so appealing in its final incarnation that they decided to live in it themselves.

Modestly innovative, it was composed of two rectangular boxes, with exterior walls made from steel-gridded frames filled with alternating solid and translucent sliding panels, giving the finished result flexibility and a play of endlessly varying light. Charles and Ray Eames specialized in practical, unfussy, and affordable design—whether it was a chair or a house—and their home would become a much-imitated icon of modern mid-century living.

RIGHT: Charles and Ray Eames gave their prototype the ultimate endorsement by choosing to make their own home in it.

BELOW: The sliding frames covering much of the exterior gave the occupants of the house plenty of options when it came to light and privacy.

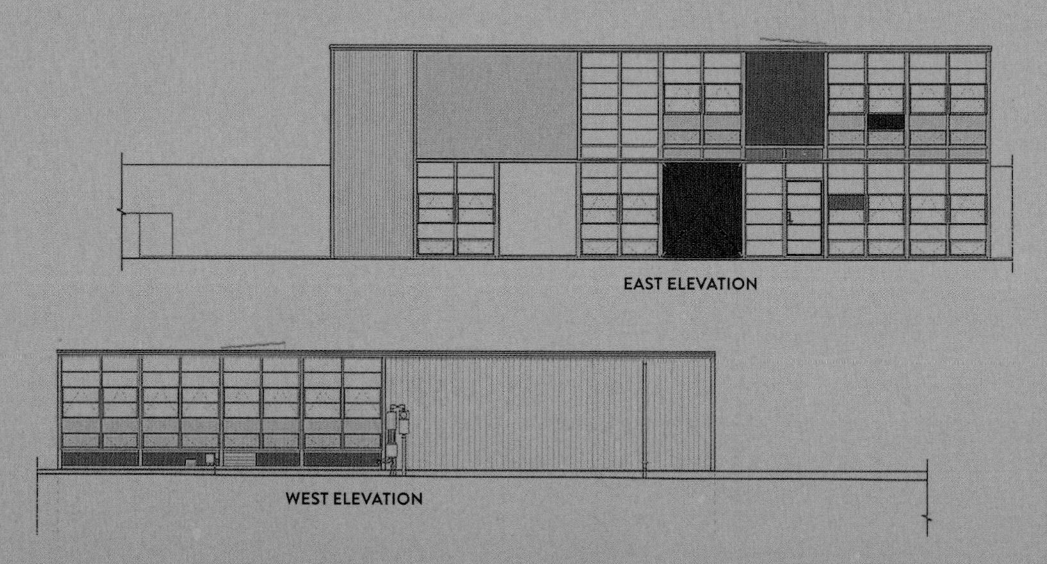

380 ART AND CULTURE

PEGGY GUGGENHEIM MUSEUM

Venice, Italy
1949

In 1949, the American heiress Peggy Guggenheim bought the eighteenth-century Palazzo Venier dei Leoni, where she would live until her death. She was already a well-known patron and collector of modern art, and had run galleries in London and New York. She knew almost every talented artist, sculptor, and writer of the time and supported many of them, claiming, "My motto was 'Buy a picture a day' and I lived up to it."

The Palazzo had never been finished—it was a long, low, white building on Venice's Grand Canal, with a curiously modern look. Guggenheim ensured her legacy by donating both the Palazzo and her art collection to the Guggenheim Foundation, which had been founded by her uncle Solomon. After she died, her art—shown in her home—became the Peggy Guggenheim Museum.

ABOVE: The unfinished nature of the single-story Palazzo Venier dei Leoni gives it a curiously modern appearance.

381 PLACE OF WORK

TELMEX BUILDING

Guadalajara, Mexico
1950

The old Telmex telecommunications building was blocking major road remodeling when Jorge Matui Remui, an engineer on the project, determined that it was easier to mount it on a platform and shift it than to demolish and rebuild it. Without disrupting the city's telecommunications for even a day, he managed to move it. His 1950 feat is marked by a bronze statue showing him bodily pushing the building into place.

DYMAXION HOUSE

Rose Hill, Kansas
1950

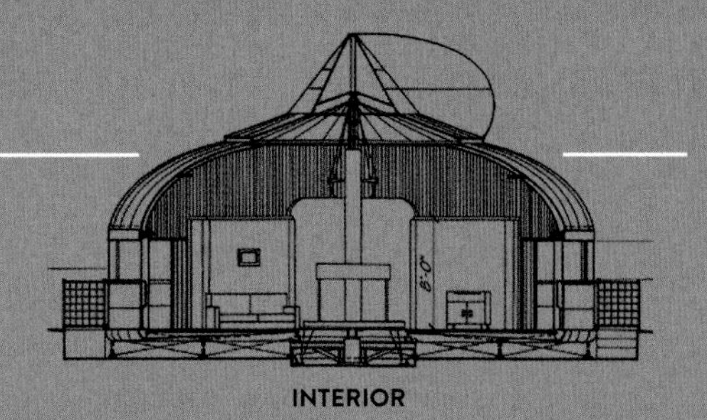

INTERIOR

The house designed as an exercise in mass production.

The architect and inventor Buckminster Fuller believed that many housing problems, particularly that of housing army veterans returning from war, could be solved if homes could be produced—and priced—like cars, and readily transported anywhere.

Dymaxion House (the name was a hybrid of three words: DYnamic, MAXimum, and TensION), was first conceived in the late 1920s and was earthquake-, tornado-, and fireproof—and energy efficient. Made in kit form, it could be sited anywhere. The structure was novel: a central stake sunk in the ground, around which the circular house was built; the aluminum roof and base was stabilized with cables, separated by a panoramic window. The high start-up cost of creating a viable production line eventually derailed the project. Rose Hill House, first shown in 1950, was one of only two prototypes ever built. Today, it can be found at the Henry Ford Museum in Dearborn, Michigan.

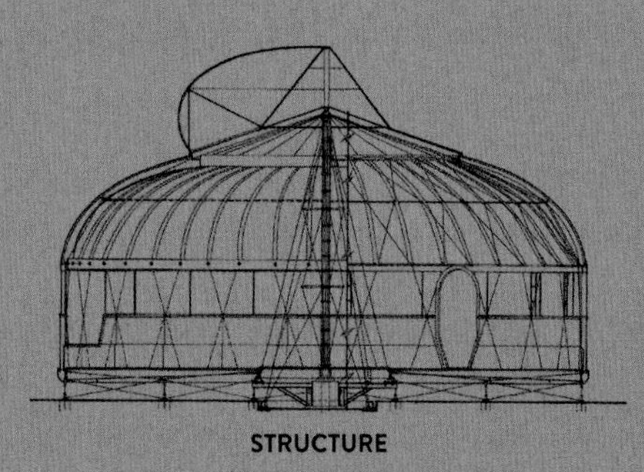
STRUCTURE

ABOVE: A cross-section of the design shows the central stabilizing pole and the double wire-wheel structure hung around it.

BELOW: Buckminster Fuller made Dymaxion House circular to minimize heat loss and to save on materials.

383 RESIDENCE/ART AND CULTURE

CAMPUS HOUSE, UNIVERSITY OF NIGERIA

Nsukka, Nigeria
1950

Whitewashed and flat-roofed, this ordinary 1950s house on the campus of the University of Nigeria, in Nsukka, has a big literary pedigree. The great writer Chinua Achebe lived here when he was a lecturer at the university, and it became the childhood home of Chimamanda Ngozi Adichie. Adichie's first two novels—*Purple Hibiscus* (2003) and *Half of a Yellow Sun* (2006)—both feature atmospheric descriptions of life in Nsukka.

ABOVE: The first indigenous university in Nigeria, the Nsukka campus, was founded in 1955, and formally inaugurated in 1960.

384 PLACE OF WORK

NIRMAL HRIDAY HOME

Kolkata, India
1952

In 1950, Mother Teresa, then an unknown Catholic nun from Albania, was given permission by the Holy See to found the Order of the Missionaries of Charity, to care for the dying poor. Nirmal Hriday—the Kalighat Home for the Dying—was the first of the many hospices she would start under the order. Housed in a disused temple, it was somewhere the destitute could be brought to die peacefully.

385 INFRASTRUCTURE AND INNOVATION

KOMSOMOLSKAYA METRO STATION

Moscow, Russia
1952

A metro system that delivered Russian history from a strongly Soviet perspective.

Moscow's underground train system opened in 1935 and, used by thousands of people every day, offered the Soviet state a powerful propaganda opportunity. Over the following decades, a number of architects devised extraordinarily decorative and elaborate schemes for the metro's stations, with the declared aim of creating "Palaces for the People." Komsomolskaya—named for the young Communists, or *komsomoltsy*—was the only station designed by Alexey Shchusev (see page 282).

At first glance, its heavily swagged, baroque-style ceiling looks more like a scheme from the era of Catherine the Great than a hymn to Soviet achievement. However, the swirling stucco frames surround mosaics depicting great generals from Russian history, with a theme of Russia's struggle for independence—entirely in keeping with the propaganda angle of the metro's role.

Shchusev was awarded the Stalin Prize for his design.

ABOVE: With its barrel-vaulted ceilings, fancy stucco ornament, and vast chandeliers, Komsomolskaya Metro Station fulfilled the Soviet "Palaces for the People" brief.

386 RESIDENCE

KIJONG DONG

Demilitarized Zone, North Korea
1953

The North Korean "peace village" of Kijong Dong was set up to give the impression of a prosperous and peaceful community. In reality, it's a propaganda village, sited between North and South Korea in the narrow buffer zone established after the Korean War. Its streets and buildings are well lit, but its school, hospital, kindergarten, and apartment blocks are eerily empty.

LEFT: An immense tower flying the North Korean flag looms over the border village of Kijong Dong.

387 PLACE OF WORK

ROYAL ENFIELD FACTORY

Chennai, India
1955

Royal Enfield motorcycles began production in 1901 in Redditch, England. In 1949, Madras Motors first imported them, and they rapidly became staples for the Indian army. In 1955, they built a plant in Tiruvottiyur, near Madras (now Chennai), to produce bikes themselves. By 1977, production had come full circle: Enfield India began to export the Enfield Bullet 350cc back to England, where they gained a cult following.

PALACE OF CULTURE AND SCIENCE

Warsaw, Poland
1955

A "gift" from the Soviet people that dominates the Warsaw skyline.

One of the last buildings designed by Lev Rudnev, one of Stalin's favorite architects, this ostentatious showpiece of Soviet achievement was built by Russian workers as a "gift of friendship" to Poland from the Soviet people. On the Polish side of the border, the "present" was largely seen as a symbol of oppression. With its highly recognizable wedding-cake style, it remains a major landmark in Warsaw.

ABOVE: The completed palace incorporated numerous traditional Polish motifs, carefully researched by Stalin's architects.

RIGHT: Long after the collapse of the Soviet Union, Warsaw's Palace of Culture and Science serves as a reminder, clearly visible from most parts of the city.

389 PLACE OF WORK

BRYANT'S GROCERY

Money, Mississippi
1955

The scene in a small-town store that led to a shocking racist murder.

Emmett Till, a 14-year-old African American boy from Chicago, was visiting relatives in the small town of Money when he stepped into Bryant's store. Carolyn Bryant, the white woman behind the counter, claimed he had "flirted" with her. Four days later, her husband and brother-in-law snatched Emmett from his great-uncle's house. Three days after that, his mutilated body was found in the Tallahatchie River.

Mamie Till-Bradley, Emmett's mother, insisted on an open coffin: horrific photographs, published in *JET* magazine, captured the nation's attention. Tried by a white jury, Bryant and his accomplice were found not guilty; Carolyn Bryant later admitted that she had invented the incident.

Emmett's murder affected a whole generation of young Black Americans, galvanizing activism in the civil rights movement. Today, the store—a roofless skeleton—is fronted by a marker on the Mississippi Freedom Trail, telling the story of Emmett Till.

ABOVE: Emmett Till's visit to Bryant's store would ultimately sign his death warrant; photographs of his horribly disfigured body prompted many to activism.

390 RELIGION AND MONUMENT

CHAPELLE NOTRE-DAME DU HAUT

Ronchamp, France
1955

Le Corbusier was the architect selected to replace an earlier pilgrim chapel that had been destroyed during World War II. The design was unlike his earlier work, which had been functionalist in form. The curve of the roof is supported by pillars outside the building's rough white concrete walls. It appears to float, and slivers of light find their way into the interior, while the south wall is pierced with deep-set windows, some of which are set with painted glass, sending vivid-colored beams inside the chapel. The end result is simple, monumental, and wholly original.

It attracted both praise and criticism—but over time, the chapel was seen as having revolutionized possibilities for ecclesiastical architecture.

391 INFRASTRUCTURE AND INNOVATION

BAIKONUR COSMODROME

Kazakhstan
1955

Located on the remote Kazakhstan steppe, construction on the Baikonur complex began early in 1955. Originally planned for the testing of intercontinental ballistic missiles, the station proved ideally suited to satellite launches and became the main base of the Soviet space program until the union broke up in 1991.

It saw, successively, the launch of the world's first artificial satellite (1957), which circled Earth three times; the flight of "space dog" Laika (1957); the first human in space, Yuri Gagarin (1961); and the first woman astronaut, Valentina Tereshkova (1963). There were also disasters, notably a huge explosion in 1960 that killed over 70 people. But the Cosmodrome has had an exceptionally long life, and helped the Soviet Union to its leading position in the early 1960s as it competed against the United States in a fiercely fought space race.

BELOW: Although parts of the Cosmodrome are abandoned, it remains largely in use today, with facilities leased out by Kazakhstan.

392 PLACE OF WORK

AALTO STUDIO

Helsinki, Finland
1956

Twenty years after he designed the Viipuri Library (see page 284), Alvar Aalto designed a studio for his architectural practice in Munkkiniemi, a wealthy suburb of Helsinki. The airy building, with a curving interior wall enclosing an open amphitheater-like space, and full of furniture of his own design, displays both his holistic approach to projects and the influence he would have over the style which would be called "mid-century modern."

BELOW: Alvar Aalto worked in the studio until his death in 1976; since 1984 it has housed the Aalto Foundation.

393 ART AND CULTURE

CINE-TEATRO RESTAURACAO

Luanda, Angola
1956

As a Portuguese colony, Angola had a strong film culture, with over 50 modernist cinemas built there by 1970. Most allowed space for socializing, as well as watching movies. The Cine-Teatro Restauracao, one of the largest, was built to a horizontal design, reminiscent of the work of Frank Lloyd Wright, by the architects Joao and Luis Garcia de Castilho. It was repurposed into the capital's National Assembly building in 1980, five years after Angola declared independence. A new government building opened in 2015, with plans to turn the building into a center for the arts announced in 2022, bringing its history full circle.

ZAISAN MEMORIAL

Ulaanbaatar, Mongolia
1956

The huge Soviet-era circular monument, officially built to mark the sacrifices of Russian soldiers in World War II, incorporates plenty of pro-Soviet propaganda, marking the historic "friendship" between the USSR and Mongolia. In the shape of a traditional Mongolian hearth, it incorporates a vast statue of a Russian soldier, victory flag in one hand and a machine gun in the other.

RIGHT: Like many monuments from the Soviet era, the memorial mixes Soviet and local—in this case, Mongolian—iconography.

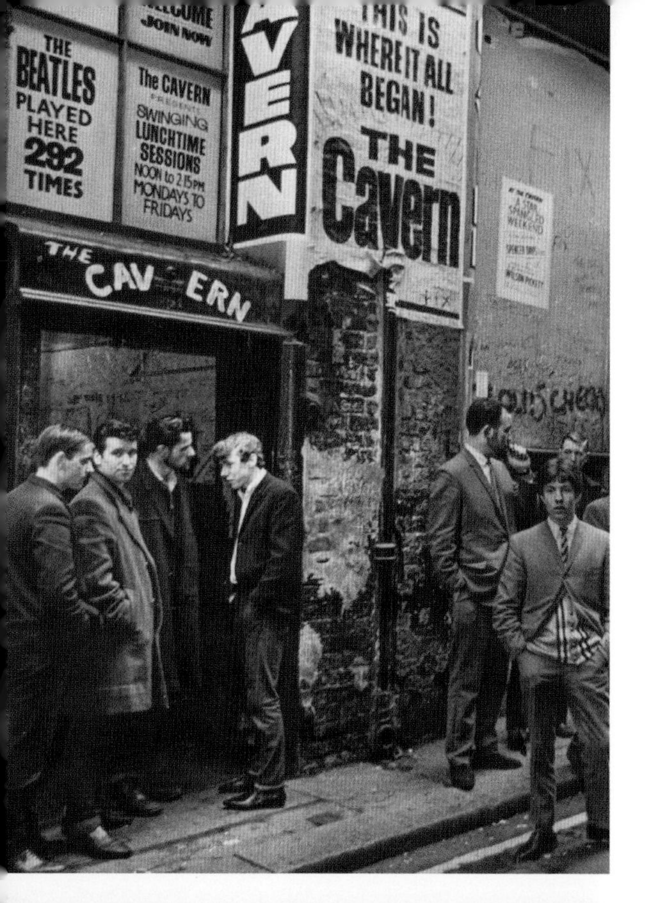

ABOVE: The Cavern's influence on the late 1950s and early 1960s music scene was out of all proportion to its size.

395 ART AND CULTURE

CAVERN CLUB

Liverpool, England
1957

Although most famous as the birthplace of the Beatles, the Cavern launched as a jazz and blues club. A change in ownership in 1959 led to acts moving toward beat—Rory Storm and the Hurricanes played here early in 1960. The Beatles made their debut Cavern performance in February 1961; later that year, their fortunes changed for good when they were spotted here by Brian Epstein, their future manager.

396 ART AND CULTURE

PRESIDENTIAL PALACE

Havana, Cuba
1959

The looming Neoclassical Presidential Palace in Havana saw the end of the brutal regime of Cuba's president Fulgencio Batista when he fled to the Dominican Republic in the early hours of January 1, 1959, after Cuban rebels—led by Che Guevara—won a notable victory against government forces at the Battle of Santa Clara. Since 1974, the palace has housed Cuba's Museum of the Revolution.

GUGGENHEIM MUSEUM

Manhattan, New York
1959

A style of museum that shocked both traditionalists and the avant-garde.

After the tycoon Solomon Guggenheim retired, he began to collect art. From the 1930s, he amassed works from many modern masters, including Kandinsky, Klee, and Chagall. In 1943, Frank Lloyd Wright was asked to design a home for the collection—a "temple of spirit," equal to the works it housed.

The end result was itself an exhibit. It marked the start of a postwar age in which museums were expected to be "characters," rather than grand expressions of wealth and status. Sitting on Fifth Avenue, the building looked like an inverted snail, a cupcake, or a washing machine, depending on which critic you read; not all were enthusiastic. Inside, paintings were displayed on a curving ramp climbing to the top of the building.

In time, the Guggenheim became one of New York's favorite museums. Wright died six months before its completion, so he never saw his vision realized.

BELOW: Frank Lloyd Wright's design for the Guggenheim Museum is as exciting from the outside as it is from the inside.

ROBBEN ISLAND

Table Bay, South Africa
1960

The prison that came to symbolize the ultimate victory of freedom over oppression.

Robben Island, located five miles off the coast of South Africa, was used variously as a prison, leper colony, and mental asylum between the mid-seventeenth and mid-twentieth centuries. From the early 1960s, it became notorious as the site of a maximum-security prison in which over 3,000 political dissidents, mostly Black men, served long sentences for opposing the apartheid regime of the minority Afrikaner government.

Nelson Mandela, a leading figure in the African National Congress, and eventually the first post-apartheid president of South Africa, was transferred here in 1963. He was detained until 1982, bar a brief "break" in Pretoria Local Prison. Walter Sisulu and Goven Mbeki were among other prominent figures in the anti-apartheid struggle who served time on Robben Island. Despite the grueling regime—bleak dormitories (in Mandela's case, a tiny cell in which he had to sleep on the floor), and days breaking rocks—the prisoners spent time educating one another, referring to the prison as "Mandela University." Mandela secretly kept autobiographical notes which, when they were discovered, cost him loss of privileges for four years.

The last political prisoners were released in 1991. After apartheid finally ended in 1994, Robben Island became a museum and visitor center.

KNOWN FOR

- A focus for the anti-apartheid movement for nearly three decades
- A place to isolate political prisoners over long periods
- An existing reminder of the apartheid system

TOP LEFT: In 1998, Nelson Mandela, now president of South Africa, took U.S. president Bill Clinton on a tour of Robben Island. They were pictured posing behind the bars of Mandela's prison cell.

RIGHT: Watchtowers, armed guards, barbed wire, and a naturally inhospitable location all ensured that no one could escape Robben Island.

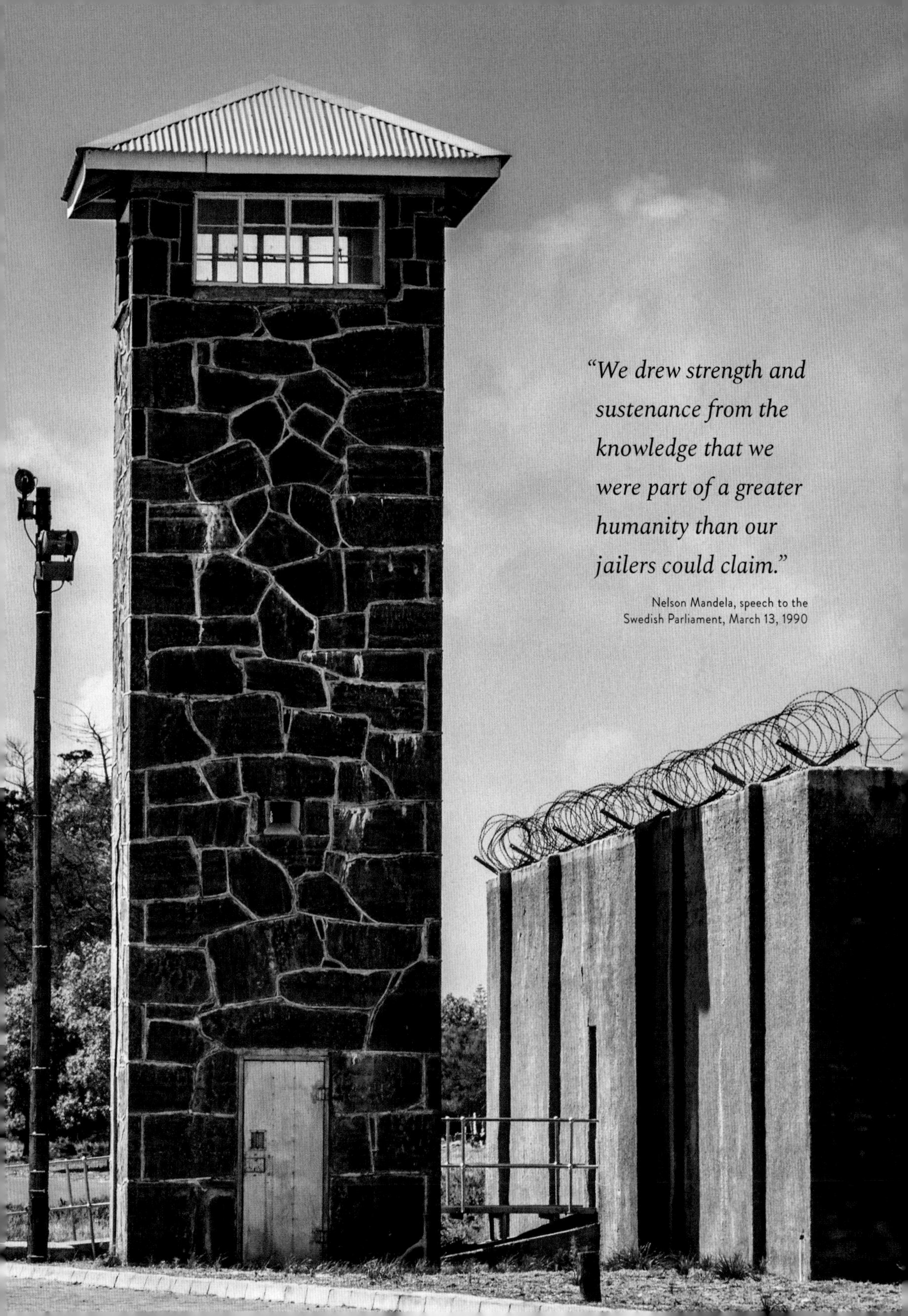

"We drew strength and sustenance from the knowledge that we were part of a greater humanity than our jailers could claim."

Nelson Mandela, speech to the Swedish Parliament, March 13, 1990

399 PLACE OF WORK

CHECKPOINT CHARLIE

Berlin, Germany
1961

The checkpoint was a marker along the Berlin Wall which separated the city—and East and West Germany—during the Cold War. In 1963, U.S. president John F. Kennedy visited, citing the wall as an example of the failure of Communism. Today, the wall's course is marked by a line of cobblestones, and the checkpoint guardhouse is in a museum.

ABOVE: Checkpoint Charlie became a symbol of the division between East and West Germany.

400 INFRASTRUCTURE AND INNOVATION

SPIRALEN TUNNEL

Norway
1961

The city of Drammen, in east Norway, is built on clay; new buildings need rock foundations for stability. When extensive quarrying started to spoil the city's appearance, the Spiralen tunnel was proposed as a better route for extracting gravel. Six loops, giving it the shape of a spring carved out of stone, allow traffic to gain height. The completed tunnel quickly became a tourist attraction when it opened in 1961. Those who drive the spiral exit to views above the spectacular Drammen valley.

401 MONUMENT

BLACK STAR GATE

Accra, Ghana
1961

Black Star Gate stands at the entrance to the immense Black Star Square, built by Kwame Nkrumah, who led Ghana (formerly the Gold Coast) to independence from Britain. As a symbol, the black star crowning it derives from that used for the Black Star shipping line, founded in 1919 by Marcus Garvey, an American civil rights leader. Its significance passed first to Ghana's own fleet, and ultimately to its flag.

402 RESIDENCE

12305 FIFTH HELENA DRIVE

Los Angeles, California
1962

Although this Spanish Revival bungalow was the last stop for Marilyn Monroe—she was found dead there on August 4, 1962—it was also, she told the press, her first real home. At the age of only 36, she had lived at no fewer than 43 addresses and, newly separated from Arthur Miller, her therapist recommended that she seek out a permanent base. She lived there for just six months.

403 ART AND CULTURE

BERLIN PHILHARMONIC HALL

Berlin, Germany
1963

The Berlin Philharmonic's original hall was bombed in World War II; the architect chosen to replace it was Hans Scharoun, whose design naturally concentrated heavily on maximizing acoustic quality. With a draped, tentlike roof, sharp interior angles, and the fact that the audience surrounded the orchestra rather than facing it, the result looked eccentric in the early 1960s but set a precedent that was soon widely imitated.

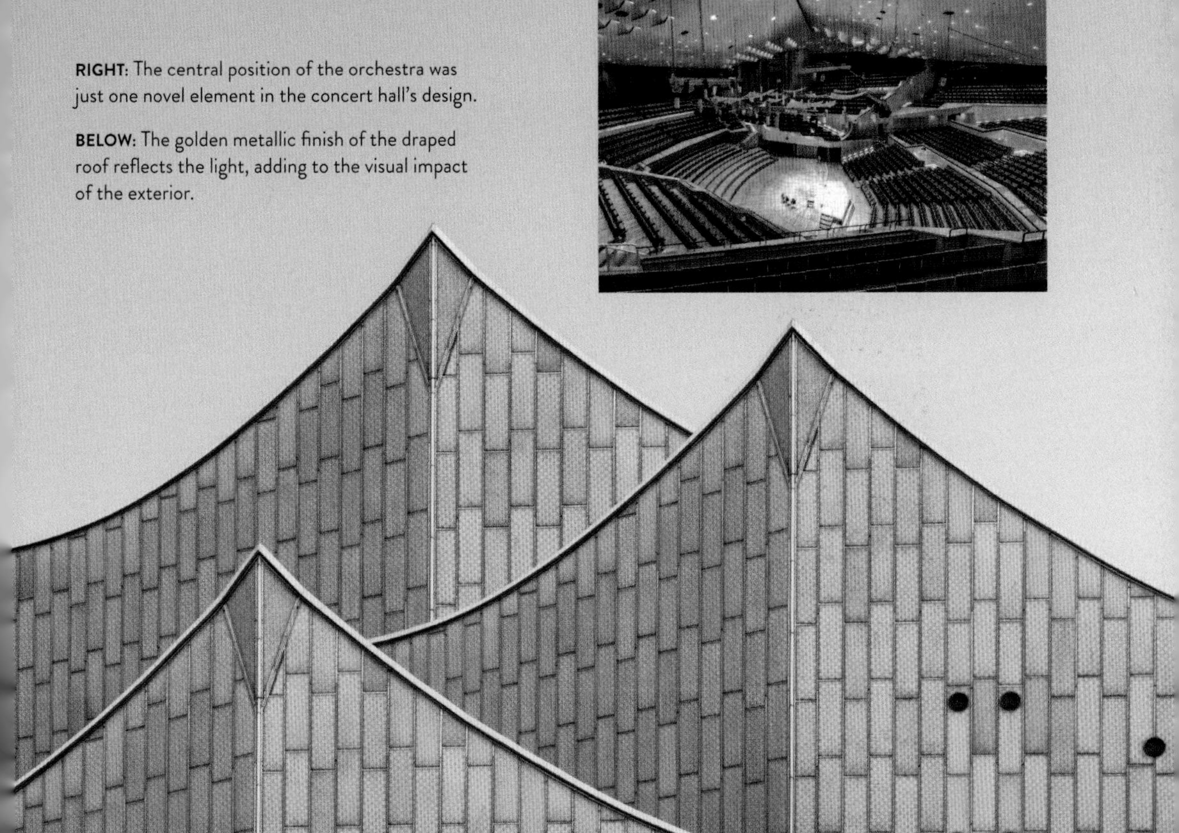

RIGHT: The central position of the orchestra was just one novel element in the concert hall's design.

BELOW: The golden metallic finish of the draped roof reflects the light, adding to the visual impact of the exterior.

ANDY WARHOL'S FACTORY

Manhattan, New York
1963

The studio where Warhol's public art and private life became indistinguishable.

When he began to produce multiple big screen prints, Andy Warhol employed assistants and took on a larger space. In all four of its incarnations, his studio was known as "the Factory" because of the production-line quality of his work which, over time, incorporated paintings, prints, photography, and movies, the latter with Warhol himself always appearing to observe rather than participate.

In the first Factory, on East 47th Street, Warhol's unique process developed over the four years he was there, and the lines between his life and work increasingly blurred. Those waiting for something to happen sat alongside those engaged in making art. After the artist Valerie Solanas shot—and nearly killed—Warhol in a fit of paranoia in 1968, the second Factory became more like a conventional studio. Here, Warhol increasingly concentrated on the business of art, becoming easily the most famous—and one of the richest—artists of his time.

"Making money is art and working is art and good business is the best art."

Andy Warhol

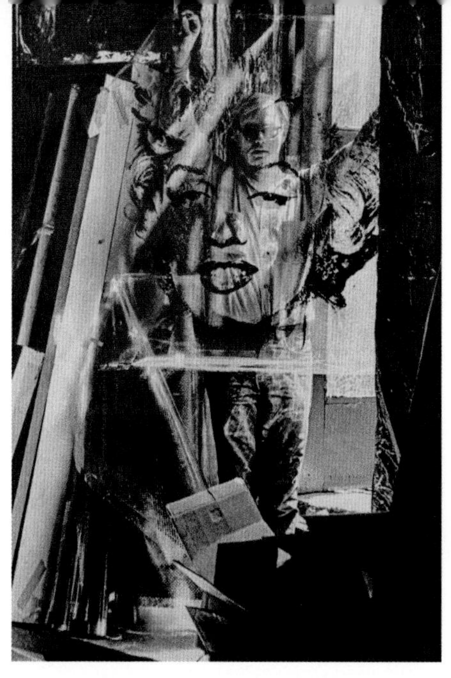

ABOVE: Andy Warhol, the ultimate observer, long outlasted the 15 minutes of fame he predicted for everyone else.

BELOW: The Factory's second incarnation was in the Decker Building at 33 Union Square West.

YOYOGI NATIONAL STADIUM

Tokyo, Japan
1964

The building that gave an enduring and elegant identity to Japan's first Olympics.

The 1964 Olympic Games marked the first time that Japan had reengaged globally after World War II, and the country made the most of the soft power inherent in hosting a major sporting event.

Central to its image was the new Yoyogi National Stadium, designed by the architect Kenzo Tange—who employed a much-admired blend of traditional Japanese vernacular forms and new construction methods. In particular, the use of steel cables to create the sweep of a pagoda-style roof was a novelty. To do this, he used techniques borrowed from suspension-bridge construction; Tange made it look as though the roofs were draped over the building. The stadium, and the Olympics it was built for, marked the start of an economic and artistic renaissance for Japan.

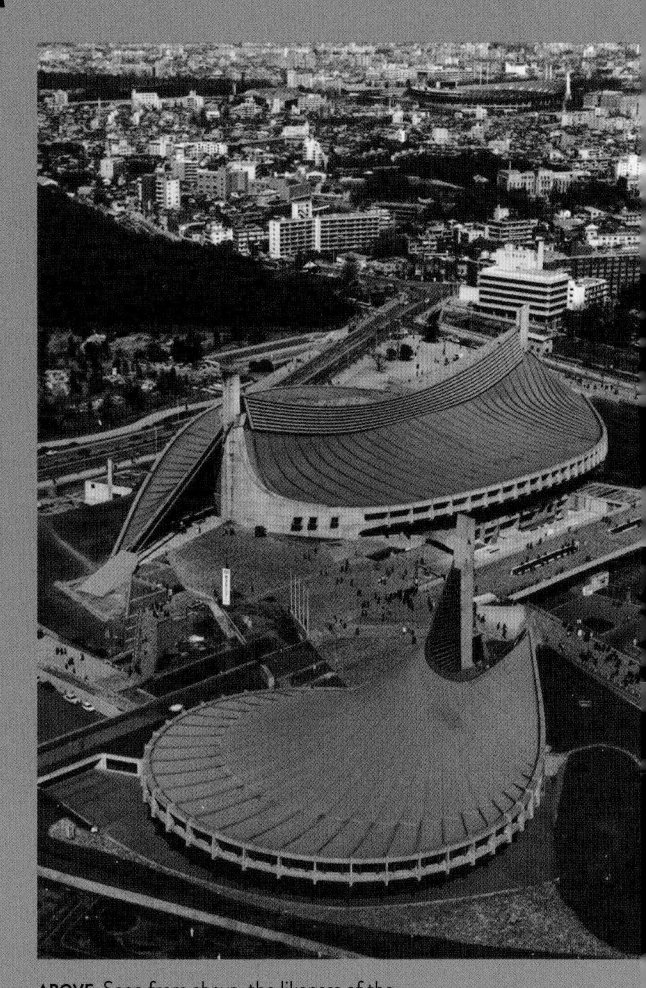

ABOVE: Seen from above, the likeness of the cable-hung roofs to the sweeping eaves of traditional Japanese architecture is unmistakable.

SWIMMING ARENA SECTION

MINI HOLLYWOOD

Almeria, Spain
1965

El Paso, the fictional town setting in the film *For a Few Dollars More*, was built in the Tabernas Desert. It was the creation of Carlo Simi, an architect working with Sergio Leone, the film's Italian director, in whose honor the term "spaghetti Western" was coined. Filming completed, the extras clubbed together and bought the set to run as a commercial attraction.

ABOVE: The mountains of southern Spain made economical stand-ins for western American locations in Sergio Leone's spaghetti Westerns.

407 INFRASTRUCTURE AND INNOVATION/MONUMENT

EDMUND PETTUS BRIDGE

Selma, Alabama
1965

The bridge where "Bloody Sunday" hastened voting reform in the American South.

On Sunday, March 7, 1965, about 600 civil rights marchers left Selma for a rally in Montgomery, Alabama's state capital, demanding an end to discriminatory practices in voting. Crossing the Pettus Bridge—named for a Civil War general and Ku Klux Klan leader—they were attacked by police, brutally beaten, and turned back. Captured on film, the attacks were watched by millions of Americans on television, prompting outrage. A second attempt—two days later—failed, and a minister from Boston who had traveled to join the marchers was murdered.

Martin Luther King Jr. petitioned the federal court to allow the march to go ahead without violence. Publicity about Bloody Sunday swelled the numbers, and 25,000 people arrived in Montgomery on March 25.

Five months later, on August 6, President Lyndon B. Johnson signed the Voting Rights Act, outlawing many of the practices that made voting hard for Black people.

RIGHT: Police attacks on unarmed marchers on the Pettus Bridge were filmed and televised, showing the reality of the civil rights struggle to a much wider audience.

SALK INSTITUTE FOR BIOLOGICAL SCIENCES

La Jolla, California
1965

When the City of San Diego gifted Jonas Salk, the scientist who discovered the polio vaccine, the site for a new institute, he briefed modernist Louis Kahn to design him a monastery dedicated to science. The austere lines of the buildings disguise the number of technical requirements they had to meet, in particular the laboratories that had to be flexible enough to meet the ever-changing demands of scientific research.

ABOVE: Louis Kahn's spare, symmetrical design and his use of rills and running water reinforce the calm atmosphere of the institute.

409 INFRASTRUCTURE AND INNOVATION

VEHICLE ASSEMBLY BUILDING

Titusville, Florida
1966

The Vehicle Assembly Building at NASA's Kennedy Space Center is designed to assemble space vehicles such as the Apollo, Saturn V, and space shuttles, and then stack them vertically onto their mobile launcher platforms, which emerge from one whole side of the building. It is the largest single-story building in the world and has been vital to space exploration.

ABOVE: The building was completed in time for the assembly of the Apollo/ Saturn V moon rocket in 1966.

410 ART AND CULTURE

PARQUE COPPELIA

Havana, Cuba
1966

The Coppelia ice-cream parlor is a noted landmark in Havana. The open, two-story pavilion has a suspended roof with eight "legs" and can accommodate over 1,000 customers at a time. It was commissioned by Fidel Castro, allegedly to prove that anything America could do, Cuba could do better. Its launch offering was a list of 26 flavors—to commemorate the date of the Cuban Revolution, July 26, 1953.

ABOVE: From a distance, the brightly colored ice-cream parlor, perched on its spindly legs, has the look of a fantasy 1960s spaceship.

411 MONUMENT

GATEWAY ARCH

St. Louis, Missouri
1966

The Gateway Arch was built to mark the "Gateway to the West"—the point from where the Lewis and Clark expedition, commissioned by Thomas Jefferson, departed in 1804 to explore the new land acquired from France in the Louisiana Purchase—and to honor the pioneers who undertook the westward expansion of America. The gleaming stainless-steel arch, built by the Finnish modernist Eero Saarinen, soars 630 feet above the Mississippi River.

ABOVE: An ingenious built-in track/elevator system enables visitors to reach the top of the arch.

412 RESIDENCE

HABITAT 67

Montreal, Canada
1967

An experimental housing project that was built as the Canadian "pavilion" for the World Expo 67, held in Montreal, Habitat 67, designed by the Israeli-Canadian architect Moshe Safdie, was made up of prefabricated concrete units arranged in pyramidal structures. It reflected a global need for dense housing that was economical with space, but which had plenty of outdoor areas nearby. Over 50 years later, it remains popular.

ABOVE: The 354 prefabricated living modules that make up Habitat 67 are interleaved with landscaped areas.

MADISON SQUARE GARDEN

Manhattan, New York
1968

The popular new arena opened at the cost of a venerable landmark.

Madison Square Garden of 1968 is the fourth incarnation of the arena. Built literally on top of Pennsylvania Station's subterranean platforms, the ground-level Beaux-Arts station building was demolished to make way for it—an act that ultimately prompted the founding of New York's Landmarks Preservation Commission. Despite this, it proved a popular location, right in the center of Manhattan, and above where the trains come in from Long Island and New Jersey, it's convenient for people throughout the tri-state area.

The new round arena was cutting-edge for its time, with a ceiling supported by cables and capacity for around 20,000 people, whether as an audience for sports or for a concert. New Yorkers quickly came to regard it with loyalty.

LEFT TOP: Despite its controversial beginnings, Madison Square Garden is accessible, well located, and popular with its hometown audience.

LEFT: Pennsylvania Station, which was demolished to make way for Madison Square Garden in 1963.

FERNSEHTURM

Berlin, Germany
1969

With its 1,200-foot height, the Fernsehturm—television tower—on Alexanderplatz was the tallest structure in Berlin when it was inaugurated, marking the 20th anniversary of the founding of the German Democratic Republic. In the divided city, it had a more-than-practical use. Its dramatically modern appearance, with a spherical revolving restaurant two-thirds up, also served to remind West Berliners of East Germany's advanced technical expertise.

LEFT: Over 50 years after its completion, the Fernsehturm still looks impressively modern, and is one of the iconic sights of Berlin.

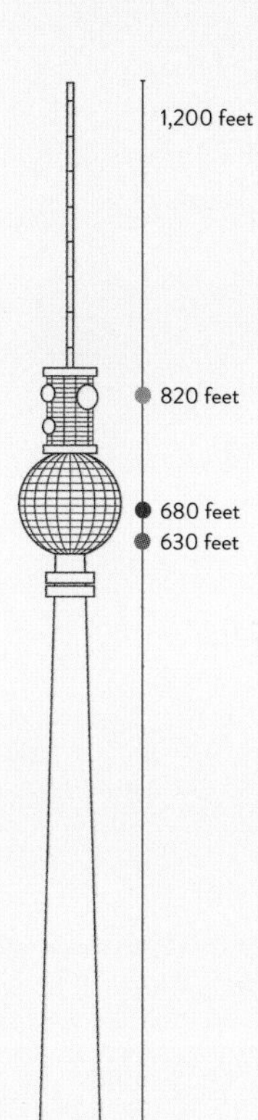

STONEWALL INN

Manhattan, New York
1969

The Stonewall uprising marked a shift in LGBTQ+ activism in the United States.

The Stonewall Inn is a gay bar in Greenwich Village, New York. In the 1960s, few establishments welcomed homosexuals, and repressive legislation made it impossible for a gay bar to obtain a liquor license. Mafia control of gay bars was a given and police raids were the norm.

The rebellion began during a routine police raid on the bar at 1:20 a.m. on June 28, 1969. This time the customers fought back. A woman, escorted out of the building in handcuffs, shouted out to bystanders, "Why don't you guys do something?" as she was bundled into a police wagon.

Watching the treatment of those arrested, the crowd became enraged. The fight spread to the surrounding streets, with chants of "Gay pride" and "Gay power." The ensuing protests lasted six days and were a turning point for the growth of gay rights groups nationally.

"This was the Rosa Parks moment, the time that gay people stood up and said 'no.' "

Lucian Truscott, *The Village Voice*

BELOW: Originally a fairly anonymous bar, Stonewall would become a legendary site in gay rights history.

BELOW RIGHT: The Pride movement quickly spread all over the world. This "Remember Stonewall" banner is being held at a Pride march in Stockholm.

416 ART AND CULTURE

MR. FREEDOM

London, England
1969

This small shop at the wrong end of Chelsea's King's Road has had an outsize influence on fashion and popular culture. In 1969 it was Mr. Freedom, selling glam rock clothes to—among others—Mick Jagger. Pop maestro Malcolm McLaren and designer Vivienne Westwood took over in 1971, giving it sequential identities. Branded first as SEX, then Seditionaries, it played a big part in the rise of punk.

417 RESIDENCE

10050 CIELO DRIVE

Los Angeles, California
1969

This remote house in Benedict Canyon attained notoriety when five people, including the film star Sharon Tate, were murdered there by members of Charles Manson's gang. It was probably a grudge crime against a creative elite that Manson felt had rejected him. Public distrust of the hippie lifestyle rose after the murders; in wider opinion, they seemed to mark an abrupt end to 1969's so-called Summer of Love.

418 ART AND CULTURE

CHELSEA HOTEL

Manhattan, New York
1969

Perhaps the most remarkable thing about the Chelsea Hotel, the bohemian hangout on West 23rd Street, was its longevity. Built in 1884, the Victorian Gothic pile hosted long-stay residents and remained comparatively inexpensive. Stanley Bard inherited part ownership from his father, David, and ran the hotel with a light hand; he was famously easygoing. It was cheap, with few rules: no wonder creatives—ranging from Dylan Thomas to Janis Joplin—were happy to stay for a while. Patti Smith left a snapshot of what life here was like in 1969, the year she moved into the hotel's tiniest room, 1017, with the photographer Robert Mapplethorpe: "It was like a doll's house in the Twilight Zone, with a hundred rooms, each a small universe."

BELOW: Musician and writer Patti Smith paid just $55 a week to stay in the smallest room at the Chelsea Hotel.

419 PLACE OF WORK

STEEL CORPORATION OFFICE BUILDING

Oruwala, Sri Lanka
1969

Attempts have been made to label the work of Geoffrey Bawa (see page 302)—one favored description was Tropical Modernism—but his output proved too varied to categorize. Despite being part-ruined, the Steel Corporation offices project the lightness and originality that mark him out as a postcolonial architectural star. Finely latticed windows and gridded walls give the impression of carved wood, but are actually built from economical precast concrete units.

BELOW: The Steel Corporation offices, extending over a reservoir, are in a poor state of repair, but still have the elegance for which Geoffrey Bawa's work is known.

420 PLACE OF WORK/INNOVATION

WILLIS TOWER

Chicago, Illinois
1970

For 20 years after its completion, the Willis Tower (originally called the Sears Tower) was the world's tallest building. It was designed by architects Skidmore, Owings & Merrill for Sears Roebuck—the world's largest retailer. Its inventive construction—a series of vertical "bundled" tubes held inside a glass exterior wall—enabled it to reach 110 stories and 1,450 feet, while retaining enough "give" to withstand Chicago's famously windy weather.

421 PLACE OF WORK

STARBUCKS

Seattle, Washington
1971

The first Starbucks store opened in Pike Place Market in 1971, selling roasted beans. The company, inspired by the belief of its owner, Howard Schulz, that he could import the coffee culture he saw in Milan, now has 32,000 stores across 80 countries. Starbucks quickly acquired plenty of imitators, although it wasn't until 2018 that its first Italian store opened, selling brewed coffee back to its roots.

WATERGATE OFFICE BUILDING

Washington, D.C.
1972

On June 17, 1972, intruders entered the offices of the Democratic National Committee in Washington's Watergate complex, searching through documents and tapping phones. Two *Washington Post* reporters traced a long, winding connection between the burglary and the reelection campaign of Republican president Richard Nixon. "Watergate" has been shorthand for scandal ever since.

BELOW: Watergate was an ordinary Washington office building until its notorious role in Richard Nixon's reelection campaign made it world famous.

423 INFRASTRUCTURE AND INNOVATION

GUOLIANG TUNNEL

Taihang Mountains, China
1972

In the past, the remote village of Guoliang could only access the outside world down precipitous flights of steps cut into the mountain. In 1972, the villagers decided to carve a tunnel, using only hand tools, to improve access. Five years later, the Guoliang Tunnel—three-quarters of a mile long—chiseled out of the sheer cliff face, is one of the most remarkable, though hair-raising, passes in China.

424 ART AND CULTURE

CBGB

Manhattan, New York
1973

The music entrepreneur and club owner Hilly Kristal opened CBGB, a live music bar on the corner where the Bowery meets Bleecker Street, to showcase the country, bluegrass, and blues styles for which it was named. It quickly took on a life of its own, becoming the natural home of punk and new wave, especially after the Mercer Arts Center, an underground music venue housed in a decrepit hotel, literally collapsed on August 3, 1973.

Early bookings included the Ramones, Patti Smith, Blondie, and Richard Hell and the Voidoids. The Ramones had the same iconic standing on the New York scene as the Sex Pistols in London—famous for their volume, their casual playing and, above all, their speed—they could get through an entire set in under 12 minutes.

The club finally closed in 2006, played out with a concert by Patti Smith.

ABOVE: The music club where many of the best-known punk and new wave bands were given their start.

SYDNEY OPERA HOUSE

New South Wales, Australia
1973

In 1957, a competition to design an opera house for Sydney was won by the Danish architect Jørn Utzon. The curved "shells" of the roof proved particularly challenging technically, and a change of government turned the project into a political hot potato, which led to Utzon's resignation. It was finally completed more than a decade late, but quickly became Sydney's most iconic landmark.

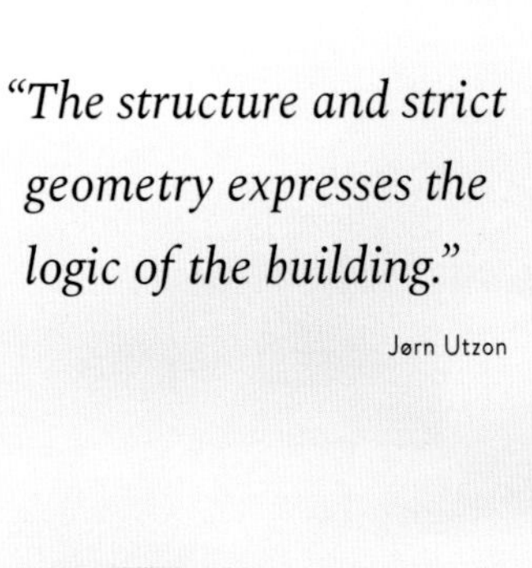

"The structure and strict geometry expresses the logic of the building."

Jørn Utzon

ABOVE: The opera house under construction in 1965.

BELOW: Over a million tiles were used on the chevrons of the roof shells, conceived to mirror the varied light in the harbor.

STADE TATA RAPHAEL

Kinshasa, Democratic Republic of the Congo
1974

Scene of the "Rumble in the Jungle"—one of the most famous boxing matches of all time.

On October 30, 1974, the boxer George Foreman defended his heavyweight championship title against Muhammad Ali at the Tata Raphael stadium in Zaire (now the Democratic Republic of the Congo); he lost in the eighth round.

Politically, the opponents were miles apart. The charismatic Ali used the publicity he gained during his first heavyweight title to declare membership of the Nation of Islam. This marked him out in 1960s America as a Black nationalist; subsequently, he forfeited the title by refusing to join the Vietnam draft. Foreman, more conventional, had his first big win against Soviet champion Jonas Cepulis at the Olympics, and celebrated by patriotically waving the American flag.

Don King, the match promoter, promised his stars $5,000,000 each; the only person to put up the money was the authoritarian president of Zaire, Mobutu Sese Seko, who saw an opportunity to champion Zaire's African identity after its years as a French colony. Holding the match there (at 4:00 a.m. so it could be shown live on American television) enabled King to promote it as a return-to-their-roots experience for Foreman and Ali.

In publicity terms, they were all winners: Ali, Foreman, and King had their fame boosted, while Mobutu got the publicity he desired for Zaire.

RIGHT: The Stade Tata Raphael, then known as Stade du 20 Mai, gets a makeover before the fight between Ali and Foreman.

KNOWN FOR

- A match with a complicated and mixed political agenda
- A major turning point in the careers of Ali and Foreman
- The first match in which Ali made use of his "rope a dope" technique to wear out his opponent

"I wanted to establish a relationship between American blacks and Africans. The fight was about racial problems, Vietnam. All of that."

Muhammad Ali

427 ART AND CULTURE

DALÍ THEATER AND MUSEUM

Catalonia, Spain
1974

Conceived during Salvador Dalí's lifetime as "the greatest Surrealist object in the world," the museum is dedicated to his work, with dozens of carefully composed surreal tableaus. Built around the core of the old theater of Figueras, ruined in the Spanish Civil War, it is also Dalí's mausoleum: a glass geodesic dome encloses the stage of the old theater, and the artist, ever present, is interred in a crypt beneath.

ABOVE: The gilded wall projections and enormous eggs along the roofline are both details used regularly by Salvador Dalí elsewhere.

428 PLACE OF WORK

HOLIDAY INN

Beirut, Lebanon
1975

A luxurious hotel built in 1973, when Beirut was a desirable travel destination, the Holiday Inn had been open for barely two years when civil war broke out. It became a prize in the so-called Battle of the Hotels; the city's lavish complexes saw pitched battles, with snipers firing from their rooftops. Fighting and subsequent looting left the hotel a decaying shell which has towered over the district ever since.

ABOVE: The Holiday Inn stands as an oppressive reminder of Beirut's civil war, which lasted from 1975 to 1990.

429 RESIDENCE

PONTE CITY

Johannesburg, South Africa
1975

The center of a neighborhood that rose, fell, and is now on the rise again.

Ponte City (now Ponte Tower) opened as a residential skyscraper—a luxury apartment block—in Hillbrow, a well-heeled district in central Johannesburg, in 1975. Its distinctive hollow-cored cylinder was the work of a young architect, Rodney Grosskopf, and it was built for an affluent, white middle class.

Five years after it opened, Hillbrow was changing. As Johannesburg acquired more of a reputation for violence, the inhabitants of Ponte City left for safer homes in the suburbs. By the close of the 1980s, the area was very run-down, and the end of apartheid in 1994 did nothing to help; Ponte had become a dangerous, high-rise slum. Slowly, through the 2010s, it began to regenerate. The building's owners started to renovate to a modest but comfortable standard. A mixture of tenants moved in: less affluent than those of the 1970s, but also more reflective of modern Johannesburg society.

RIGHT: The changing fortunes of Ponte City—from luxury apartments to slum, then back to modest-but-respectable living quarters—have, to some extent, mirrored the story of Johannesburg itself.

430 RESIDENCE/ART AND CULTURE

GREY GARDENS

Long Island, New York
1975

Home to "Big" and "Little" Edie Beale—aunt and cousin of Jackie Onassis—Grey Gardens and its occupants were the stars of a widely admired cult movie directed by the avant-garde Maysles brothers. The film observed the impoverished life of the eccentric pair in the decrepit mansion, dreaming of the glories of their socialite past. The film is still shown as an accomplished example of cinema verité.

431 RESIDENCE/ART AND CULTURE

56 HOPE ROAD

Kingston, Jamaica
1975

In 1972, Chris Blackwell signed the reggae band Bob Marley and the Wailers to his label, Island Records. Three years later, Marley acquired Blackwell's house at Hope Road as part of his contract negotiations for the album *Natty Dread.* Built in the 1800s, it was big enough for Marley to build a recording studio there. After his break from the Wailers, he recorded most of his solo music here.

Marley didn't live at Hope Road full time, but he spent large chunks of time there, when he had a break from his punishing touring schedule. He kept an open house, for playing and rehearsing.

In a wealthy part of Kingston, the house is just up the road from the home of Jamaica's prime minister. If anyone mocked him for that, Marley joked, "I've brought the ghetto uptown," referring to his roots in poverty-stricken Trench Town, where he'd grown up.

LEFT: "Little" Edie Beale, one of the eccentric stars of Grey Gardens, poses—wearing a fur coat from more prosperous days—in front of her dilapidated home.

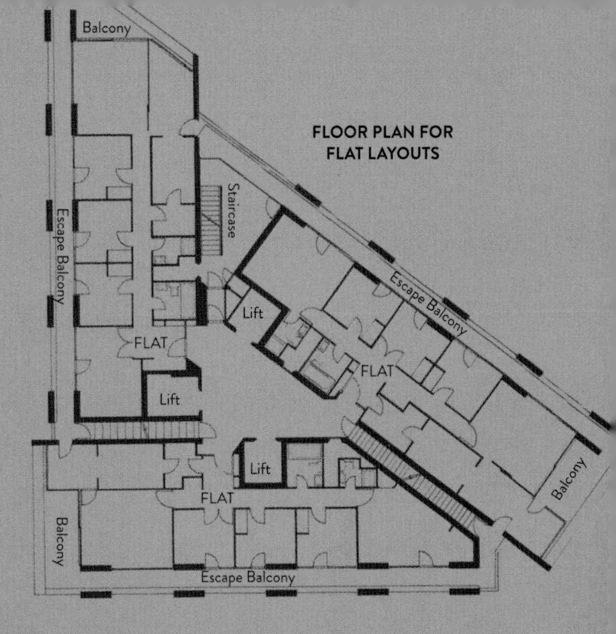

432 RESIDENCE

BARBICAN ESTATE

London, England
1976

Part of the regeneration of an area of London bombed in World War II, the 35-acre estate incorporated 2,000 flats, an arts center, and a school, laid out with plenty of landscaping and largely pedestrianized. The Brutalist style—named in part for the use of then-cheap rough-finish concrete—wasn't universally popular, but perceptions of the estate changed over time, taking it from a utilitarian to a desirable living space.

ABOVE LEFT: While the Barbican blocks are unapologetically Brutalist in style, the layouts of the flats inside are conventional.

LEFT: Arched windows at the top of the block are echoed by unusual inverted arches on the ground floor.

CENTRE POMPIDOU

Paris, France
1977

The arts center that set a new standard of originality in public building.

The idea for a new arts center came from the conservative president Georges Pompidou, one of a number of public building projects planned for Paris at the start of the new decade after one in which the city—and its image—had been damaged by extensive riots. The winners of the competition to design it were Renzo Piano and Richard Rogers, both architects who would go on to have distinguished careers.

Their vision was unprecedented: a building that carried its essential amenities in bright tubes and pipes wrapped around the exterior, leaving the inside uncluttered. In low-rise Paris, it could also be seen from a considerable distance away. It was fresh. It offered many challenges during the build, and when it finally opened in 1977 it was greeted with a mixed response, finding both fans and critics. Over time it has become a well-loved stalwart of Parisian culture.

BELOW: The bright colors used for the exterior pipework stand out against the more traditional muted grays of the Parisian skyline.

434 ART AND CULTURE

STUDIO 54

Manhattan, New York
1977

The club that marked the high point of the disco era.

Although it lasted only three years, Studio 54's reputation as New York's greatest nightspot long outlived the club itself. Opened by Steve Rubell and Ian Schrager on April 26, 1977, it was carefully managed to appear as exclusive as possible—crammed with the famous and the beautiful. Great music was as infamous as the legendary drug use and sex exploits. The quintessential Studio 54 moment was Bianca Jagger's arrival—on a white horse led by a naked man covered in glitter.

In 1979, Rubell was reported saying the club had cleared $7,000,000 in its first year. Studio 54 was raided on New Year's Eve, and Rubell and Schrager ended up in jail. On February 7, 1980, they held one last party before the doors closed for good. Self-consciously decadent and too successful for its own good, Studio 54 epitomized a moment of excess at the turn of the 1980s.

"It's a dictatorship at the door and a democracy on the dancefloor."

Andy Warhol

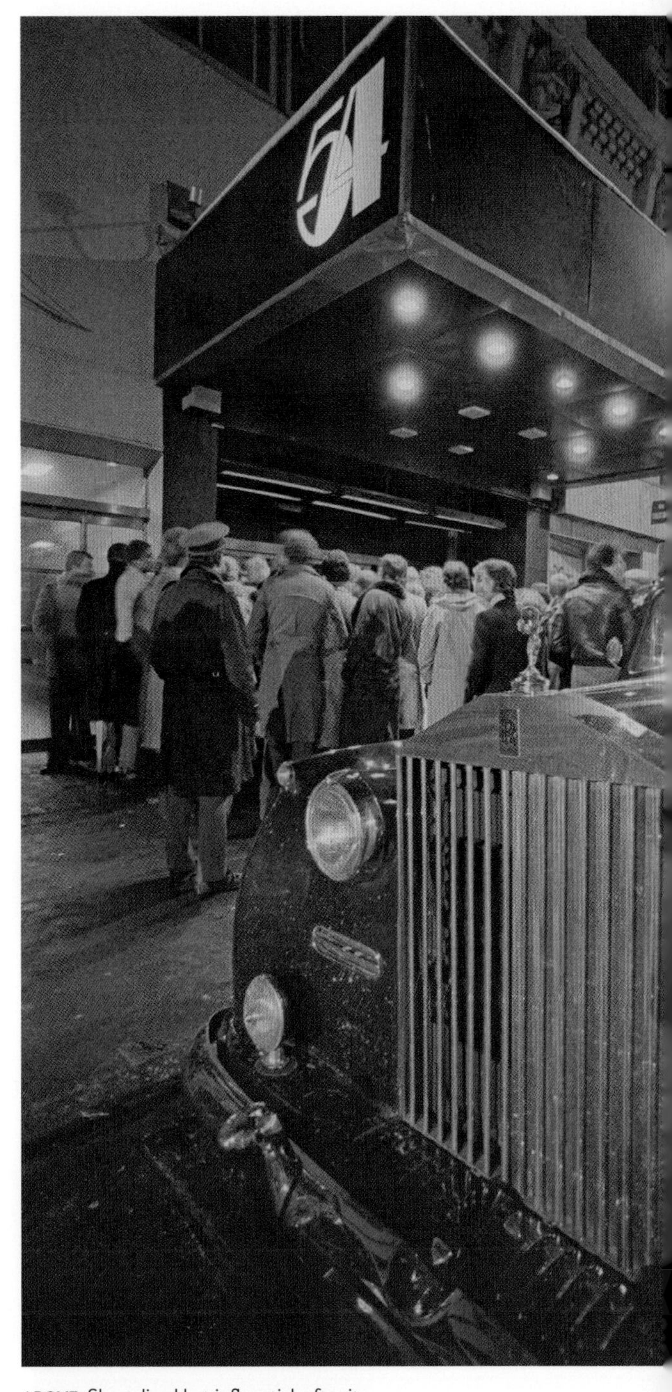

ABOVE: Short-lived but influential, after its closure Studio 54 was widely written about, cementing its decadent reputation.

435 RESIDENCE

HACIENDA NÁPOLES

Puerto Triunfo, Colombia
1978

The drug lord's estate that typified cocaine-fueled 1970s living.

When the infamous Colombian narcotics kingpin Pablo Escobar bought Hacienda Nápoles in 1978, it was an unremarkable estate with 5,000 acres. Escobar quickly adapted it to suit him, building multiple pools, a dinosaur sculpture park (its sculptures built around real dinosaur fossils), a bull ring, and a private zoo. The main gateway was topped by a replica of the Piper Cub plane that carried his first ever cocaine shipment to the United States.

Escobar was shot by Colombian police in 1993, and the state ultimately took over Nápoles, reinventing it as a wholesome day out for the public, including a butterfly farm. The animals from the private zoo were sold off. Famously, four breeding hippos escaped, and have since thrived in the nearby Magdalena River Basin—a current herd of around 100 serves as a reminder of Escobar's playground.

"We asked around and of course they were all coming from Hacienda Nápoles . . . Everything happened because of the whim of a villain."

Carlo Valderrama, Webconserva charity, commenting on the Magdalena River's hippo problem

ABOVE: For two decades after Pablo Escobar's death his estate crumbled, the interiors looted, and swimming pools filled with scummy water. Eventually the grounds were reclaimed by the government, cleaned up, and converted into a park for public use.

436 RESIDENCE

JONESTOWN

Guyana
1978

On November 18, 1978, over 900 people belonging to the People's Temple, a utopian cult led by the "Reverend" Jim Jones, died in a mass murder/suicide at Jonestown, the community he had founded in the Guyanese jungle. They had drunk Kool-Aid with cyanide on the orders of Jones, who shot himself. Jonestown has been intensively studied as the most extreme example of destructive manipulation by a charismatic leader.

437 RESIDENCE

DAKOTA BUILDING

Manhattan, New York
1980

On December 8, 1980, John Lennon was shot dead at the entrance to the Dakota Building. Although the association with Lennon's murder added to its fame, it has its own story. When it was built in 1884, it was so far west in the city that critics jibed "It might as well be in Dakota!"—unwittingly naming it. Luxuriously appointed, it made apartment dwelling—previously associated with the poor—fashionable for the rich and famous.

438 ART AND CULTURE

AUDITORIUM, KANDY ARTS CENTRE

Kandy, Sri Lanka
1980

Minnette de Silva was a Sri Lankan Modernist, an admirer of Le Corbusier, and also of traditional Sinhalese architecture. De Silva very much pursued her own style, and was one of the first to blend modern structures and building techniques with traditional details and finishes, using local artisans. This airy two-story auditorium, part open to the elements, seats up to 1,000 people. It is one of her few surviving buildings.

ABOVE: De Silva's auditorium was her last major project, and combined tradition with modernity—the raised timber roof helped ventilation and let in additional light.

NATIONAL HEROES ACRE

Harare, Zimbabwe
1981

Built to commemorate the guerrilla patriots who fought for Zimbabwe's independence, the silhouette of the monument is in the shape of two AK-47 rifles, above which is the Tomb of the Unknown Soldier, featuring three heroic figures. The style of the tomb is familiar from the monuments of North Korea. It was commissioned from Mansudae Studio, a North Korean company best known for their monumental statuary of the Kim family.

ABOVE: Black granite tiers, referencing the walls of Great Zimbabwe (see page 100), lead to a 130-foot-tall obelisk overlooking Harare, topped by an eternal flame.

RIGHT: Studio Mansudae has created many major monuments in Africa, with works in Luanda and Kinshasa as well as Harare.

MEMORIAL NECRÓPOLE ECUMÊNICA

Santos, Brazil
1983

A high-rise cemetery that may be a sign of things to come.

Architecturally, the Necrópole in Santos, a coastal town south of São Paulo, is unremarkable. It looks like a bland hotel in a modern resort. Inside, it's different: a multistory columbarium takes the place of a conventional graveyard, incorporating a crematorium, crypts, and a chapel. At 32 stories, it's the world's tallest cemetery. Increased demand means that it's constantly growing upward, with hundreds of niches on every floor. It's surrounded by landscaped gardens, and there's a restaurant on the roof. Prices vary: the most desirable niches, with mountain views, are the most expensive.

Its founder, Pepe Altstut, who started out in construction, believes this high-rise city for the dead represents the face of the future. "It's natural," he says, "that those who occupy apartments in life, should do so in death, too."

BELOW: In cities where land is scarce and expensive, old-style cemeteries may be on their way out.

SLOVAK RADIO

Bratislava, Slovakia
1983

The brutal-looking introverted pyramid, held in a rusted metal grid, was originally conceived in 1967. It was planned as one of a number of large public buildings in a park, around a grand central boulevard in Bratislava. Czechoslovakia left the USSR, and the political landscape changed before the scheme could be implemented, but Slovak Radio was built, opening in 1983, and broadcasting regularly from 1985. Perhaps surprisingly considering its extreme shape, it also holds a concert hall that can seat an audience of over 500.

Although its style was dated even before it was completed, and it makes regular appearances on "world's ugliest buildings" lists, Slovak Radio is held in affection by many Bratislavians and is an instantly recognizable landmark from vantage points all across the city.

BELOW: The building was granted Slovakian National Monument status in 2018, cementing its standing among Bratislava's landmarks.

CHERNOBYL NUCLEAR POWER PLANT

Pripyat, Ukraine
1984

Site of the worst disaster in the history of nuclear power.

Number 4 was the last of the Chernobyl Nuclear Power Plant's reactors to start operations in 1984. On April 26, 1986, errors during a test caused a power surge. Reactor 4 overheated, and two explosions blew its lid off, throwing out a cloud of radiation 400 times larger than that released by the atomic bomb at Hiroshima.

Two workers were killed in the explosion, and another 28 died from radiation poisoning. Over 350,000 people—including the entire population of Pripyat, the town built to serve the plant—were evacuated. The cloud of radioactivity spread as far as Sweden before the Soviet government admitted to the accident two days later. The cleanup set a huge exclusion zone around the plant and encased the reactor in a concrete-and-steel sarcophagus. President Mikhail Gorbachev later wrote that the Chernobyl disaster was an important factor in the breakup of the Soviet Union.

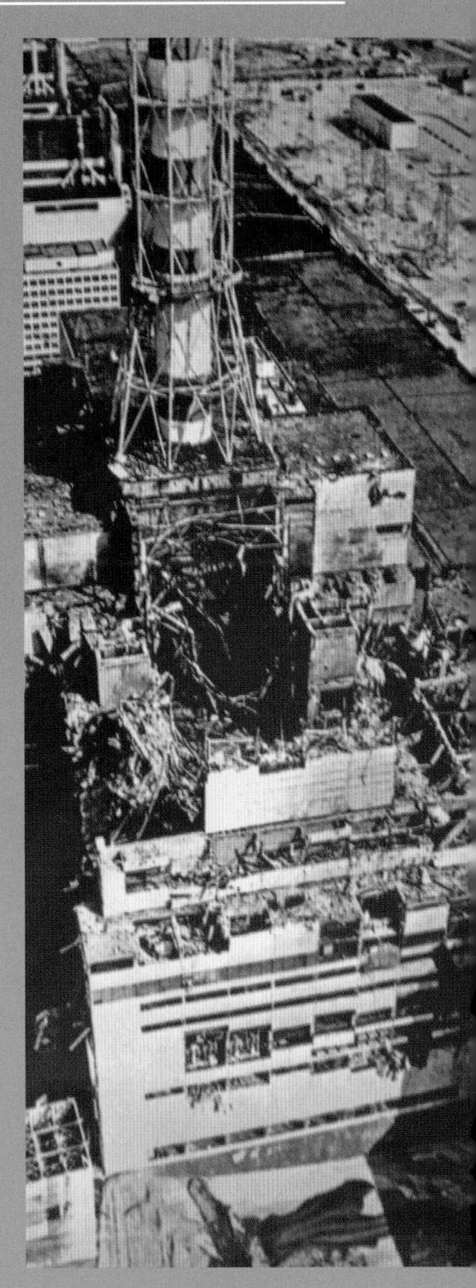

ABOVE: The catastrophic meltdown at Reactor 4, seen from above shortly after the disaster.

"For the first time, the Soviet leadership allowed the media to pursue serious public debates about nuclear dangers. The result was a surge of anti-nuclear sentiments in the Soviet Union. Gorbachev . . . immediately sensed that Chernobyl would increase anti-nuclear momentum in the West."

Vladislav M. Zubok, Russian historian, writing on the long-term effects of the Chernobyl catastrophe

INTERNATIONAL SPACE STATION

Low Earth Orbit
1984

The challenges of setting up a permanent working laboratory in space.

In 1984, President Ronald Reagan announced that NASA would build a long-term research station in space. Then called "Freedom," it was renamed the International Space Station (ISS) as more countries agreed to pool resources and increase the project's scope. It took 30 separate missions, involving five different space agencies, to make the ISS a reality. The initial unit launch for the space build took place in November 1998 from Baikonur Cosmodrome (see page 313), when Russia sent up the first control module. In December of that year, a connecting module was launched by the United States. Astronauts connected them in space, and more modules were added on subsequent missions. By 2009, the ISS was fully operational. Since the first mission, it has been continuously occupied, astronauts serving "shifts" of around six months.

The ISS operates at an altitude of about 250 miles and continually orbits the Earth, each circuit taking 90 minutes. End-to-end, it measures over 350 feet. It's used for general scientific research, as well as testing systems for future space missions. The United States has committed to funding until 2030, while Russia has indicated that it intends to build its own station and will withdraw from the ISS in 2024.

RIGHT: Astronauts Sergey Prokopyev and Dmitri Petelin on a spacewalk outside the Nauka laboratory module in May 2023.

BELOW: The entire space station: the central canisters are where the astronauts live and work, while the flat "sails" are solar panels used to collect energy.

KNOWN FOR

- Uniting the efforts of five agencies: NASA (United States), Roscosmos (Russia), JAXA (Japan), ESA (Europe), and CSA (Canada), making it a truly international collaboration
- Being entirely assembled in space
- Pooling the resources and knowledge of all space-going nations

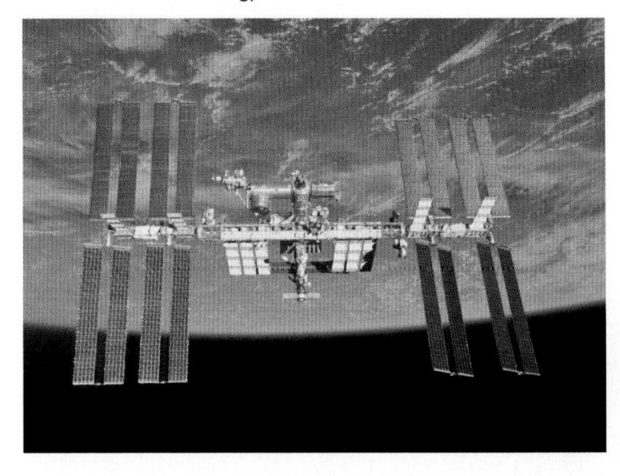

"It's like building a ship in the middle of the ocean from the keel up. You've got to float and you've got to sail. All this has to occur while you're actually building the ship, and that's what the station is like."

Mike Suffredini, NASA station program manager

444 MONUMENT

LAS POZAS

San Luis Potosi, Mexico
1984

This sculpture garden was built in the Mexican jungle by Edward James, an eccentric British author and enthusiast for surrealism. By the time of his death in 1984, around 150 local people had helped him realize his vision. This included elaborate "ruins," terraces, and staircases that lead nowhere. Taken as a whole, despite its date, the impression is that of an ancient city, overrun by nature.

ABOVE: The inspiration for Las Pozas ranged from Mayan ruins to classical Greek and Roman temples.

445 RELIGION AND MONUMENT

WAT PA MAHA CHEDI KAEW TEMPLE

Sisaket Province, Thailand
1986

In 1984, a group of monks began to collect the trash, specifically glass beer bottles, littering the countryside. With the support of local schools, over a million bottles were gathered within a couple of years. By 1986, the "temple of a million bottles" was completed; green (imported) and brown (local) bottles were laid into a cement base in neat geometrical patterns, while the bottle caps were used to create sacred art around the statue of Buddha inside. The collection continues, and new buildings continue to be added.

ABOVE: Predominantly green and brown, the bottles are set into cement in a range of decorative geometric patterns.

446 ART AND CULTURE

CHINATI FOUNDATION

Marfa, Texas
1986

An art museum in which works of art and the surrounding land are inextricably linked.

Conceived on a large desert site near Marfa by the artist Donald Judd, the contemporary art museum is based around a sprawling collection of buildings, many from the 1940s, repurposed from an ex-military base, Fort D. A. Russell. The result took form as an outdoor/indoor liminal space that, in the magical desert landscape, has proved inspirational for artists ever since.

"Somewhere a portion of contemporary art has to exist as an example of what the art and its context were meant to be. Somewhere . . . a strict measure must exist for the art of this time and place."

Donald Judd, *Statement for the Chinati Foundation*, 1987

ABOVE: Donald Judd originally conceived Chinati as a showcase both for his own work and that of two fellow artists, Dan Flavin and John Chamberlain.

HYSOLAR RESEARCH INSTITUTE

Stuttgart, Germany
1987

The Deconstructivist design that galvanized a new solar research building.

When Günter Behnisch—whose groundbreaking style had become known as Deconstructivism—was commissioned to design a new center for solar research at the University of Stuttgart, cost was an important factor. The building must be effective as a lab, but also economical. His response has been compared to an explosion: the laboratories were housed in prefabricated containers, while the walls and roof around them took sharp angles, as though they were falling outward. The whole was then linked by a red pipe, which runs the length of the building.

The effect was impressive but unsettling. By the early 2000s, the solar research unit had moved and the building was falling into disrepair. Since 2009, it has been entirely renovated, and today it houses the university's Visualization Research Center.

BELOW: The research building retains its striking looks, although after it changed function some of its more radical aspects became decorative rather than practical.

MUSÉE D'ORSAY

Paris, France
1987

The station that transformed into one of the greatest museums in Paris.

Gare d'Orsay was built to serve the 1900 World Expo in Paris. The mundane needs of an intercity station, serving southwest France, were concealed behind a handsome stone facade. Victor Laloux's design complemented the upmarket seventh arrondissement in which it was located. When World War II broke out, its life as a station drew to an end: the platforms were too short for the new longer trains.

After it closed, it was sequentially a dispatch depot, a film set, and an auction house, until President Giscard d'Estaing proposed that the redundant—but beautiful—building could be brought together with the city's need for a museum to display its important art from the second half of the nineteenth century. The conversion took a decade. It retained many original features, including the facade—with its central clock—and arched glazed ceiling. It made an ideal home for the art of Van Gogh, Monet, Seurat, and others.

"The station is superb and looks like a Palais des Beaux-Arts."

Edouard Detaille, French artist, prophesying the Gare d'Orsay's future when it first opened in 1900

RIGHT: A highly successful conversion—the Musée d'Orsay combines the airiness of the original building with large, light gallery areas.

449 POLITICS AND NATIONAL DEFENSE

PARLIAMENT HOUSE

Canberra, Australia
1988

The new parliament building was notable not only for its size but also for the references to Australia's culture and history that are integrated into the design, including a pool, built of South Australian black granite. The "cathedral," an open space using the rock Parliament is built on as the floor, and the 345-million-year-old local fossil, known as "Shawn the Prawn," is embedded in a tile in the entrance hall.

BELOW: Over 90 percent of the materials for the new building—six times larger than Australia's old parliament—were sourced within Australia.

450 ART AND CULTURE

LOUVRE PYRAMID

Paris, France
1989

Designed to ease congestion in the entrance to the Louvre Museum, the 71-foot glass pyramid, designed by Chinese-American architect I. M. Pei, shares the classical dimensions of the Great Pyramid of Giza (see page 21). Unashamedly modern, it didn't gain immediate favor. Parisians felt that it desecrated the classical facade of the Louvre. Paris is famous for successfully assimilating contemporary structures, and ultimately the Louvre Pyramid became a destination in its own right.

451 RELIGION AND MONUMENT

NOTRE DAME DE LA PAIX

Yamoussoukro, Ivory Coast
1989

The outsized basilica that towers over the small city of Yamoussoukro.

Yamoussoukro was the birthplace of the first president of Ivory Coast, Félix Houphouët-Boigny, who declared this backwater his country's capital in 1983. In the early 1980s, Ivory Coast was rich, largely through cocoa exports, and Houphouët-Boigny took advantage of the new wealth by commissioning a number of projects. These included a grandiose palace for himself, and Notre Dame de la Paix, which towers over the land around it.

On seeing the design, the pope requested the church be built a symbolic fraction shorter than St. Peter's in Rome; however, an immense gold cross ensured Notre Dame became the tallest church in the world. By the time it was consecrated in 1989, the boom was over and Ivory Coast was much poorer. Houphouët-Boigny died in 1993. His country's business center never transferred from Abidjan, its traditional commercial hub, so Notre Dame de la Paix's congregations remain dwarfed by its scale.

"This project from Houphouët was fundamentally driven by his faith. He had a deal with Ivory Coast, but most of all he had a deal with God."

Pierre Fakhoury, architect of Notre Dame de la Paix

ABOVE: The dome of Notre Dame de la Paix can be seen for miles across the flat country that surrounds Yamoussoukro.

BERLIN WALL

Berlin, Germany
1989

The historic moment that marked the end of the Cold War.

Built in 1961 to divide East Berlin from the West, the wall was deemed necessary by the Soviet-allied East German authorities as ever-increasing numbers of East Berliners were leaving East Germany. It came to be used—particularly by Western leaders—as a symbol of the division within Europe.

By the 1980s, the Soviet Union was in economic collapse. Its leader, Mikhail Gorbachev, worked to forge closer links with the West, introducing policies of *glasnost* and *perestroika*—openness and restructuring—for the disintegrating Eastern Bloc. The changes came too late. With other members, in particular Poland and Hungary, powering their own democratic movements, East Germans took to the streets to demand more democratic government.

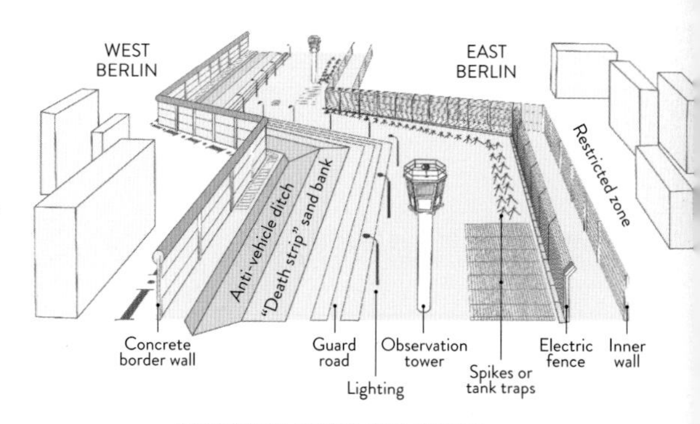

STRUCTURE OF THE BERLIN WALL

In November 1989, around 500,000 people collected in East Berlin to protest. On November 9, a policy granting new travel freedoms for East Berliners was accidentally announced early; this caused massive crowds to flock to the wall. The guards, intimidated, opened the six checkpoints, letting people through. They stood back and watched as they climbed the wall and began to dismantle it. As a barrier to freedoms, the wall was finished, although the last of it was not demolished until late 1991.

KNOWN FOR

- The moment when an intended loosening of borders broke them wide open
- The first step toward the reunification of Germany, which would happen less than a year later
- A late signal to the Soviet Union of the final failure of the socialist system

ABOVE: The elaborate safeguards of the Berlin Wall ensured that it was impossible to cross.

RIGHT: November 9, 1989: a huge crowd of Berliners arrived at the wall, the checkpoints were opened, and large numbers of people stood on top of it, celebrating their new freedoms.

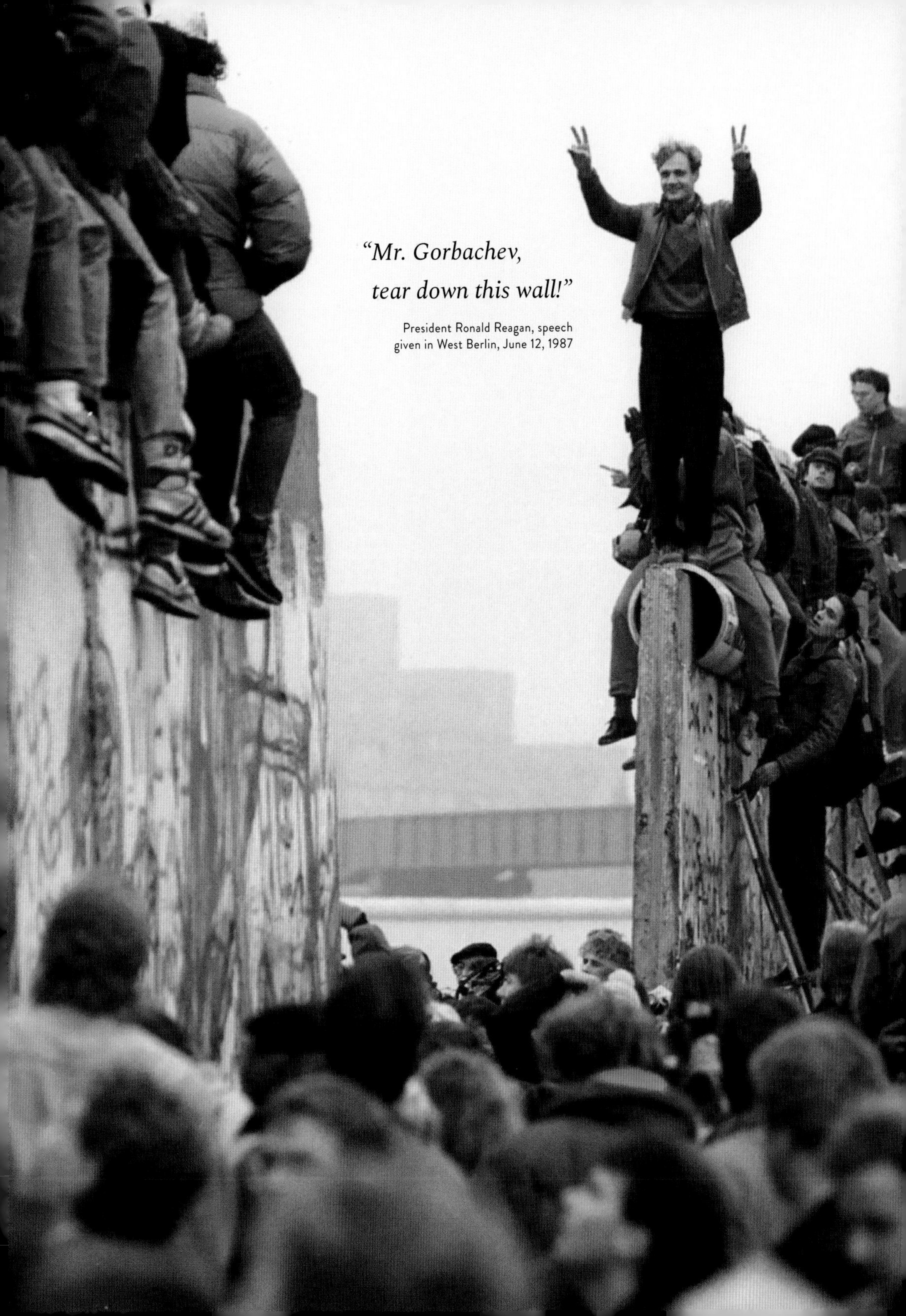

"Mr. Gorbachev,
tear down this wall!"

President Ronald Reagan, speech
given in West Berlin, June 12, 1987

BANK OF CHINA TOWER

Hong Kong, China
1990

The building—four conjoined towers of different heights, with zigzag braces lit up—was the response of architect I. M. Pei (see page 357) to the bank's commission for a super-high skyscraper. The design evolved in response to the need for a lot of offices on a site with a small footprint, that was stable enough to withstand the weather in a typhoon-prone country. At 1,209 feet, it is still one of Hong Kong's tallest buildings.

> *"Probably the most innovative skyscraper structure built anywhere to date."*
>
> Peter Blake, architect and critic, 1991

LEFT: The spiky outline of Pei's bank building has been compared to a twisted sheaf of upright bamboo stems.

FREE UNIVERSITY OF THE ENVIRONMENT

Paraná, Brazil
1992

A not-for-profit foundation which offers free lessons for all on ecological and environmental issues.

Founded in Curitiba, a city of 1.6 million people, also known as "the ecological capital of Brazil," the Free University of the Environment is built in an abandoned stone quarry and made from recycled wooden telephone poles. Innovatively designed with a minimal global footprint, and a consciously ecological agenda, its aim is to educate Curitiba's population: helping to make their city both green and sustainable.

BELOW: The university center is set in the lush forested grounds of Zaninelli Park in Curitiba.

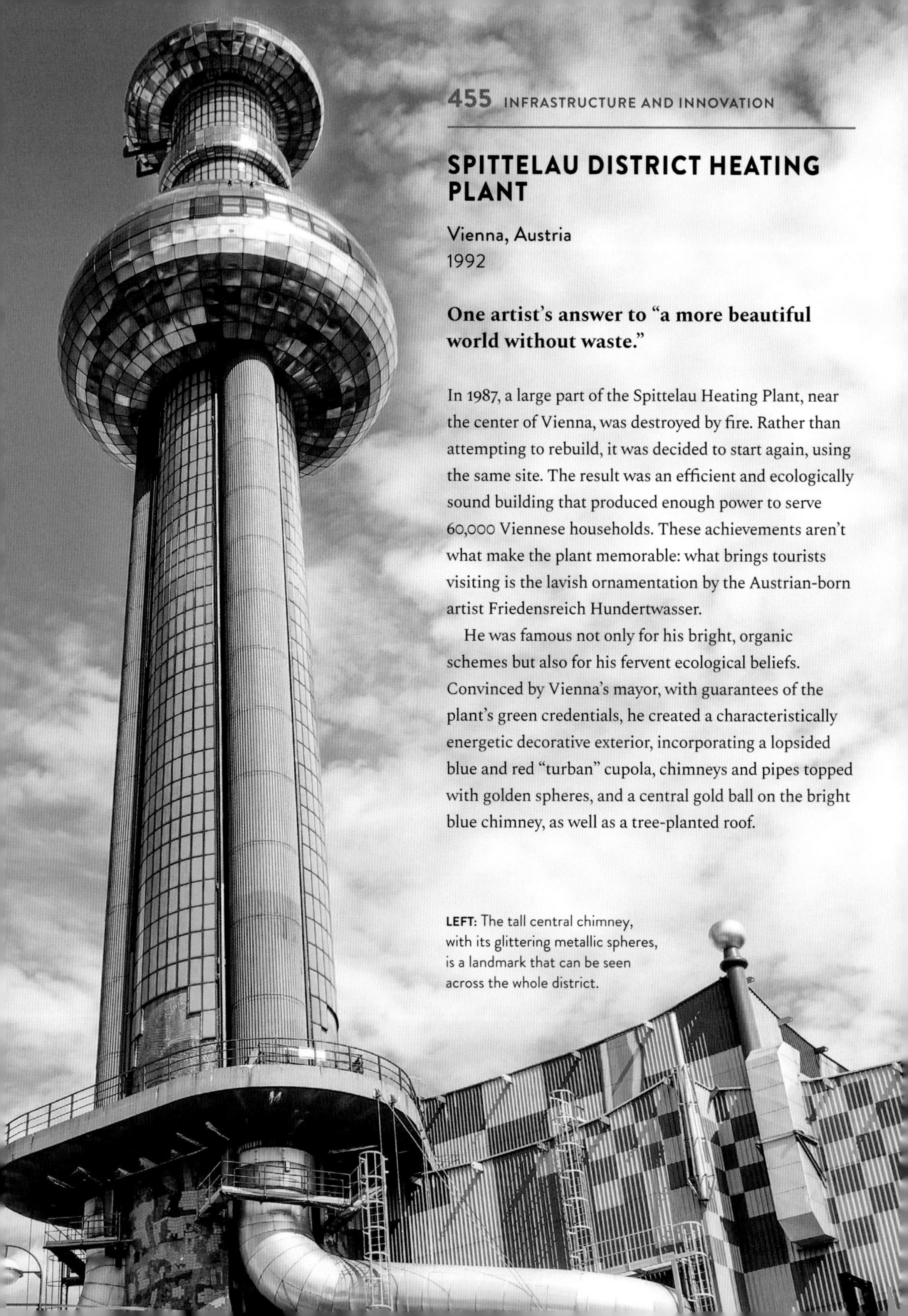

SPITTELAU DISTRICT HEATING PLANT

Vienna, Austria
1992

One artist's answer to "a more beautiful world without waste."

In 1987, a large part of the Spittelau Heating Plant, near the center of Vienna, was destroyed by fire. Rather than attempting to rebuild, it was decided to start again, using the same site. The result was an efficient and ecologically sound building that produced enough power to serve 60,000 Viennese households. These achievements aren't what make the plant memorable: what brings tourists visiting is the lavish ornamentation by the Austrian-born artist Friedensreich Hundertwasser.

He was famous not only for his bright, organic schemes but also for his fervent ecological beliefs. Convinced by Vienna's mayor, with guarantees of the plant's green credentials, he created a characteristically energetic decorative exterior, incorporating a lopsided blue and red "turban" cupola, chimneys and pipes topped with golden spheres, and a central gold ball on the bright blue chimney, as well as a tree-planted roof.

LEFT: The tall central chimney, with its glittering metallic spheres, is a landmark that can be seen across the whole district.

456 RESIDENCE

MARIKA-ALDERTON HOUSE

Yirrkala, Northern Territory, Australia
1994

A landmark case established the entitlement of Aboriginal people to their traditional lands, but left the government in control of funds, design, materials, and construction. The house of Banduk Marika, an Aboriginal leader, and her partner, Mark Alderton, bypassed the process that tended to fix on whichever design was cheapest. Instead they commissioned an impressive, airy prefabricated home. Planned as a prototype, it may be the first of many.

457 INFRASTRUCTURE AND INNOVATION

CHANNEL TUNNEL

English Channel
1994

A tunnel linking Britain and France had been talked of since the days of Napoleon, but it wasn't until the 1980s that engineering advances made it possible. In 1986, Britain and France signed a treaty agreeing to the project running under the English Channel between Folkestone in Kent and Sangatte, near Calais. Work began in 1987, employing 13,000 workers, and a great deal of heavy machinery, to dig from both sides. The "breakthrough" date—when the workers met in the middle—came on December 1, 1990. The project took another four years to finish; it comprises three linked passages, one for the trains going in each direction, and a service tunnel. The tunnel was formally opened on May 6, 1994, by Queen Elizabeth II and the French president, François Mitterrand.

BELOW: It took three years for the two halves of the tunnel to meet at a midpoint, in an engineering tour de force.

HÔTEL DES MILLE COLLINES

Kigali, Rwanda
1994

The hotel that became a place of refuge for hundreds during the Rwanda genocide.

In 1994, the Hôtel des Mille Collines in Kigali was owned by the Belgian airline Sabena. When the plane of Rwandan president Juvenal Habyarimana was shot down at Kigali airport on April 6, rumors that it had been a Tutsi-run assassination sparked a tribal genocide carried out by the Hutus. Sabena evacuated European staff from the hotel, and a new manager, Paul Rusesabagina, was left in charge.

It is said that Rusesabagina offered shelter to thousands of Tutsis, who were being slaughtered, but that he also kept communications open with the local Hutu militias, bribing them to keep his hotel guests safe. Other versions tell a much darker story, claiming that Tutsis had to pay generously for their safety. What isn't disputed is that 1,268 people were protected at the Mille Collines, at a time when they would almost certainly have been killed outside.

"It was not the largest genocide in the history of the world, but it was the fastest and most efficient."

Paul Rusesabagina,
An Ordinary Man: An Autobiography

BELOW: United Nations peacekeepers evacuated foreign guests at the start of the genocide, but across most of the country, Tutsis were left to fend for themselves.

DANCING HOUSE

Prague, Czech Republic
1996

The architects—the Canadian-American Frank Gehry and the Croatian-Czech Vlado Milunić—conceived a Deconstructivist design in which a dynamic "dancing" part leaned into an upright. It symbolizes the country's transition from a communist state to a democracy. Its original nickname, "Fred and Ginger," eventually gave way to the Dancing House. The latter was thought to sound less "Hollywood" in historic Prague.

ABOVE: The site of Dancing House had been derelict since the previous building was destroyed when the United States bombed Prague in 1945.

LEFT: The upright concrete tower was originally designated "Fred," while its leaning-glass partner was "Ginger."

460 INFRASTRUCTURE AND INNOVATION

PARANAL OBSERVATORY

Cerro Paranal, Chile
1996

Chile's Atacama Desert offers ideal conditions for space research: dry, clear nights at high altitude. The Paranal mountaintop was donated by the Chilean government to the European Southern Observatory. The station, 8,645 feet above sea level, was inaugurated in 1996. With a VLT (Very Large Telescope) and four smaller partner telescopes, it has both cutting-edge technology and the perfect site for modern astronomy.

ABOVE: The observatory is sited in one of the driest areas on Earth, which is also subject to an absolute minimum of light pollution.

461 ART AND CULTURE

BAJA FILM STUDIOS

Baja California, Mexico
1996

Built by Twentieth Century Fox, these Rosarito studios were needed for the production of the film *Titanic* in 1988, which called for larger tanks—so-called wet set—than were used for any previous film. The site, directly overlooking the Pacific, means that the studio's largest tank can be lined up with the ocean horizon so that they blend visually for a convincing impression. Today, 25 years later, Baja Studios remains the favored location for many sea-themed movies.

ABOVE: Since the late 1980s, the majority of movies that call for scenes set on the high seas have been filmed in the vast tanks of the Baja Film Studios.

VIDHAN BHAVAN STATE ASSEMBLY BUILDING

Madhya Pradesh, India
1996

The impressive state government center that manages to maintain a human scale.

The Indian architect Charles Correa built the State Assembly to replace a formal, colonial-era building. Located on a hill overlooking Bhopal, Madhya Pradesh's capital city, it occupies a large site that Correa divided into nine squares, used for different functions, including spaces for the Lower and Upper Houses, a joint Assembly Hall, a library, and all the necessary administration spaces.

The form of the Assembly was influenced by the mandala—the ancient Hindu concept of the organization of the universe—and its design concentrates on the links between human-sized spaces, with plenty of appealing detail, including some notable murals, but lacking in oversized built-to-impress elements. Everything has its place, much of the site is open to the sky, and the only standout larger building is the domed Assembly Hall, which makes a conscious reference to the ancient Buddhist stupa at nearby Sanchi.

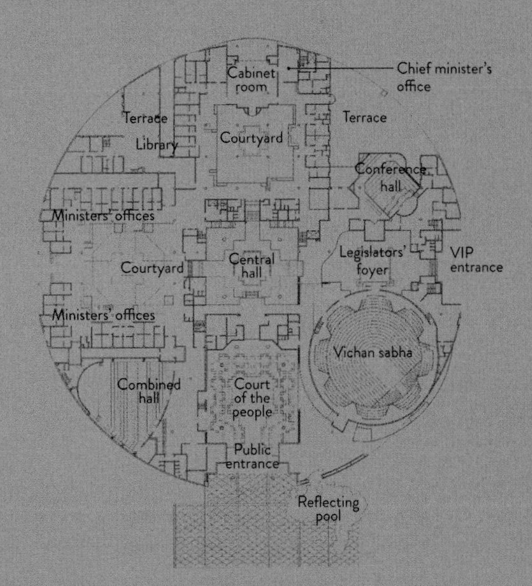

GROUND FLOOR PLAN

ABOVE: The four "corner" squares of the plan are dedicated to halls for the upper and lower houses, a combined hall to accommodate both, and cabinet rooms and offices for the state ministers and officials.

BELOW: The circular wall surrounding the Assembly Building conceals a complex site that incorporates nine separate compartments, each with its own courtyards and gardens.

463 PLACE OF WORK

PETRONAS TOWERS

Kuala Lumpur, Malaysia
1997

Designed by the Argentinian-American architect Cesar Pelli, the Petronas Towers serve as headquarters for the oil company. They are linked by a sky bridge halfway up, and are the tallest paired towers in the world. Despite their modernity, in cross-section they reference the Rub el-Hizb, a traditional Islamic symbol based on two squares placed crosswise over one another, with circles on each intersection between the two—a nod to Malaysia's Islamic identity.

464 ART AND CULTURE

GLOBE THEATRE

London, England
1997

Shakespeare's Globe is a modern replica of the original Globe Theatre, where many of Shakespeare's plays were first performed, usually in the round. The director Sam Wanamaker championed the need for a new/old theater for over 20 years. The first Globe burned down in 1599; the replica, as close as modern safety rules could allow, opened with a performance of *Henry V*.

465 INFRASTRUCTURE AND INNOVATION

CAMPO VOLANTIN BRIDGE

Bilbao, Spain
1998

A graceful design from the Valencian architect Santiago Calatrava, the pedestrian bridge is in the shape of a parabolic arch from which the glass-floored walkway is suspended by cables. Unusually, it became the subject of a lawsuit when Bilbao commissioned a new walkway off one side of the bridge, designed by fellow architect Arata Isozaki. Calatrava sued the city for spoiling the artistic integrity of his design. He ultimately won.

ABOVE: Campo Volantin Bridge is light and elegant in form, characteristic of Calatrava.

OPPOSITE: A different company was hired for each tower, and they were encouraged to race one another to finish.

6 2000–2020

ØRESUND BRIDGE AND DROGDEN TUNNEL

Sweden and Denmark
2000

The iconic link between Sweden and Denmark, which has affected the fortunes of both.

A direct transportation connection between the two Scandinavian countries had been discussed for at least a century before being agreed on in 1991. The bridge/tunnel link took five years to complete. It included the construction of an artificial island, Peberholm, at which the bridge ends and the tunnel—which covers the last stretch to Copenhagen—begins. It was a huge engineering challenge. The design had to accommodate a stretch of water famous for its stormy weather, large ships needed to pass underneath, and planes taking off from Kastrop Airport in Denmark had to be considered. The result was a spare, elegant structure, and offered the bonus of a large nature reserve on the uninhabited Peberholm.

The link has made commuting between the countries easy. It has commercially benefited both, in particular the area around Malmö. However, it has caused some tensions, notably in 2015, when border controls were imposed during an unprecedented refugee crisis in Europe.

BELOW: The bridge runs for an unbroken five miles from the Swedish coast to the island of Peberholm, from where the tunnel takes traffic the remaining two and a half miles to Denmark.

GANDO SCHOOL

Gando, Burkina Faso
2001

A simple and imaginative archetype for sustainable building.

The award-winning Gando School was the first project of its architect, Diébédo Francis Kéré. Kéré grew up in Gando, and each day he had to travel nearly 25 miles to get to school. He wanted his village to have a school of its own. The building needed to be economical, both to construct and to maintain.

Kéré's solution was a building of clay bricks: cheap to make, easy to assemble, and helpful in controlling the temperature inside in a very hot climate. However, clay deteriorates quickly in the rainy season, so while the classrooms have clay roofs pierced with holes to manage airflow, above is a second suspended roof of tin sheeting, to keep the rain off. Local people engaged with the project, and were encouraged to collect stones for the foundations and fetch water for brick production. The result is a well-ventilated, appealing school that offers a model for further local building.

"In my culture everyone has to put his path to push the community forward, so I started to build a school."

Diébédo Francis Kéré, architect of Gando School

BELOW: The tin roofs that top the earthen rooms ensure that the clay bricks won't degrade during the seasonal rains.

468 PLACE OF WORK

CITY HALL

Amsterdam, Netherlands
2001

Just after midnight on April 1, 2001, the mayor of Amsterdam, Job Cohen, oversaw the weddings of four same-sex couples in City Hall. They were the first legal same-sex marriages in the world, after the Netherlands became the first country to grant gay partners the same legal rights as heterosexual couples. Over two decades later, 33 other countries have followed the example set by the Netherlands.

469 PLACE OF WORK

ONE WORLD TRADE CENTER

Manhattan, New York
2001

The destruction of the Twin Towers on September 11, 2001, had far-reaching consequences. The worst terrorist attack ever perpetrated in America, it killed nearly 3,000 people; it changed both the skyline and the mindset of many New Yorkers. It led to the invasion of Afghanistan, in the so-called War on Terror, just a month later.

ABOVE LEFT: In 2002 an art installation, *Tribute in Light*, marked the anniversary of the fall of the World Trade Center in the form of two towers of light beams.

ABOVE: One World Trade Center opened in November 2014, topping out at a height of 1,776 feet.

THE EDEN PROJECT

Cornwall, England
2001

Sited in a disused quarry, the Eden Project was originally conceived as a way to re-create distant climates—and their flora—in the world's largest greenhouses. With a structure based on soap bubbles, the two sequences of interlinked domes were made from honeycombed steel skeletons overlaid with high-tech "skins" of plastic, successfully creating both rainforest and Mediterranean microclimates, with an abundance of plants and a self-contained runoff system for conserving water.

ABOVE: Each of the two biomes—one re-creating rainforest and the other Mediterranean conditions—is made up of several linked "bubble" domes.

INTERNATIONAL LIBRARY OF CHILDREN'S LITERATURE

Tokyo, Japan
2002

Tokyo's Imperial Library of 1906 was built in a Western style. To modernize it for its new role as a center of children's literature, the architect Tadeo Ando added two glass cubes—the first marking the new entrance, and the second superimposed on the original facade at third-floor level, giving the resulting space a liminal quality, or—in Japanese terms—an *engawa*: a space between the old and the new.

ABOVE: Parts of the original Imperial Library building have been enclosed in modern glass walls, perfectly marrying the old with the new.

PALESTINIAN PARLIAMENT

Abu Dis, Jerusalem
2003

Simultaneously unfinished and ruined, the parliament building never served its purpose.

The building that was to be a parliament for a new Palestinian state is in Abu Dis, on the outskirts of Jerusalem. In 1993, the Palestine Liberation Organization (PLO) and Yitzhak Rabin, then prime minister of Israel, signed an agreement on the principles of self-government for Palestine. The agreement, subsequently dubbed the Oslo Peace Accords, led the PLO to believe that before long they would have a state—and, by extension, a parliament—of their own. Construction of the building began in 1996, designed by the Palestinian-Jordanian architect Ja'afar Tuqan. In 2003, the Oslo Peace Accords collapsed, and the so-called Second Intifada—a Palestinian revolt against Israeli occupation—broke out. Work on the parliament ceased.

Today, the wreck sits behind a tall concrete wall. Some Palestinians disliked the choice of site. They believed they deserved a parliament in the center of Jerusalem, not on the road leading out of it. Meanwhile, the building has been given to Al-Quds University, in the hope that at some point funds may be found to convert it into a public amenity, such as a cultural center.

ABOVE: U.S. president Bill Clinton cheerleads a handshake between Israeli prime minister Yitzhak Rabin and Yasser Arafat, PLO chairman, at the 1993 signing of the Oslo Accords in Washington, D.C.

RIGHT: The parliament was built at a time of optimism, but has become a symbol of the dashed hopes of the Palestinian people.

> *"The capital of Palestine is Jerusalem."*
>
> Mohammed Faroun, Abu Dis resident

KNOWN FOR

- A grim symbol of failed Palestinian hopes for self-government
- A reminder that Abu Dis was too peripheral a site for a parliament
- It has never been used in more than 20 years, and stands only as a ruin

473 PLACE OF WORK

GOOGLEPLEX

Mountain View, California
2004

By 2004, the search engine Google, founded by Larry Page and Sergey Brin, needed more space. The move to the "Googleplex" offered employees a raft of amenities, from free food and gym facilities to a crèche and a pets-welcome policy. Natural light, glass partitions, and small areas—indoors and out—designed around group working all boosted creativity. The Googleplex quickly became a model for modern employers.

474 ART AND CULTURE

ORDRUPGAARD MUSEUM EXTENSION

Ordrupgaard, Denmark
2005

Housed in the grounds of the museum's main building, an early twentieth-century mansion, the extension at Ordrupgaard was the first building in northern Europe by the celebrated British-Iraqi architect Zaha Hadid. With a low, curvy outline in black concrete—giving it the nickname "the Beached Whale"—the building's large side facades are entirely glazed, reflecting its wooded surroundings and grounding it in its setting.

ABOVE: With the new extension, "Zaha Hadid has managed to capture the special spirit of the site," said the director of Ordrupgaard, Anne-Birgitte Fonsmark.

475 PLACE OF WORK

GORILLA GUARDIANS VILLAGE

Volcanoes National Park, Rwanda
2005

The village was founded by a park ranger who realized that poachers who preyed on critically endangered mountain gorillas needed alternative ways to make a living in the tough rural economy. The village is staffed by reformed poachers, who act as tourist guides and offer insights into Rwanda's culture. The successful initiative has made guarding the gorillas a profitable—as well as an environmentally and ethically desirable—choice.

476 INFRASTRUCTURE AND INNOVATION

UMHLANGA PIER

Kwa Zulu Natal, South Africa
2007

Designed by architect Andre Duvenage, the pier is a local attraction. The superstructure imitates the ribs of a whale. The primary reason for building it was to disguise the troughlike culvert underneath it, which acts not only as a support but also gets rid of stormwater, cleaning the water in the vicinity and helping to avoid stagnant pools from polluting the popular beach.

BELOW: Seen from a distance, it's easy to spot the resemblance of the pier's arches to the ribs of a whale.

477 ART AND CULTURE

THREE SHADOWS PHOTOGRAPHY ART CENTER

Beijing, China
2007

Although Ai Weiwei's international fame comes mainly through his art, it was as an architect that he designed Three Shadows, Beijing's first privately owned center for photography. It was founded by the photographers RongRong and Inri on the site of an old car mechanics workshop, in the bohemian Chaoyang district. Textured walls of reused brick around an open courtyard reference the rapidly disappearing buildings of old Beijing.

478 INFRASTRUCTURE AND INNOVATION

SMART TUNNEL

Kuala Lumpur, Malaysia
2007

The multitasking tunnel that can convert to a drain.

Kuala Lumpur has long been subject to flash flooding: two large rivers run through it, its tropical location means that it is subject to frequent heavy rainfall, and climate change has increased the frequency of major storms. SMART, an acronym for Stormwater Management and Road Tunnel, describes the innovative design that works to ease traffic jams in Kuala Lumpur's famously overcrowded city center, and which also acts as a stormwater drain.

The tunnel has three operating modes. With low or no rainfall, the two-level highway through the tunnel—one level for each direction—stays open. When there is slight flooding, the highway remains open and the floodwater drains through a bypass channel underneath it. If heavy rain persists, the highway closes and—once the last vehicle has exited the tunnel—a sluice opens to allow the flood to drain through the whole tunnel. Experts assert that the tunnel saves the city from flash floods several times a year.

LEFT: Between 2021 and 2022, the internal gallery space at Three Shadows was remodeled and updated.

SVALBARD GLOBAL SEED VAULT

Spitsbergen, Norway
2008

The home of the world's most remote seed bank.

A tunnel entrance, topped by a gleaming illuminated panel by the artist Dyveke Sanne, leads straight into the hillside. Designed by the Norwegian architect Peter Soderman, the vault has three parts. Inside, the tunnel leads down to a chamber, giving access to a small triple vault in which the seeds are kept.

Svalbard is likely to warm over future decades but is predicted to remain under permafrost—so even in the event of a power failure, the seeds would remain frozen. The seeds are backup supplies, duplicates of others stored in more riskily located banks. The collection, already comprising well over a million seed varieties, represents most of the crops in the world, vacuum-packed in aluminum bags, and stored in boxes at a steady -0.4°F. It is an insurance against agricultural disasters. The seeds of any and every country are included in the vault, regardless of regime or political color: a Noah's Ark for global agriculture.

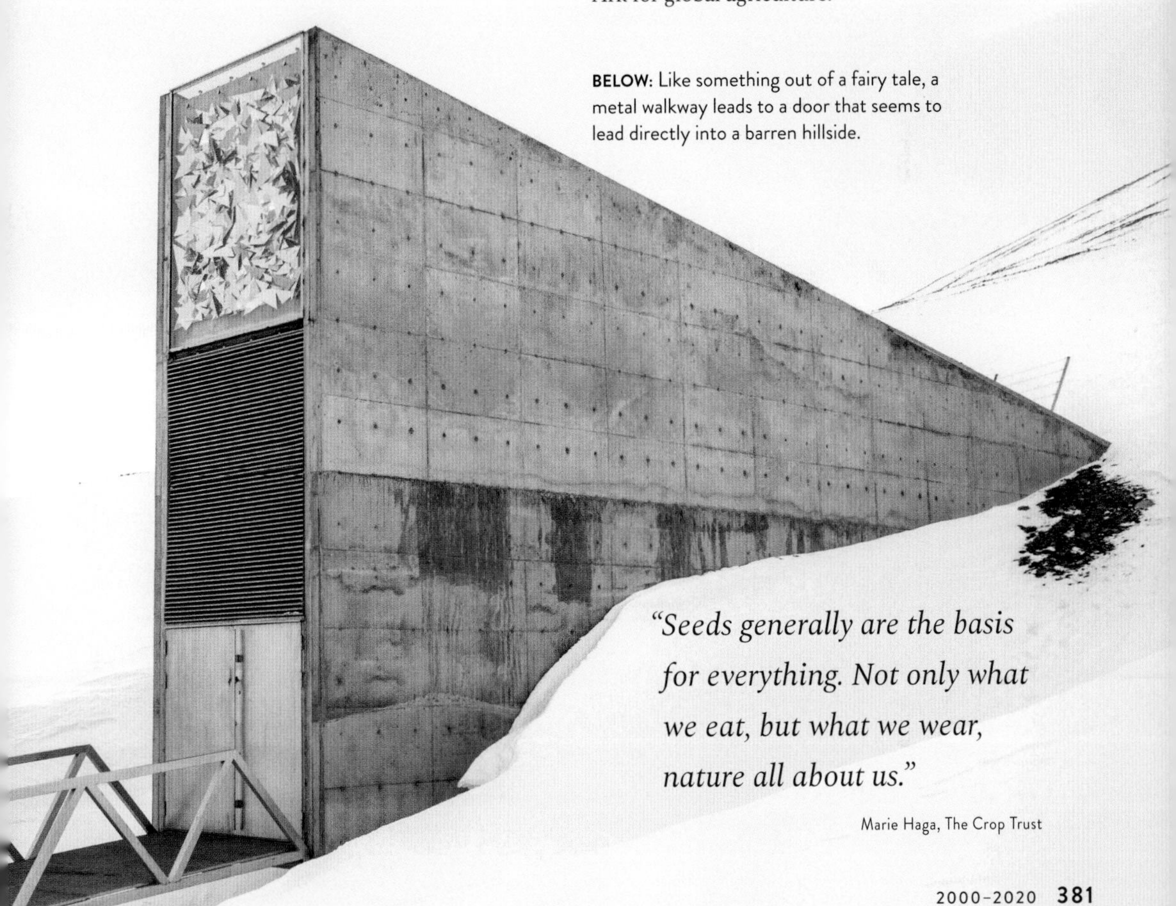

BELOW: Like something out of a fairy tale, a metal walkway leads to a door that seems to lead directly into a barren hillside.

"Seeds generally are the basis for everything. Not only what we eat, but what we wear, nature all about us."

Marie Haga, The Crop Trust

480 INFRASTRUCTURE AND INNOVATION

LARGE HADRON COLLIDER

Mayrin, Switzerland
2008

Housed in an underground tunnel between France and Switzerland, the Large Hadron Collider was built by the European Organization for Nuclear Research (CERN). Planned since 1984, its function is to test the theories of particle physics. It aimed to re-create the conditions of the big bang by enabling particles to collide at immensely high speeds and temperatures, which many scientists believe holds the secret of how objects gain mass.

481 PLACE OF WORK

BURJ KHALIFA

Dubai, United Arab Emirates
2010

Currently the world's tallest building, the Burj Khalifa, a luxury hotel, is well known for the technical achievement of its construction. The end result looks like a dhow—a traditional sailing boat—in full sail. It was designed by architects Skidmore, Owings & Merrill, who also designed the Willis Tower (see page 332), the previous tallest building. The footprint of the Burj Khalifa—three curving parts united into a single tower—is unlike any other.

LEFT: The glittering cladding of the Burj Khalifa is made up of aluminum and stainless-steel panels.

AFRICAN RENAISSANCE MONUMENT

Dakar, Senegal
2010

A controversial landmark built in the midst of an economic crisis.

The African Renaissance Monument—a bronze group comprising a man, woman, and child—leans eagerly forward over the Atlantic. At 160 feet high, it stands in a hilltop position outside Dakar. Commissioned by President Abdoulaye Wade, it celebrated the 50-year anniversary of Senegal's independence from France.

The African Renaissance was a concept, dating back to the 1940s, of the African nations uniting as a single global force. It was the idea behind the African Union, a coalition of 55 African states which was founded in 2001.

The monument received unfavorable reviews. It cost $27 million at a time when 47 percent of Senegalese people were living below the poverty line, and the near nudity of the two adult figures didn't go down well with a largely Muslim population. Nor did it represent Senegalese creativity: it was designed by the Romanian-French artist Virgil Magherusan, and constructed by the North Korean company Mansudae.

RIGHT: The monument's figures have the hyper-heroic look characteristic of works produced by North Korea's Mansudae company.

"Africa has arrived in the twenty-first century standing tall and more ready than ever to take its destiny into its hands."

President Abdoulaye Wade of Senegal, speaking at the monument's unveiling, April 3, 2010

483 INFRASTRUCTURE AND INNOVATION

DANYANG–KUNSHAN BRIDGE

Xiangcheng/Suzhou/Jiangsu, China
2011

At 104 miles long, the bridge spans three Chinese provinces. It was built at a cost of more than $8.5 billion to improve transportation along the Yangtze River Delta. The greatest challenge was to manage a secure structure of such a length that could adapt around a number of different levels. Earthquake resistance, tornado defenses, and ship-collision avoidance are all built in.

484 ART AND CULTURE

JANE'S CAROUSEL

Brooklyn, New York
2011

Jane's Carousel—originally the Idora Park Merry-go-round—was made in 1922. This vintage fairground ride is originally from Youngstown, Ohio, and was bought by David Walentas and his wife Jane (after whom it was later renamed) in 1984. Together, they spent the next two decades restoring all 48 horses and their surroundings to their original condition.

Today, it's one of the attractions of Brooklyn Bridge Park. It sits at the riverside, just by the piers of the Brooklyn Bridge, in a transparent granite, steel, and acrylic "jewel box" designed by the French architect Jean Nouvel, which serves as a display case to protect it, and enables it to remain open to the public year-round.

BELOW: A marriage of old and new in Brooklyn Bridge Park.

485 RESIDENCE

RIKUZENTAKATA HOME-FOR-ALL

Rikuzentakata, Japan
2011

The Home-for-All initiative to provide more community spaces—from kindergartens to meeting places—was started by a group of architects in response to the effects of the devastating earthquake and tsunami that hit Japan in 2011. The coastal town of Rikuzentakata has a particularly striking example, built around huge cedar uprights like a house on stilts, but also referencing driftwood serendipitously washed onto the shore.

486 RESIDENCE/ART AND CULTURE

ABEOKUTA FOREST HOME

Ogun State, Nigeria
2012

Wole Soyinka—playwright, poet, novelist, and the first African Nobel Laureate—has lived and worked all over the world. At times he has been exiled from Nigeria because of his fearless political outspokenness, yet his home remains close to Abeokuta, his birthplace. It is his base in the forest outside the city.

Set in 10 acres of mostly forested land, his handsome brick-and-wood house is filled with the books and art he has collected over a lifetime. His creation of a retreat has been fully realized over the last decade, with the addition of an annex for visiting artists, and an amphitheater for live performances. The forest around the retreat has been carefully managed to minimize the carbon footprint of the property, including the installation of solar panels.

With the work of the Wole Soyinka Foundation, Soyinka is not only helping artists to create work in the present, but also guaranteeing his legacy.

LEFT: Home-for-All projects were designed to be modest in cost and beneficial to their communities.

THREE GORGES DAM

Hubei, China
2012

An extraordinary engineering achievement, with pros and cons.

The Three Gorges Dam had two objectives: to produce electricity, and to alleviate unexpected flooding. It always had supporters: Mao had been an enthusiast but couldn't afford it. Even when it was eventually approved in 1992, it was a political hot potato: one third of legislators voted against it.

The largest hydroelectric dam in the world, it bridges the Yangtze River, stretching 7,660 feet wide, with a height of 607 feet. Completed in 2006, it reached full generating capacity in 2012. The dam's electricity reduced the need for coal-fueled power, and its reservoir allows shipping to sail inland to Chongqing, cutting road traffic.

On the downside, 1.3 million people were displaced, many landscapes and archaeological sites were obliterated, and the surrounding environment has been irreparably damaged. The displacement of sediment in the river has resulted in more landslides; some scientists believe the landscape is now unstable, making earthquakes more likely.

"When it comes to environmental change, the implementation of the Three Gorges Dam and reservoir is the great granddaddy of all changes."

George Davis, a tropical medicine specialist

BELOW: It's estimated that over 1,500 villages and towns were flooded as a side effect of the completion of the immense Three Gorges Dam.

488 PLACE OF WORK

RANA PLAZA FACTORY

Dhaka, Bangladesh
2013

The tragedy that led to a greater awareness of the real cost of fast fashion.

On the morning of April 24, 2013, Rana Plaza, an eight-story commercial building on the outskirts of Dhaka, suddenly collapsed. Inside, 1,134 workers were killed instantly and an estimated 2,000 more suffered life-changing injuries. Rana Plaza housed a clothing factory where machinists put together garments for many well-known global brands. When it emerged that concerns about the substandard building had been raised for some time, it caused international scandal. Textile workers had been laboring in dangerous conditions for subsistence pay. In the West, both brands and their consumers had to examine their conscience about the real cost of cheap clothes.

A decade later, after hard campaigning by the garment workers' unions, some safety protections have been put in place, but pay is still poor. Global awareness of both the human and the ecological price of fast fashion still has a long way to go.

"We still haven't heard of a brand putting their hand up, saying, 'I shall produce less, and I shall make better clothes, made by people who are adequately paid.'"

Orsola De Castro, of advocacy group Fashion Revolution

ABOVE: Textile workers were forced back to work despite large cracks appearing in the walls of the Rana Plaza; just days later it collapsed, prompting an international scandal.

MAKOKO FLOATING SCHOOL

Lagos, Nigeria
2013

Although it's sometimes referred to as the Venice of Africa, in reality Makoko is an acutely poor community living in houses on stilts in the Lagos lagoon, with almost no public services. The innovative Floating School is part of a regeneration plan: a simple, A-frame wooden structure—designed for low ecological impact—buoyed by plastic barrels. In 2016, the original structure collapsed in heavy rains.

"A powerful demonstration, be it in Lagos or in Venice, that architecture, at once iconic and pragmatic, can amplify the importance of education."

Awards of the Biennale Architettura, 2016

RIGHT: The simple design of the Floating School made it an affordable solution for a school, although the structure proved too lightweight to withstand a torrential rainy season.

490 ART AND CULTURE

MIRANTE DO GAVIÃO LODGE

Rio Negro, Brazil
2014

On the banks of the Rio Negro, near the edge of the remote Anavihanas National Park, Mirante do Gavião—or Hawk's Eyrie—is an eco-lodge set up to have as low an impact on the surrounding landscape as possible. It has been meticulously built with local materials.

The architects, Atelier O'Reilly, are specialists in sustainable building. They modeled the roofs on the upturned hulls of the river craft used by the indigenous people of the Amazon.

Ventilation is important in such a hot, humid environment, and the surfaces—balconies, wooden walkways, and roofs—are all raised clear of other surfaces, ensuring that there's good airflow around the lodge buildings. Inside, the textiles and furniture have been created in collaboration with local craftspeople.

RIGHT: Dense planting on the towers helps to keep the apartments inside cool.

491 INFRASTRUCTURE AND INNOVATION

BOSCO VERTICALE

Milan, Italy
2014

One of the most successful examples of "green wall" building, Bosco Verticale—or Vertical Forest—is a pair of reinforced concrete residential towers with facades covered in over 20,000 trees, shrubs, and smaller plants. The plants improve air quality and keep the temperature inside the towers stable. Additionally, solar panels and water recycling help to minimize the project's energy footprint.

492 INFRASTRUCTURE AND INNOVATION

THE EDGE

Amsterdam, Netherlands
2015

PLP Architecture designed next-generation offices for the Amsterdam headquarters of Deloitte: the Edge. This fifteen-story building manages its own energy needs to a very high level. In sustainability credentials tests, the Edge scored an impressive 98.3 percent.

Covered with solar panels, it also has rainwater collection, and an aquifer thermal energy system to regulate the building's temperature. Thousands of sensors calculate where energy can be temporarily shut down. An app will direct you to a parking space when you arrive, and let you know which space you'll be working in: the ultimate hot-desking.

493 ART AND CULTURE

SMITHSONIAN MUSEUM OF AFRICAN AMERICAN HISTORY AND CULTURE

Washington, D.C.
2016

The drive for a museum dedicated to the African American experience is more than a century old, but in 2003 it was finally approved. The completed building and grounds are full of cultural references to both African and African American cultures and communities. The building's inverted, stepped pyramid echoes the symbol of a West African Yoruba crown; the bronze panels decorating it recall the wrought ironwork made by enslaved Americans.

BELOW: The museum is enclosed in an impressive cage of elaborate wrought-metal panels.

494 ART AND CULTURE

SUMIDA HOKUSAI MUSEUM

Tokyo, Japan
2016

Katsushika Hokusai is the artist and printmaker known—even by those who aren't familiar with Japanese art—for the iconic print *The Great Wave off Kanagawa*. He lived most of his life in the Sumida district of Tokyo, where the museum celebrates his achievements.

The architect Kazuyo Sejima created a simple, blocky four-story building entirely wrapped in an aluminum skin, reflecting the sky. Because the eighteenth- and nineteenth-century prints that comprise most of Hokusai's work are fragile, it was important that the museum shouldn't be flooded with too much light. Sejima's sleek solution was to install glass only on the inside of the V-shapes and slits where the units and angles of the building lean into one another.

495 RELIGION AND MONUMENT

BAHÁ'Í TEMPLE OF SOUTH AMERICA

Santiago, Chile
2016

Technically and visually innovative, the Bahá'í Temple is one of a series of eight new temples built for the Bahá'í faith on sites all over the world. The building is formed of nine twisted "wings," made from thousands of angled panels of marble and glass, which reflect light both within and around them. The curving shape of each piece gives the temple the look of an opening flower bud.

ABOVE: The flower-bud structure of the temple fits well into the landscaped gardens around it.

LEFT: The museum's design carefully filters light to the interior, helping to protect the priceless print collections.

496 ART AND CULTURE

DANDAJI LIBRARY

Dandaji, Niger
2019

Conceived and built jointly by Niamey-based architects Atelier Masomi and ecological architecture specialists Studio Chahar, the library was an imaginative—but simple—conversion of the village's near-derelict "melting" mosque. A mezzanine floor—of wood and metal—was added to the original adobe construction. Opposite, a new mosque was built from locally made compressed-earth bricks, prompting a natural traffic between the library (for work), and the mosque (for prayer).

497 INFRASTRUCTURE AND INNOVATION

JEWEL

Singapore Changi Airport, Singapore
2019

Conceived to reinforce Changi as a popular stop-off point for long-haul travelers, Jewel is an extensive entertainment and retail complex. Far more unusually, it offers travelers a substantial green landscape, including the "rain vortex"—the world's tallest indoor waterfall—cascading through a central skylight in the roof, and the so-called Shisheido Forest Valley, a botanical garden on an impressively large scale.

ABOVE LEFT: Once stabilized, the original niches of the mosque could be used to hold the bookshelves of the new library.

LEFT: Jewel is a unique—and successful—experiment in marrying a transportation hub with a major greenscaping project, to the benefit of both.

498 POLITICS AND NATIONAL DEFENSE

EU PARLIAMENT BUILDING

Brussels, Belgium
2020

Completed in 1995, the Paul-Henri Spaak building houses the parliamentary debating chamber for members of the EU, as well as the president's offices. It was here, on January 31, 2020, that the UK formally left the union, the first country in its sixty-two-year history to do so.

499 PLACE OF WORK

HUANAN SEAFOOD WHOLESALE MARKET

Hubei Province, China
2020

The wet market in Wuhan became notorious as the likely origin of the coronavirus pandemic that exploded, first across China, then globally. It sold live animals of many different species. It is thought that the virus jumped cross-species into people. Wuhan was certainly the epicenter of the outbreak, but a competing theory holds that the virus "escaped" from the Wuhan Institute of Virology. The market closed permanently on January 1, 2020.

500 PLACE OF WORK

PRINCETON SCHOOL OF PUBLIC AND INTERNATIONAL AFFAIRS

Princeton, New Jersey
2020

Originally named for Woodrow Wilson, the 35th president of the United States, the name became a source of controversy in the twenty-first century when Wilson's racist views were subjected to critical reevaluation. In 2020, the murder of George Floyd by police, and the subsequent outrage expressed by the Black Lives Matter movement, prompted Princeton to remove Wilson's name from the school—just one of many institutions to reconsider their naming policy.

BELOW: The Black Lives Matter protests prompted demands for the removal of controversial names and dedications from many campus buildings all over the world.

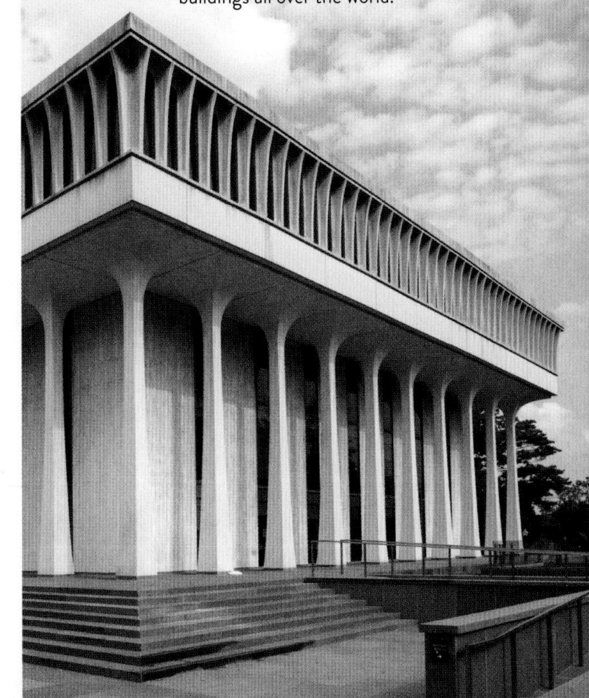

INDEX

U

V

W

X

Y

Z

PICTURE CREDITS

The publisher would like to thank the following for the permission to reproduce copyright material. T = top, B = bottom, L = left, C = center, R = right

agefotostock: 119R De Agostini/Icas94; 144T Jerónimo Alba; 168B CSP_Morphart; 326R Edwin Remsberg; 385 Edmund Sumner/VIEW
Alamy: 5BR, 238B, 307T Volgi archive; 7 Xinhua; 10BLScience History Images; 12–13 Greatstock; 17 markferguson2; 21B Science History Images; 26L Photo 12; 27, 199, 357 Hemis; 28R Top Photo Corporation; 31B, 34, 49C Classic Image; 33B robertharding; 37T EU/BT; 43T Adam Eastland; 46B Album; 55LT Danvis Collection; 71T PRISMA ARCHIVO; 87B, 149T Antiqua Print Gallery; 93 Florilegius; 94 Ariadne Van Zandbergen; 96T Xinhua; 111CL Antiqua Print Gallery; 114–115 Neil Baylis; 121B Gado Images; 144B STOCKFOLIO®; 182B Andre M. Chang; 213R GRANGER – Historical Picture Archive; 231 Artokoloro; 244L numb; 248T History and Art Collection; 251 GC Stock; 257L Kim Karpeles; 258R parkerphotography; 263 Jessie/ Stockimo; 267 Science History Images; 271 (inset) INTERFOTO; 274L Peter Cavanagh; 283 ZUMA Press, Inc.; 288 NurPhoto SRL; 289B Robert Wyatt; 292R Globe Stock Premium; 298 Prisma by Dukas Presseagentur GmbH; 301 imageBROKER; 302R wanderluster; 307B Everett Collection Historical; 314 Nick Harrison; 316T Keystone Press; 318, 337, 359 Associated Press; 322T PA Images; 334 Andia; 338R dpa picture alliance archive; 380 Christian J Kober; 381 Cultura RM
American Academy in Rome: 252 Image courtesy of the American Academy in Rome, Institutional Archive
atelier masōmī: 392T James Wang, courtesy of atelier masōmī
Barbican Living: 341TR
Charles Correa Foundation: 238L, 367T, 367B © Charles Correa, courtesy Charles Correa Foundation
City of Sydney Archives: 335 (inset) Len Stone Photograph Collection, courtesy of the City of Sydney Archives
Creative Commons: 19 CC BY-SA 4.0/Tjp finn; 26R CC BY 3.0/youssef_alam; 42 CC BY-SA 4.0/ Zhangzhugang; 63BL CC0 1.0/Bigjap; 65T CC BY-SA 3.0/Ssriram mt; 65B CC BY-SA 3.0/Raja1111; 71BL&BR CC BY-SA 4.0/Olaf Væring (1837–1906)/ Kulturhistorisk museum, UiO (Museum of Cultural History, part of the University of Oslo, Norway); 84R CC BY-SA 4.0/Megginede; 101L CC BY-SA 4.0/Zaid isam; 107B CC BY-SA 4.0/Igor Pinigin; 110 CC BY-SA 4.0/Alexander Leisser; 111T CC BY 2.0/ Manuele Zunelli; 111CR CC BY-SA 3.0/Vladsinger; 116 CC BY-SA 3.0/ Franzfoto; 146 CC BY-SA 3.0/ Dmadeo; 155L CC BY-SA 4.0/ P.Cikovac; 186 CC BY-SA 4.0/Bestbudbrian; 193 CC BY-SA 3.0/ Diuturno; 211 inset CC BY-SA 4.0/W. Bulach; 214L CC BY-SA 3.0/Samadolfo; 222 CC BY-SA 3.0/ Sagrada Família (oficial); 229L CC BY-SA 4.0/ Spudgun67; 245L CC BY-SA 2.0/Rod Waddington; 262R CC BY-SA 3.0/Wiiii; 269L CC BY-SA 4.0/ Thomas Ledl; 280 CC BY-SA 4.0/gillfoto; 284R CC BY 4.0/Ninaraas; 285L CC-BY-SA 3.0/Bundesarchiv, Bild 183-R82532; 290 CC BY 2.0/Paul Mannix; 311L CC-BY-SA-3.0/Fortepan/Éva Román; 330L CC BY-SA 2.0 /Andie Nordgren; 333 CC BY-SA 3.0/ Florian Hirzinger - www.fh-ap.com; 345 CC BY-SA 4.0/JanManu; 346T CC BY-SA 2.0/ilf_; 349 CC BY-SA 2.0/ IAEA Imagebank; 353 CC BY-SA 3.0/ John Cummings; 363 CC BY-SA 3.0/Tambo; 366L CC BY 4.0/ESO; 366R CC BY-SA 2.0/Comisión Mexicana de Filmaciones; 373 CC BY-SA 3.0/ GandoIT; 376 Vince Musi/The White House; 378 CC BY 2.0/jelm6; 386 CC BY-SA 2.0/Dan Kamminga
Dennis Historical Society: 142
Frances Loeb Library, Harvard: 238T, 323B Tange, Kenzō (1913–2005). The Kenzo Tange Archive, Gift of Takako Tange, 2011. Yoyogi Gymnasium (Tokyo). Folder A051-006. Courtesy of the Frances Loeb Library, Harvard University Graduate School of Design
Getty Images: 10TR, 21C Historical Picture Archive; 10–11 DEA/ICAS94; 14, 244R Westend61; 29T Dorling Kindersley; 40L Print Collector; 53T DE AGOSTINI PICTURE LIBRARY; 56R DEA PICTURE LIBRARY; 104 DEA/J. L. CHARMET; 130B duncan1890; 139 Nastasic; 154–155, 171 Sepia Times; 164BR Peter Dazeley; 167 Smith Collection/ Gado; 183 Popperfoto; 194L The Washington Post; 196 Fairfax Media Archives; 200B Mark Kolbe; 203 Krista Few; 206 UniversalImagesGroup; 218B Print Collector; 226L Photo 12; 245R Wallace Marly; 253 Universal History Archive; 266, 279T, 325B Bettmann; 272R Denver Post; 275L ullstein bild Dtl.; 296L Pierre Jahan; 297 Photo Researchers; 303B New York Daily News; 308 Terence Spencer/ Popperfoto; 323T Three Lions; 340 Hulton Archive; 342 Johannes Mann; 343 antoinette norcia; 344R Bloomberg; 346B JEKESAI NJIKIZANA; 347 Anadolu Agency; 364 Scott Peterson; 377 AHMAD GHARABLI
iStock: 25 antonbelo; 39R Nnehring; 85L ZU_09; 96B iStock; 109L antiqueimgnet; 117T ilbusca; 120 Pyrosky; 158L bauhaus1000; 201L Orietta Gaspari; 221 ilbusca; 235B clu; 247 oversnap; 356 Mlenny
Kathleen Steeden: 341TL
Libraries Tasmania: 200T Libraries Tasmania, Online collection, PWD266-1-1778
Library of Congress: 176–177T, 205T, 208, 210, 227R, 233R, 236TL, 236TR, 236BL, 242, 286 [Carol M. Highsmith], 287, 304T&B, 328B, 393
Library of Virginia: 136R
Memphis Press-Scimitar newspaper morgue, Special Collections Department, University of Memphis Libraries: 312
NASA: 350, 351
NLE Works: 388
RCAHMS (Scotland) Inventory of Stirling: 161BR Courtesy of the Records of the Royal Commission on the Ancient and Historical Monuments of Scotland (RCAHMS), Edinburgh, 1960 © Crown Copyright: HES
Sebastian Posingis: 332
Shutterstock: 3, 48, 80T, 135T, 170T, 173T Morphart Creation; 5T Nicku; 15 R.M. Nunes; 20T pql89; 20B M. Vinuesa; 24L, 29B, 143L, 143R Homo Cosmicos; 24R Timofeev Vladimir; 28L Jess Kraft; 30R TripDeeDee Photo; 31T pio3; 32 Kite_rin; 35T Erika Bisbocci; 37B warasit phothisuk; 38L Damian Byrne; 38R prochasson Frederic; 41 Truba7113; 43B Grisha Bruev; 44 LouieLea; 45, 66, 74–75, 102T Marzolino; 46T Flo K; 47 Anibal Trejo; 49T Stefano Tammaro; 51 BearFotos; 52L Diego Grandi; 52R Massimo Salesi; 53B, 106 saiko3p; 54 Kevin Standage; 55LB J_J; 55R Travel Turkey; 56L YusufAslan; 57 PhotoZeli; 58 Harmony Video Production; 59 Alla Lla; 60 Mazur Travel; 61B Aleksandr Medvedkov; 62T Leonid Andronov; 62B Luciano Mortula - LGM; 63T Reimar; 63TL&R Vector Tradition; 64B Mikhail Markovskiy; 67 lladyjane; 69 Leonid Andronov; 70 Adel Newman; 72 Myriam B; 73 JoaLacerda; 76 Richard Cavalleri; 77L windcoast; 77R Joseph Thomas Photography; 78B Linda Szeto; 79 Christophe Cappelli; 80B Munzir Rosdi; 83 Matyas Rehak; 84L Anton_Ivanov; 85R Travelvolo; 86 CREO327; 88L Ralf Broskvar; 88R Eric Valenne geostory; 89B Sergii Figurnyi; 90L Wangkun Jia; 90R photo_jeongh; 95L Ondrej Bucek; 95R Isogood_patrick; 97 Ricardo Barata; 98L Richie Chan; 98R DemarK; 99, 136L, 162, 136L, 162, 179BR, 254, 259 (inset), 260L, 326L Everett Collection; 100 HandmadePictures; 103L b-hide the scene; 103R Avigator Fortuner; 105 Erlantz P.R; 107T Olga Popova; 108 rongyiquan; 111B Nowaczyk; 118R Radek Sturgolewski; 119L Bill Perry; 122 Luis Overlander; 123L Erlantz P.R; 123R ImagesofIndia; 125 Nicholas Courtney; 126 dimbar76; 127T canadastock; 128 Sergii Figurnyi; 129 padchas; 131 TNShutter; 132T Roman Babakin; 134 Matyas Rehak; 137 KKKvintage; 138 Mohamed Reedi; 141 mamahoohooba; 147 Ramunas Bruzas; 148 PhotoFires; 152R makinajp; 153 Hakat; 156 Nexajai; 158R tolobalaguer.com; 159 Mario Hagen; 160–161 Ulmus Media; 161T siete_vidas; 164BL Photosite; 165 Simon Annable; 166 Diego Grandi; 168T Ilona Lablaika; 169 Paul Daniels; 170B Goekce; 172 Mikhail Gnatkovskiy; 174 Andrey_Popov; 174 (inset) SAHAS2015; 179T Dmitry Naumov; 180 high fliers; 181 PhotoJuli86; 184 I Wei Huang; 185R Daniel Avram; 187 Sean Pavone; 189B HVRIS; 190 riekephotos; 191 Lao Ma; 192 Zack Frank; 194R rightclickstudios; 204L Polsq1; 207 little_larc; 209 Alexey Fedorenko; 211 anek.soowannaphoom; 214R tr3gin; 217 Evgeniya Uvarova; 219 Brian Logan Photography; 220 Jeremy Richards; 223 Ttstudio; 228T apiguide; 229R canadastock; 230 NaughtyNut; 232 Hein Nouwens; 233L melissamn; 235TL marina rodyukova; 235TR KOV777; 236BR Nagel Photography; 237 smpoly; 238–239 CoolR; 240 Anna_plucinska; 241 Introspective Design; 243R Drop of Light; 248B Lukas Bischoff Photograph; 249 Claudio Divizia; 255 Ion Mes; 256 Chris971; 257R Rbgarcia; 258L Diego Grandi; 259 Da-ga; 264 Lois GoBe; 268 Carlos Yudica; 270 Cinematographer; 271 Leo_tronico; 272L AlexCorv; 273B Studio MDF; 274R nito; 275R Marco Rubino; 276 Matej Kastelic; 277L La_Mar; 277R EQRoy; 278R Matyas Rehak; 281 Lorena Huerta; 289T Nils Versemann; 292L Marques; 294 Kagai19927; 295 Keitma; 296R Pamela Brick; 297 (inset) Adrinson Yanes Hernandez; 299 Danny Ye; 302L Maria Amador; 303T Ritu Manoj Jethani; 305 V Can; 306 travelview; 309 Minute of love; 313 kaiser-v; 315 Pises Tungittipokai; 316B Claudio Divizia; 321 (inset) posztos; 322B Alizada Studios; 324 Fotomicar; 325T Andriy Blokhin; 327R Mircea Costina; 328T valerii eidlin; 329 (inset) tur-illustration; 331 pxl.store; 338L Taras Verkhovynets; 339 Felix Lipov; 344L Jess Kraft; 352L Marcos Botelho Jr; 352R Ben Reeves; 354 struvictory; 362 Igor Plotnikov; 369 Eleni Mavrandoni; 370TR&BL 4Alona; 372 BABAROGA; 375R yu_photo; 382 Tomasz Czajkowski; 383 Dereje; 387 Sk Hasan Ali; 390T Kit Leong; 391T NataliaCatalina.com; 391B cowardlion
Unsplash: 1 Gábor Molnár; 2 Sam Balye; 21T Dario Morandotti; 22–23 K. Mitch Hodge; 39L Stamatina Kiriazou; 68T Carolina Nichitin; 81 Mario La Pergola; 92 Adarsh Baraiya; 109R Victor Malyushev; 112 Mario La Pergola; 113 farin sadiq; 145 Akash Pratap Singh; 148 (inset) Hannah Falk; 150 Rahul Viswanath; 212–213 samuel hanna; 224–225 Tim Hüfner; 250 Ilya Sosyniuk; 261 Mike Hsieh; 279B Nationaal Archief; 285R Emil Widlund; 291 Bradley Pritchard Jones; 311R Jacek Jabłoński; 317 Brandon W; 319 Grant Durr; 321 Simone Hutsch; 327L Chris Hardy; 329 Juan Giraudo; 330R Karly Jones; 335 Jesse Hammer; 341B Kate Olfans; 348 Martin Katler; 355 Tim Wildsmith; 360 Chapman Chow; 361 Patrick Miyaoka; 365 Alice; 368 Nazarizal Mohammad; 374L Olga Subach; 374R Radu Lin; 375L Benjamin Elliott; 379 Marlin Clark; 384 Vicente García Pérez; 389 Max van den Oetelaar; 392B Pang Yuhao
Wellcome Collection: 114TL, 127B, 133L, 273T

Front cover images (left to right, top to bottom): Shutterstock/M. Shcherbyna; Shutterstock/ TNShutter; wikicommons; Shutterstock/Drop of Light; Unsplash/Dario Morandotti; Shutterstock/ Marzolino; Unsplash/Pratap Singh; Unsplash/Emil Widlund
Back cover images (left to right): Shutterstock/padchas; Unsplash/Chris Hardy; Shutterstock/ Travelvolo; Shutterstock/ Nicholas Courtney Shutterstock/siete_vidas

While every effort has been made to credit photographers, The Bright Press would like to apologize should there have been any omissions or errors, and would be pleased to make the appropriate correction for future editions of the book.